Boost C++ Application Development Cookbook

Over 80 practical, task-based recipes to create applications using Boost libraries

Antony Polukhin

[PACKT] open source*
PUBLISHING   community experience distilled

BIRMINGHAM - MUMBAI

Boost C++ Application Development Cookbook

First published: August 2013

Production Reference: 1210813

Published by Packt Publishing Ltd.
Livery Place
35 Livery Street
Birmingham B3 2PB, UK.

ISBN 978-1-84951-488-0

www.packtpub.com

Cover Image by Suresh Mogre (suresh.mogre.99@gmail.com)

Credits

Author

Antony Polukhin

Reviewers

Béla Tibor Bartha

Paul A. Bristow

Acquisition Editor

Akram Hussain

Lead Technical Editor

Arun Nadar

Technical Editors

Sampreshita Maheshwari

Vivek Pillai

Hardik B. Soni

Copy Editors

Adithi Shetty

Laxmi Subramanian

Gladson Monterio

Brandt D'Mello

Sayanee Mukherjee

Alfida Paiva

Aditya Nair

Project Coordinator

Anugya Khurana

Proofreader

Stephen Silk

Indexer

Monica Ajmera Mehta

Graphics

Abhinash Sahu

Ronak Druv

Production Coordinator

Conidon Miranda

Cover Work

Conidon Miranda

About the Author

Antony Polukhin was born in Russia. As a child, he could speak the Russian and Hungarian languages and learned English at school. Since his school days, he was participating in different mathematics, physics, and chemistry competitions and winning them.

He was accepted into University twice: once for taking part in a city mathematics competition and again for gaining high score in an internal Universities mathematics and physics challenge. In his university life, there was not a year when he did not participate in an exam: he gained 'A's in all disciplines by writing highly difficult programs for each teacher. He met his future wife in university and graduated with honors.

For more than three years, he worked in a VoIP company developing business logic for a commercial alternative to Asterisc. During those days he started contributing to Boost and became a maintainer of the Boost.LexicalCast library. He also started making translations to Russian for Ubuntu Linux at that time.

Today, he develops a query engine for graph-oriented databases and continues to contribute to the open source. You may find his code in Boost libraries such as Any, LexicalCast, TypeTraits, Variant, and others.

He has been happily married for a year now.

I would like to thank my family, especially my wife, Irina Polukhina, for drawing sketches of pictures and diagrams all through the book. Great thanks to Paul Anthony Bristow for reviewing this book and getting through the insane number of commas that I used in the first drafts. I would also like to thank all of the people from the Boost community for writing those great libraries and for opening an amazing word of C++ for me.

About the Reviewers

Béla Tibor Bartha is a professional software engineer working on various technologies and languages. Although in the last four years he's been working on iOS and OS X applications, C++ is his old passion along with game development as personal projects.

Paul A. Bristow is a long-time member of the Boost community (and contributor to Boost. Math) who has watched with amusement and amazement at how C++ has been made to do so many wonderful things that it was never designed to do (many of which are nicely demonstrated in this book).

www.PacktPub.com

Support files, eBooks, discount offers and more

You might want to visit www.PacktPub.com for support files and downloads related to your book.

Did you know that Packt offers eBook versions of every book published, with PDF and ePub files available? You can upgrade to the eBook version at www.PacktPub.com and as a print book customer, you are entitled to a discount on the eBook copy. Get in touch with us at service@packtpub.com for more details.

At www.PacktPub.com, you can also read a collection of free technical articles, sign up for a range of free newsletters and receive exclusive discounts and offers on Packt books and eBooks.

http://PacktLib.PacktPub.com

Do you need instant solutions to your IT questions? PacktLib is Packt's online digital book library. Here, you can access, read and search across Packt's entire library of books.

Why Subscribe?

- ▸ Fully searchable across every book published by Packt
- ▸ Copy and paste, print and bookmark content
- ▸ On demand and accessible via web browser

Free Access for Packt account holders

If you have an account with Packt at www.PacktPub.com, you can use this to access PacktLib today and view nine entirely free books. Simply use your login credentials for immediate access.

Table of Contents

Preface

A few years ago one of my friends was looking for a book about the Boost libraries. I asked him "Why don't you read the documentation?". His answer was, "I do not know much and I do not know where to start. Boost is huge; I have no time to read all about it."

Well, that was a good hint but such a book would be of interest only to beginners. Professionals would find nothing interesting in it unless I added some C++11 stuff and compared the existing Boost libraries with the new C++ standard.

I could also add answers to common questions that arise in Boost mailing lists but are hard to find or not covered by the documentation. Spice it up with performance notes and we'd get a book that would be interesting to almost everyone.

This book will take you through a number of clear, practical recipes that will help you to take advantage of some readily available solutions.

Boost C++ Application Development Cookbook starts out teaching the basics of the Boost libraries that are now mostly part of C++11 and leave no chance for memory leaks. Managing resources will become a piece of cake. We'll see what kind of work can be done at compile time and what Boost containers can do. Do you think multithreading is a burden? Not with Boost. Do you think writing portable and fast servers is impossible? You'll be surprised! Compilers and operating systems differ too much? Not with Boost. From manipulating images to graphs, directories, timers, files, and strings – everyone will find an interesting topic.

You will learn everything needed for the development of high-quality, fast, and portable applications. Write a program once and you can use it on Linux, Windows, Mac OS, and Android operating systems.

What this book covers

Chapter 1, Starting to Write Your Application, covers some recipes for everyday use. We'll see how to get configuration options from different sources and what can be cooked up using some of the datatypes introduced by Boost library authors.

Chapter 2, *Converting Data*, explains how to convert strings, numbers, and user-defined types to each other, how to safely cast polymorphic types, and how to write small and large parsers right in C++ source files.

Chapter 3, *Managing Resources*, provides guidance to easily managing resources and how to use a datatype capable of storing any functional objects, functions, and lambda expressions. After reading this chapter your code will become more reliable and memory leaks will become history.

Chapter 4, *Compile-time Tricks*, walks you through some basic examples on how Boost libraries can be used in compile-time checking, for tuning algorithms and in other metaprogramming tasks.

Chapter 5, *Multithreading*, discusses threads and everything connected with them.

Chapter 6, *Manipulating Tasks*, explains that we can split all of the processing, computations, and interactions to functors (tasks) and process each of those tasks almost independently. Moreover, we need not block on some slow operations such as receiving data from socket or waiting for timeout, but instead provide a callback task and continue processing other tasks.

Chapter 7, *Manipulating Strings*, covers different aspects of changing, searching, and representing strings. We'll see how some common string-related tasks can easily be done using Boost libraries.

Chapter 8, *Metaprogramming*, is devoted to some cool and hard-to-understand metaprogramming methods. Those methods are not for everyday use, but they will be a real help for development of generic libraries.

Chapter 9, *Containers*, covers Boost containers and everything directly connected to them. This chapter provides information about Boost classes that can be used in everyday programming and that will make your code much faster and development of new applications easier.

Chapter 10, *Gathering Platform and Compiler Information*, provides different helper macros used to detect compiler, platform, and Boost features. Those macros are widely used across Boost libraries and are essential for writing portable code that is able to work with any compiler flags.

Chapter 11, *Working with the System*, takes a closer look at the filesystem and at creating and deleting files. We'll see how data can be passed between different system processes, how to read files with maximum speed, and how to do other tricks.

Chapter 12, *Scratching the Tip of the Iceberg*, is devoted to some of those big libraries, giving the basics to start with. Some of the Boost libraries are small and meant for everyday use, others require a separate book to describe all of their features.

What you need for this book

To run the examples in this book, the following software will be required:

▸ **C++ compiler**: Any modern, popular C++ compiler will be suitable

▸ **IDE**: QtCreator is recommended as an IDE

▸ **Boost**: You should have a full build of Boost 1.53

▸ **Miscellaneous tools**: Graphviz (any version) and libpng (latest version)

Note that if you are using Linux, all of the required software except Boost can be found in the repository.

Who this book is for

This book is great for developers who are new to Boost, and who are looking to improve their knowledge of Boost and see some undocumented details or tricks. It's assumed that you will have some experience in C++ already, as well as being familiar with the basics of STL. A few chapters will require some previous knowledge of multithreading and networking. You are expected to have at least one good C++ compiler and compiled version of Boost (1.53.0 or later is recommended), which will be used during the exercises within this book.

Conventions

In this book, you will find a number of styles of text that distinguish between different kinds of information. Here are some examples of these styles, and an explanation of their meaning.

Code words in text, database table names, folder names, filenames, file extensions, pathnames, dummy URLs, user input, and Twitter handles are shown as follows: "It means that you can catch almost all Boost exceptions using `catch (const std::exception& e)`."

A block of code is set as follows:

```cpp
#include <boost/variant.hpp>
#include <iostream>
#include <vector>
#include <string>

int main()
{
    typedef boost::variant<int, const char*, std::string> my_var_t;
    std::vector<my_var_t> some_values;
    some_values.push_back(10);
    some_values.push_back("Hello there!");
```

```
some_values.push_back(std::string("Wow!"));
std::string& s = boost::get<std::string>(some_values.back());
s += " That is great!\n";
std::cout << s;
return 0;
}
```

New terms and **important words** are shown in bold.

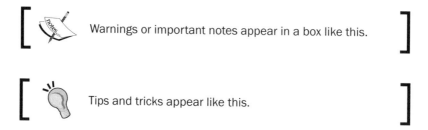

Warnings or important notes appear in a box like this.

Tips and tricks appear like this.

Reader feedback

Feedback from our readers is always welcome. Let us know what you think about this book—what you liked or may have disliked. Reader feedback is important for us to develop titles that you really get the most out of.

To send us general feedback, simply send an e-mail to feedback@packtpub.com, and mention the book title via the subject of your message.

If there is a topic that you have expertise in and you are interested in either writing or contributing to a book, see our author guide on www.packtpub.com/authors.

Customer support

Now that you are the proud owner of a Packt book, we have a number of things to help you to get the most from your purchase.

Downloading the example code

You can download the example code files for all Packt books you have purchased from your account at http://www.packtpub.com. If you purchased this book elsewhere, you can visit http://www.packtpub.com/support and register to have the files e-mailed directly to you.

Errata

Although we have taken every care to ensure the accuracy of our content, mistakes do happen. If you find a mistake in one of our books—maybe a mistake in the text or the code—we would be grateful if you would report this to us. By doing so, you can save other readers from frustration and help us improve subsequent versions of this book. If you find any errata, please report them by visiting http://www.packtpub.com/submit-errata, selecting your book, clicking on the **errata submission form** link, and entering the details of your errata. Once your errata are verified, your submission will be accepted and the errata will be uploaded on our website, or added to any list of existing errata, under the Errata section of that title. Any existing errata can be viewed by selecting your title from http://www.packtpub.com/support.

Piracy

Piracy of copyright material on the Internet is an ongoing problem across all media. At Packt, we take the protection of our copyright and licenses very seriously. If you come across any illegal copies of our works, in any form, on the Internet, please provide us with the location address or website name immediately so that we can pursue a remedy.

Please contact us at copyright@packtpub.com with a link to the suspected pirated material.

We appreciate your help in protecting our authors, and our ability to bring you valuable content.

Questions

You can contact us at questions@packtpub.com if you are having a problem with any aspect of the book, and we will do our best to address it.

1
Starting to Write Your Application

In this chapter we will cover:

- ▶ Getting configuration options
- ▶ Storing any value in a container/variable
- ▶ Storing multiple chosen types in a container/variable
- ▶ Using a safer way to work with a container that stores multiple chosen types
- ▶ Returning a value or flag where there is no value
- ▶ Returning an array from a function
- ▶ Combining multiple values into one
- ▶ Reordering the parameters of a function
- ▶ Binding a value as a function parameter
- ▶ Using the C++11 move emulation
- ▶ Making a noncopyable class
- ▶ Making a noncopyable but movable class

Introduction

Boost is a collection of C++ libraries. Each library has been reviewed by many professional programmers before being accepted to Boost. Libraries are tested on multiple platforms using many compilers and the C++ standard library implementations. While using Boost, you can be sure that you are using one of the most portable, fast, and reliable solutions that is distributed under a license suitable for commercial and open source projects.

Many parts of Boost have been included in C++11, and even more parts are going to be included in the next standard of C++. You will find C++11-specific notes in each recipe of this book.

Without a long introduction, let's get started!

In this chapter we will see some recipes for everyday use. We'll see how to get configuration options from different sources and what can be cooked up using some of the datatypes introduced by Boost library authors.

Getting configuration options

Take a look at some of the console programs, such as `cp` in Linux. They all have a fancy help, their input parameters do not depend on any position, and have a human readable syntax, for example:

```
$ cp --help
```

```
Usage: cp [OPTION] ... [-T] SOURCE DEST
  -a, --archive             same as -dR --preserve=all
  -b                        like --backup but does not accept an argument
```

You can implement the same functionality for your program in 10 minutes. And all you need is the `Boost.ProgramOptions` library.

Getting ready

Basic knowledge of C++ is all you need for this recipe. Remember that this library is not a header-only, so your program will need to link against the `libboost_program_options` library.

How to do it...

Let's start with a simple program that accepts the number of apples and oranges as input and counts the total number of fruits. We want to achieve the following result:

```
$ our_program -apples=10 -oranges=20
Fruits count: 30
```

Perform the following steps:

1. First of all, we need to include the `program_options` header and make an alias for the `boost::program_options` namespace (it is too long to type it!). We would also need an `<iostream>` header:

```
#include <boost/program_options.hpp>
#include <iostream>
namespace opt = boost::program_options;
```

2. Now we are ready to describe our options:

```
// Constructing an options describing variable and giving
// it a textual description "All options" to it.
opt::options_description desc("All options");

// When we are adding options, first parameter is a name
// to be used in command line. Second parameter is a type
// of that option, wrapped in value<> class.
// Third parameter must be a short description of that
// option
desc.add_options()
    ("apples", opt::value<int>(), "how many apples do you have")
    ("oranges", opt::value<int>(), "how many oranges do you have")
;
```

3. We'll see how to use a third parameter a little bit later, after which we'll deal with parsing the command line and outputting the result:

```
// Variable to store our command line arguments
opt::variables_map vm;

// Parsing and storing arguments
opt::store(opt::parse_command_line(argc, argv, desc), vm);
opt::notify(vm);
std::cout << "Fruits count: "
    << vm["apples"].as<int>() + vm["oranges"].as<int>()
    << std::endl;
```

That was simple, wasn't it?

4. Let's add the `--help` parameter to our option's description:

```
("help", "produce help message")
```

5. Now add the following lines after `opt::notify(vm);`, and you'll get a fully functional help for your program:

    ```
    if (vm.count("help")) {
        std::cout << desc << "\n";
        return 1;
    }
    ```

    Now, if we call our program with the `--help` parameter, we'll get the following output:

    ```
    All options:
      --apples arg          how many apples do you have
      --oranges arg         how many oranges do you have
      --help                produce help message
    ```

    As you can see, we do not provide a type for the option's value, because we do not expect any values to be passed to it.

6. Once we have got through all the basics, let's add short names for some of the options, set the default value for apples, add some string input, and get the missing options from the configuration file:

    ```
    #include <boost/program_options.hpp>
    // 'reading_file' exception class is declared in errors.hpp
    #include <boost/program_options/errors.hpp>
    #include <iostream>
    namespace opt = boost::program_options;

    int main(int argc, char *argv[])
    {
        opt::options_description desc("All options");
        // 'a' and 'o' are short option names for apples and
        // oranges 'name' option is not marked with
        // 'required()', so user may not support it
        desc.add_options()
            ("apples,a", opt::value<int>()->default_value(10),
                "apples that you have")
            ("oranges,o", opt::value<int>(), "oranges that you have")
            ("name", opt::value<std::string>(), "your name")
            ("help", "produce help message")
        ;
        opt::variables_map vm;
        // Parsing command line options and storing values to 'vm'
    ```

```
opt::store(opt::parse_command_line(argc, argv, desc), vm);
  // We can also parse environment variables using
  // 'parse_environment' method
  opt::notify(vm);
  if (vm.count("help")) {
      std::cout << desc << "\n";
      return 1;
  }
  // Adding missing options from "aples_oranges.cfg"
  // config file.
  // You can also provide an istreamable object as a
  // first parameter for 'parse_config_file'
  // 'char' template parameter will be passed to
  // underlying std::basic_istream object
  try {
    opt::store(
      opt::parse_config_file<char>("apples_oranges.cfg", desc),
      vm
    );
  } catch (const opt::reading_file& e) {
      std::cout
          << "Failed to open file 'apples_oranges.cfg': "
          << e.what();
  }
  opt::notify(vm);
  if (vm.count("name")) {
    std::cout << "Hi," << vm["name"].as<std::string>() << "!\n";
  }

  std::cout << "Fruits count: "
      << vm["apples"].as<int>() + vm["oranges"].as<int>()
      << std::endl;
  return 0;
}
```

When using a configuration file, we need to remember that its syntax differs from the command-line syntax. We do not need to place minuses before the options. So our `apples_oranges.cfg` option must look like this:

`oranges=20`

How it works...

This example is pretty trivial to understand from code and comments. Much more interesting is what output we get on execution:

```
$ ./our_program --help
All options:
  -a [ --apples ] arg (=10) how many apples do you have
  -o [ --oranges ] arg      how many oranges do you have
  --name arg                your name
  --help                    produce help message

$ ./our_program
Fruits count: 30

$ ./our_program -a 10 -o 10 --name="Reader"
Hi,Reader!
Fruits count: 20
```

There's more...

The C++11 standard adopted many Boost libraries; however, you won't find `Boost.ProgramOptions` in it.

See also

> ▸ Boost's official documentation contains many more examples and shows more advanced features of `Boost.ProgramOptions`, such as position-dependent options, nonconventional syntax, and more. This is available at the following link:
>
> http://www.boost.org/doc/libs/1_53_0/doc/html/program_options.html

Downloading the example code

You can download the example code files for all Packt books that you have purchased from your account at http://www.PacktPub.com. If you purchased this book elsewhere, you can visit http://www.PacktPub.com/support and register to have the files e-mailed directly to you.

Storing any value in a container/variable

If you have been programming in Java, C#, or Delphi, you will definitely miss the ability to create containers with the `Object` value type in C++. The `Object` class in those languages is a basic class for almost all types, so you are able to assign (almost) any value to it at any time. Just imagine how great it would be to have such a feature in C++:

```cpp
#include <iostream>
#include <vector>
#include <string>
#include <auto_ptr.h>

int main()
{
    typedef std::auto_ptr<Object> object_ptr;
    std::vector<object_ptr> some_values;
    some_values.push_back(new Object(10));
    some_values.push_back(new Object("Hello there"));
    some_values.push_back(new Object(std::string("Wow!")));
    std::string* p =
        dynamic_cast<std::string*>(some_values.back().get());
    assert(p);

    (*p) += " That is great!\n";
    std::cout << *p;
    return 0;
}
```

Getting ready

We'll be working with the header-only library. Basic knowledge of C++ is all you need for this recipe.

How to do it...

In such cases, Boost offers a solution, the `Boost.Any` library, which has an even better syntax:

```cpp
#include <boost/any.hpp>
#include <iostream>
#include <vector>
#include <string>
```

```
int main()
{
    std::vector<boost::any> some_values;
    some_values.push_back(10);
    const char* c_str = "Hello there!";
    some_values.push_back(c_str);
    some_values.push_back(std::string("Wow!"));
    std::string& s =
        boost::any_cast<std::string&>(some_values.back());
    s += " That is great!\n";
    std::cout << s;
    return 0;
}
```

Great, isn't it? By the way, it has an empty state, which could be checked using the `empty()` member function (just as in STL containers).

You can get the value from `boost::any` using two approaches:

```
boost::any variable(std::string("Hello world!"));

//#1: Following method may throw a boost::bad_any_cast exception
// if actual value in variable is not a std::string
std::string s1 = boost::any_cast<std::string>(variable);

//#2: If actual value in variable is not a std::string
// will return an NULL pointer
std::string* s2 = boost::any_cast<std::string>(&variable);
```

How it works...

The `boost::any` class just stores any value in it. To achieve this it uses the **type erasure** technique (close to what Java or C# does with all of its types). To use this library, you do not really need to know its internal implementation, so let's just have a quick glance at the type erasure technique. `Boost.Any`, on assignment of some variable of type `T`, constructs a type (let's call it `holder<T>`) that may store a value of the specified type `T`, and is derived from some internal base-type placeholder. A placeholder has virtual functions for getting `std::type_info` of a stored type and for cloning a stored type. When `any_cast<T>()` is used, `boost::any` checks that `std::type_info` of a stored value is equal to `typeid(T)` (the overloaded placeholder's function is used for getting `std::type_info`).

There's more...

Such flexibility never comes without a cost. Copy constructing, value constructing, copy assigning, and assigning values to instances of `boost::any` will call a dynamic memory allocation function; all of the type casts need to get **runtime type information** (**RTTI**); `boost::any` uses virtual functions a lot. If you are keen on performance, see the next recipe, which will give you an idea of how to achieve almost the same results without dynamic allocations and RTTI usage.

Another disadvantage of `Boost.Any` is that it cannot be used with RTTI disabled. There is a possibility to make this library usable even with RTTI disabled, but it is not currently implemented.

> Almost all exceptions in Boost derive from the `std::exception` class or from its derivatives, for example, `boost::bad_any_cast` is derived from `std::bad_cast`. It means that you can catch almost all Boost exceptions using `catch (const std::exception& e)`.

See also

- ▸ Boost's official documentation may give you some more examples, and it can be found at `http://www.boost.org/doc/libs/1_53_0/doc/html/any.html`

- ▸ The *Using a safer way to work with a container that stores multiple chosen types* recipe for more info on the topic

Storing multiple chosen types in a variable/ container

Are you aware of the concept of unrestricted unions in C++11? Let me tell you about it in short. **C++03 unions** can only hold extremely simple types of data called POD (plain old data). So in C++03, you cannot, for example, store std::string or std::vector in a union. C++11 relaxes this requirement, but you'll have to manage the construction and destruction of such types by yourself, call in-place construction/destruction, and remember what type is stored in a union. A huge amount of work, isn't it?

Getting ready

We'll be working with the header-only library, which is simple to use. Basic knowledge of C++ is all you need for this recipe.

How to do it...

Let me introduce the Boost.Variant library to you.

1. The Boost.Variant library can store any of the types specified at compile time; it also manages in-place construction/destruction and doesn't even require the C++11 standard:

```cpp
#include <boost/variant.hpp>
#include <iostream>
#include <vector>
#include <string>

int main()
{
    typedef boost::variant<int, const char*, std::string>
      my_var_t;
    std::vector<my_var_t> some_values;
    some_values.push_back(10);
    some_values.push_back("Hello there!");
    some_values.push_back(std::string("Wow!"));
    std::string& s = boost::get<std::string>(some_values.back());
    s += " That is great!\n";
    std::cout << s;
    return 0;
}
```

   Great, isn't it?

2. Boost.Variant has no empty state, but has an empty() function, which always returns false. If you do need to represent an empty state, just add some trivial type at the first position of the types supported by the Boost.Variant library. When Boost.Variant contains that type, interpret it as an empty state. Here is an example in which we will use a boost::blank type to represent an empty state:

```
typedef boost::variant<boost::blank, int, const char*,
        std::string> my_var_t;
// Default constructor will construct an
// instance of boost::blank
my_var_t var;
// 'which()' method returns an index of a type,
// currently held by variant.
assert(var.which() == 0); // Empty state
var = "Hello, dear reader";
assert(var.which() != 0);
```

3. You can get a value from a variant using two approaches:

```
boost::variant<int, std::string> variable(0);
// Following method may throw a boost::bad_get
// exception if actual value in variable is not an int
int s1 = boost::get<int>(variable);
// If actual value in variable is not an int
// will return an NULL pointer
int* s2 = boost::get<int>(&variable);
```

How it works...

The boost::variant class holds an array of characters and stores values in that array. Size of the array is determined at compile time using sizeof() and functions to get alignment. On assignment or construction of boost::variant, the previous values are in-place destroyed, and new values are constructed on top of the character array using the new placement.

There's more...

The Boost.Variant variables usually do not allocate memory in a heap, and they do not require RTTI to be enabled. Boost.Variant is extremely fast and used widely by other Boost libraries. To achieve maximum performance, make sure that there is a trivial type in the list of supported types, and that this type is at the first position.

 Boost.Variant is not a part of the C++11 standard.

- The *Using a safer way to work with a container that stores multiple chosen types* recipe

- Boost's official documentation contains more examples and descriptions of some other features of `Boost.Variant`, and can be found at:

  `http://www.boost.org/doc/libs/1_53_0/doc/html/variant.html`

Using a safer way to work with a container that stores multiple chosen types

Imagine that you are creating a wrapper around some SQL database interface. You decided that `boost::any` will perfectly match the requirements for a single cell of the database table. Some other programmer will be using your classes, and his task would be to get a row from the database and count the sum of the arithmetic types in a row.

Here's how the code would look:

```
#include <boost/any.hpp>
#include <vector>
#include <string>
#include <typeinfo>
#include <algorithm>
#include <iostream>

// This typedefs and methods will be in our header,
// that wraps around native SQL interface
typedef boost::any cell_t;
typedef std::vector<cell_t> db_row_t;

// This is just an example, no actual work with database.
db_row_t get_row(const char* /*query*/) {
    // In real application 'query' parameter shall have a 'const
    // char*' or 'const std::string&' type? See recipe Using a
    // reference to string type in Chapter 7, Manipulating Strings
    // for an answer.
    db_row_t row;
    row.push_back(10);
    row.push_back(10.1f);
    row.push_back(std::string("hello again"));
    return row;
}
```

```
// This is how a user will use your classes
struct db_sum: public std::unary_function<boost::any, void> {
private:
    double& sum_;
public:
    explicit db_sum(double& sum)
        : sum_(sum)
    {}

    void operator()(const cell_t& value) {
        const std::type_info& ti = value.type();
        if (ti == typeid(int)) {
            sum_ += boost::any_cast<int>(value);
        } else if (ti == typeid(float)) {
            sum_ += boost::any_cast<float>(value);
        }
    }
};

int main()
{
    db_row_t row = get_row("Query: Give me some row, please.");
    double res = 0.0;
    std::for_each(row.begin(), row.end(), db_sum(res));
    std::cout << "Sum of arithmetic types in database row is: " << res
<< std::endl;
    return 0;
}
```

If you compile and run this example, it will output a correct answer:

```
Sum of arithmetic types in database row is: 20.1
```

Do you remember what your thoughts were when reading the implementation of `operator()`? I guess they were, "And what about double, long, short, unsigned, and other types?". The same thoughts will come to the mind of a programmer who will use your interface. So you'll need to carefully document values stored by your `cell_t`, or read the more elegant solution described in the following sections.

Getting ready

Reading the previous two recipes is highly recommended if you are not already familiar with the `Boost.Variant` and `Boost.Any` libraries.

How to do it...

The `Boost.Variant` library implements a visitor programming pattern for accessing the stored data, which is much safer than getting values via `boost::get<>`. This pattern forces the programmer to take care of each variant type, otherwise the code will fail to compile. You can use this pattern via the `boost::apply_visitor` function, which takes a visitor functional object as the first parameter and a variant as the second parameter. Visitor functional objects must derive from the `boost::static_visitor<T>` class, where `T` is a type being returned by a visitor. A visitor object must have overloads of `operator()` for each type stored by a variant.

Let's change the `cell_t` type to `boost::variant<int, float, string>` and modify our example:

```
#include <boost/variant.hpp>
#include <vector>
#include <string>
#include <iostream>

// This typedefs and methods will be in header,
// that wraps around native SQL interface.
typedef boost::variant<int, float, std::string> cell_t;
typedef std::vector<cell_t> db_row_t;

// This is just an example, no actual work with database.
db_row_t get_row(const char* /*query*/) {
    // See the recipe "Using a reference to string type"
    // in Chapter 7, Manipulating Strings
    // for a better type for 'query' parameter.
    db_row_t row;
    row.push_back(10);
    row.push_back(10.1f);
    row.push_back("hello again");
    return row;
}


// This is how code required to sum values
// We can provide no template parameter
// to boost::static_visitor<> if our visitor returns nothing.
struct db_sum_visitor: public boost::static_visitor<double> {
    double operator()(int value) const {
        return value;
    }
```

```
        double operator()(float value) const {
            return value;
        }
        double operator()(const std::string& /*value*/) const {
            return 0.0;
        }
    };

    int main()
    {
        db_row_t row = get_row("Query: Give me some row, please.");
        double res = 0.0;
        db_row_t::const_iterator it = row.begin(), end = row.end();
        for (; it != end; ++it) {
            res += boost::apply_visitor(db_sum_visitor(), *it);
        }
        std::cout << "Sum of arithmetic types in database row is: "
                  << res << std::endl;
        return 0;
    }
```

How it works...

The `Boost.Variant` library will generate a big `switch` statement at compile time, each case of `which` will call a visitor for a single type from the variant's list of types. At runtime, the index of the stored type can be retrieved using `which()`, and a jump to the correct case in the switch will be made. Something like this will be generated for `boost::variant<int, float, std::string>`:

```
    switch (which())
    {
    case 0: return visitor(*reinterpret_cast<int*>(address()));
    case 1: return visitor(*reinterpret_cast<float*>(address()));
    case 2: return visitor(*reinterpret_cast<std::string*>(address()));
    default: assert(false);
    }
```

Here, the `address()` function returns a pointer to the internal storage of `boost::variant<int, float, std::string>`.

There's more...

If we compare this example with the first example in this recipe, we'll see the following advantages of `boost::variant`:

 ▸ We know what types a variable can store

 ▸ If a library writer of the SQL interface adds or modifies a type held by a variant, we'll get a compile-time error instead of incorrect behavior

See also

 ▸ After reading some recipes from *Chapter 4, Compile-time Tricks*, you'll be able to make the visitor object so generic that it will be able to work correctly even if the underlying types change

 ▸ Boost's official documentation contains more examples and a description of some other features of `Boost.Variant`, and is available at the following link:

    `http://www.boost.org/doc/libs/1_53_0/doc/html/variant.html`

Returning a value or flag where there is no value

Imagine that we have a function that does not throw an exception and returns a value or indicates that an error has occurred. In Java or C# programming languages, such cases are handled by comparing a return value from a function value with a null pointer; if it is null then an error has occurred. In C++, returning a pointer from a function confuses library users and usually requires dynamic memory allocation (which is slow).

Getting ready

Only basic knowledge of C++ is required for this recipe.

How to do it...

Ladies and gentlemen, let me introduce you to the `Boost.Optional` library using the following example:

The `try_lock_device()` function tries to acquire a lock for a device, and may succeed or not depending on different conditions (in our example it depends on the `rand()` function call). The function returns an optional variable that can be converted to a Boolean variable. If the returned value is equal to Boolean `true`, then the lock is acquired, and an instance of a class to work with the device can be obtained by dereferencing the returned optional variable:

```cpp
#include <boost/optional.hpp>
#include <iostream>
#include <stdlib.h>

class locked_device {
    explicit locked_device(const char* /*param*/) {
        // We have unique access to device
        std::cout << "Device is locked\n";
    }
public:
    ~locked_device () {
        // Releasing device lock
    }

    void use() {
        std::cout << "Success!\n";
    }
    static boost::optional<locked_device> try_lock_device() {
        if (rand()%2) {
            // Failed to lock device
            return boost::none;
        }
        // Success!
        return locked_device("device name");
    }
};

int main()
{
    // Boost has a library called Random. If you wonder why it was
    // written when stdlib.h has rand() function, see the recipe
    // "Using a true random number generator in Chapter 12,
    // Scratching the Tip of the Iceberg
    srandom(5);
```

```
    for (unsigned i = 0; i < 10; ++i) {
        boost::optional<locked_device> t
                    = locked_device::try_lock_device();
        // optional is convertible to bool
        if (t) {
            t->use();
            return 0;
        } else {
            std::cout << "...trying again\n";
        }
    }
    std::cout << "Failure!\n";
    return -1;
}
```

This program will output the following:

```
...trying again
...trying again
Device is locked
Success!
```

 The default constructed optional variable is convertible to a Boolean variable holding false and must not be dereferenced, because it does not have an underlying type constructed.

How it works...

The Boost.Optional class is very close to the boost::variant class but for only one type, boost::optional<T> has an array of chars, where the object of type T can be an in-place constructor. It also has a Boolean variable to remember the state of the object (is it constructed or not).

There's more...

The Boost.Optional class does not use dynamic allocation, and it does not require a default constructor for the underlying type. It is fast and considered for inclusion in the next standard of C++. The current boost::optional implementation cannot work with C++11 **rvalue** references; however, there are some patches proposed to fix that.

The C++11 standard does not include the Boost.Optional class; however, it is currently being reviewed for inclusion in the next C++ standard or in C++14.

See also

▶ Boost's official documentation contains more examples and describes advanced features of Boost.Optional (like in-place construction using the factory functions). The documentation is available at the following link:

```
http://www.boost.org/doc/libs/1_53_0/libs/optional/doc/html/
index.html
```

Returning an array from a function

Let's play a guessing game! What can you tell about the following function?

```
char* vector_advance(char* val);
```

Should return values be deallocated by the programmer or not? Does the function attempt to deallocate the input parameter? Should the input parameter be zero-terminated, or should the function assume that the input parameter has a specified width?

And now, let's make the task harder! Take a look at the following line:

```
char ( &vector_advance( char (&val)[4] ) )[4];
```

Please do not worry; I've also been scratching my head for half an hour before getting an idea of what is happening here. vector_advance is a function that accepts and returns an array of four elements. Is there a way to write such a function clearly?

Getting ready

Only basic knowledge of C++ is required for this recipe.

How to do it...

We can rewrite the function like this:

```
#include <boost/array.hpp>
typedef boost::array<char, 4> array4_t;
array4_t& vector_advance(array4_t& val);
```

Here, boost::array<char, 4> is just a simple wrapper around an array of four char elements.

This code answers all of the questions from our first example and is much more readable than the second example.

How it works...

The first template parameter of `boost::array` is the element type, and the second one is the size of an array. `boost::array` is a fixed-size array; if you need to change the array size at runtime, use `std::vector` or `boost::container::vector` instead.

The `Boost.Array` library just contains an array in it. That is all. Simple and efficient. The `boost::array<>` class has no handwritten constructors and all of its members are public, so the compiler will think of it as a POD type.

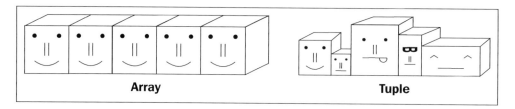

Array   **Tuple**

There's more...

Let's see some more examples of the usage of `boost::array`:

```
#include <boost/array.hpp>
#include <algorithm>

// Functional object to increment value by one
struct add_1 : public std::unary_function<char, void> {
    void operator()(char& c) const {
        ++ c;
    }
    // If you're not in a mood to write functional objects,
    // but don't know what does 'boost::bind(std::plus<char>(),
    // _1, 1)' do, then read recipe 'Binding a value as a function
    // parameter'.
};

typedef boost::array<char, 4> array4_t;
array4_t& vector_advance(array4_t& val) {
    // boost::array has begin(), cbegin(), end(), cend(),
    // rbegin(), size(), empty() and other functions that are
    // common for STL containers.
    std::for_each(val.begin(), val.end(), add_1());
    return val;
}
```

```
int main() {
    // We can initialize boost::array just like an array in C++11:
    // array4_t val = {0, 1, 2, 3};
    // but in C++03 additional pair of curly brackets is required.
    array4_t val = {{0, 1, 2, 3}};

    // boost::array works like a usual array:
    array4_t val_res;          // it can be default constructible and
    val_res = vector_advance(val);   // assignable
    // if value type supports default construction and assignment

    assert(val.size() == 4);
    assert(val[0] == 1);
    /*val[4];*/ // Will trigger an assert because max index is 3
    // We can make this assert work at compile-time.
    // Interested? See recipe 'Checking sizes at compile time'
    // in Chapter 4, Compile-time Tricks.'
    assert(sizeof(val) == sizeof(char) * array4_t::static_size);
    return 0;
}
```

One of the biggest advantages of `boost::array` is that it provides exactly the same performance as a normal C array. People from the C++ standard committee also liked it, so it was accepted to the C++11 standard. There is a chance that your STL library already has it (you may try to include the `<array>` header and check for the availability of `std::array<>`).

See also

- Boost's official documentation gives a complete list of the `Boost.Array` methods with a description of the method's complexity and throw behavior, and is available at the following link:

  `http://www.boost.org/doc/libs/1_53_0/doc/html/boost/array.html`

- The `boost::array` function is widely used across recipes; for example, refer to the *Binding a value as a function parameter* recipe

Combining multiple values into one

There is a very nice present for those who like `std::pair`. Boost has a library called `Boost.Tuple`, and it is just like `std::pair`, but it can also work with triples, quads, and even bigger collections of types.

Getting ready

Only basic knowledge of C++ and STL is required for this recipe.

How to do it...

Perform the following steps to combine multiple values in to one:

1. To start working with tuples, you need to include a proper header and declare a variable:

    ```
    #include <boost/tuple/tuple.hpp>
    #include <string>

    boost::tuple<int, std::string> almost_a_pair(10, "Hello");
    boost::tuple<int, float, double, int> quad(10, 1.0f, 10.0, 1);
    ```

2. Getting a specific value is implemented via the `boost::get<N>()` function, where `N` is a zero-based index of a required value:

    ```
    int i = boost::get<0>(almost_a_pair);
    const std::string& str = boost::get<1>(almost_a_pair);
    double d = boost::get<2>(quad);
    ```

    The `boost::get<>` function has many overloads and is used widely across Boost. We have already seen how it can be used with other libraries in the *Storing multiple chosen types in a container/variable* recipe.

3. You can construct tuples using the `boost::make_tuple()` function, which is shorter to write, because you do not need to fully qualify the tuple type:

    ```
    using namespace boost;

    // Tuple comparison operators are
    // defined in header "boost/tuple/tuple_comparison.hpp"
    // Don't forget to include it!
    std::set<tuple<int, double, int> > s;
    s.insert(make_tuple(1, 1.0, 2));
    s.insert(make_tuple(2, 10.0, 2));
    s.insert(make_tuple(3, 100.0, 2));
    ```

```
// Requires C++11
auto t = make_tuple(0, -1.0, 2);
assert(2 == get<2>(t));
// We can make a compile-time assert for type
// of t. Interested? See chapter 'compile-time tricks'
```

4. Another function that makes life easy is `boost::tie()`. It works almost as `make_tuple`, but adds a nonconst reference for each of the passed types. Such a tuple can be used to get values to a variable from another tuple. It can be better understood from the following example:

```
boost::tuple<int, float, double, int> quad(10, 1.0f, 10.0, 1);
int i;
float f;
double d;
int i2;

// Passing values from 'quad' variables
// to variables 'i', 'f', 'd', 'i2'
boost::tie(i, f, d, i2) = quad;
assert(i == 10);
assert(i2 == 1);
```

How it works...

Some readers may wonder why we need a tuple when we can always write our own structures with better names, for example, instead of writing `boost::tuple<int, std::string>`, we can create a structure:

```
struct id_name_pair {
    int id;
    std::string name;
};
```

Well, this structure is definitely more clear than `boost::tuple<int, std::string>`. But what if this structure is used only twice in the code?

The main idea behind the tuple's library is to simplify template programming.

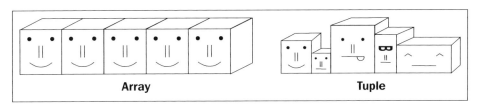

Array   **Tuple**

There's more...

A tuple works as fast as `std::pair` (it does not allocate memory on a heap and has no virtual functions). The C++ committee found this class to be very useful and it was included in STL; you can find it in a C++11-compatible STL implementation in the header file `<tuple>` (don't forget to replace all the `boost::` namespaces with `std::`).

The current Boost implementation of a tuple does not use variadic templates; it is just a set of classes generated by a script. There is an experimental version that uses C++11 rvalues and an emulation of them on C++03 compilers, so there is a chance that Boost 1.54 will be shipped with faster implementation of tuples.

See also

  ▶ The experimental version of tuples can be found at the following link:

      `http://svn.boost.org/svn/boost/sandbox/tuple-move/`

  ▶ Boost's official documentation contains more examples, information about performance, and abilities of `Boost.Tuple`. It is available at the following link:

      `http://www.boost.org/doc/libs/1_53_0/libs/tuple/doc/tuple_users_guide.html`

  ▶ The *Converting all tuple elements to strings* recipe in *Chapter 8, Metaprogramming,* shows some advanced usages of tuples

Reordering the parameters of function

This recipe and the next one are devoted to a very interesting library, whose functionality at first glance looks like some kind of magic. This library is called `Boost.Bind` and it allows you to easily create new functional objects from functions, member functions, and functional objects, also allowing the reordering of the initial function's input parameters and binding some values or references as function parameters.

Getting ready

Knowledge of C++, STL algorithms, and functional objects is required for this recipe.

How to do it...

  1. Let's start with an example. You are working with a vector of integral types provided by some other programmer. That integral type has only one operator, `+`, but your task is to multiply a value by two. Without `bind` this can be achieved with the use of a functional object:

```
class Number{};
inline Number operator + (Number, Number);

// Your code starts here
struct mul_2_func_obj: public std::unary_function<Number, Number>
{
    Number operator()(Number n1) const {
        return n1 + n1;
    }
};

void mul_2_impl1(std::vector<Number>& values) {
    std::for_each(values.begin(), values.end(), mul_2_func_obj());
}
```

With `Boost.Bind`, it would be as follows:

```
#include <boost/bind.hpp>
#include <functional>

void mul_2_impl2(std::vector<Number>& values) {
    std::for_each(values.begin(), values.end(),
        boost::bind(std::plus<Number>(), _1, _1));
}
```

2. By the way, we can easily make this function more generic:

```
template <class T>
void mul_2_impl3(std::vector<T>& values) {
    std::for_each(values.begin(), values.end(),
        boost::bind(std::plus<T>(), _1, _1));
}
```

How it works...

Let's take a closer look at the `mul_2` function. We provide a vector of values to it, and for each value it applies a functional object returned by the `bind()` function. The `bind()` function takes in three parameters; the first parameter is an instance of the `std::plus<Number>` class (which is a functional object). The second and third parameters are placeholders. The placeholder `_1` substitutes the argument with the first input argument of the resulting functional object. As you might guess, there are many placeholders; placeholder `_2` means substituting the argument with the second input argument of the resulting functional object, and the same also applies to placeholder `_3`. Well, seems you've got the idea.

There's more...

Just to make sure that you've got the whole idea and know where bind can be used, let's take a look at another example.

We have two classes, which work with some sensor devices. The devices and classes are from different vendors, so they provide different APIs. Both classes have only one public method `watch`, which accepts a functional object:

```
class Device1 {
private:
    short temperature();
    short wetness();
    int illumination();
    int atmospheric_pressure();
    void wait_for_data();
public:
    template <class FuncT>
    void watch(const FuncT& f) {
        for(;;) {
            wait_for_data();
            f(
                temperature(),
                wetness(),
                illumination(),
                atmospheric_pressure()
            );
        }
    }
};

class Device2 {
private:
    short temperature();
    short wetness();
    int illumination();
    int atmospheric_pressure();
    void wait_for_data();
public:
    template <class FuncT>
    void watch(const FuncT& f) {
        for(;;) {
```

```
            wait_for_data();
            f(
                wetness(),
                temperature(),
                atmospheric_pressure(),
                illumination()
            );
        }
    }
};
```

The `Device1::watch` and `Device2::watch` functions pass values to a functional object in a different order.

Some other libraries provide a function, which is used to detect storms, and throws an exception when the risk of a storm is high enough:

```
void detect_storm(int wetness, int temperature, int atmospheric_
pressure);
```

Your task is to provide a storm-detecting function to both of the devices. Here is how it can be achieved using the `bind` function:

```
        Device1 d1;
        // resulting functional object will silently ignore
        // additional parameters passed to function call
        d1.watch(boost::bind(&detect_storm, _2, _1, _4));
        ...
        Device2 d2;
        d2.watch(boost::bind(&detect_storm, _1, _2, _3));
```

The `Boost.Bind` library provides good performance because it does not use dynamic allocations and virtual functions. It is useful even when the C++11 lambda functions are not usable:

```
template <class FuncT>
void watch(const FuncT& f) {
    f(10, std::string("String"));
    f(10, "Char array");
    f(10, 10);
}

struct templated_foo {
    template <class T>
```

```
        void operator()(T, int) const {
            // No implementation, just showing that bound
            // functions still can be used as templated
        }
    };

    void check_templated_bind() {
        // We can directly specify return type of a functional object
        // when bind fails to do so
        watch(boost::bind<void>(templated_foo(), _2, _1));
    }
```

Bind is a part of the C++11 standard. It is defined in the `<functional>` header and may slightly differ from the `Boost.Bind` implementation (however, it will be at least as effective as Boost's implementation).

See also

  ▶   The *Binding a value as a function parameter* recipe says more about the features of `Boost.Bind`

  ▶   Boost's official documentation contains many more examples and descriptions of advanced features. It is available at the following link:

      `http://www.boost.org/doc/libs/1_53_0/libs/bind/bind.html`

Binding a value as a function parameter

If you work with the STL library a lot and use the `<algorithm>` header, you will definitely write a lot of functional objects. You can construct them using a set of STL adapter functions such as `bind1st`, `bind2nd`, `ptr_fun`, `mem_fun`, and `mem_fun_ref`, or you can write them by hand (because adapter functions look scary). Here is some good news: `Boost.Bind` can be used instead of all of those functions and it provides a more human-readable syntax.

Getting ready

Read the previous recipe to get an idea of placeholders, or just make sure that you are familiar with C++11 placeholders. Knowledge of STL functions and algorithms is welcomed.

How to do it...

Let's see some examples of the usage of `Boost.Bind` along with traditional STL classes:

  1.   Count values greater than or equal to 5 as shown in the following code:

```
boost::array<int, 12> values
    = {{1, 2, 3, 4, 5, 6, 7, 100, 99, 98, 97, 96}};

std::size_t count0 = std::count_if(values.begin(), values.end(),
    std::bind1st(std::less<int>(), 5));
std::size_t count1 = std::count_if(values.begin(), values.end(),
    boost::bind(std::less<int>(), 5, _1));
assert(count0 == count1);
```

2. This is how we could count empty strings:

```
boost::array<std::string, 3>  str_values
    = {{"We ", "are", " the champions!"}};
count0 = std::count_if(str_values.begin(), str_values.end(),
    std::mem_fun_ref(&std::string::empty));
count1 = std::count_if(str_values.begin(), str_values.end(),
    boost::bind(&std::string::empty, _1));
assert(count0 == count1);
```

3. Now let's count strings with a length less than 5:

```
// That code won't compile! And it is hard to understand
//count0 = std::count_if(str_values.begin(),
//str_values.end(),
//std::bind2nd(
//    std::bind1st(
//        std::less<std::size_t>(),
//        std::mem_fun_ref(&std::string::size)
//    )
//, 5
//));
// This will become much more readable,
// when you get used to bind
count1 = std::count_if(str_values.begin(), str_values.end(),
    boost::bind(std::less<std::size_t>(),
    boost::bind(&std::string::size, _1), 5));
assert(2 == count1);
```

4. Compare the strings:

```
std::string s("Expensive copy constructor of std::string will be
called when binding");
count0 = std::count_if(str_values.begin(), str_values.end(),
    std::bind2nd(std::less<std::string>(), s));
count1 = std::count_if(str_values.begin(), str_values.end(),
    boost::bind(std::less<std::string>(), _1, s));
assert(count0 == count1);
```

How it works...

The `boost::bind` function returns a functional object that stores a copy of the bound values and a copy of the original functional object. When the actual call to `operator()` is performed, the stored parameters are passed to the original functional object along with the parameters passed at the time of call.

There's more...

Take a look at the previous examples. When we are binding values, we copy a value into a functional object. For some classes this operation is expensive. Is there a way to bypass copying?

Yes, there is! And the `Boost.Ref` library will help us here! It contains two functions, `boost::ref()` and `boost::cref()`, the first of which allows us to pass a parameter as a reference, and the second one passes the parameter as a constant reference. The `ref()` and `cref()` functions just construct an object of type `reference_wrapper<T>` or `reference_wrapper<const T>`, which is implicitly convertible to a reference type. Let's change our previous examples:

```
#include <boost/ref.hpp>
...
std::string s("Expensive copy constructor of std::string now "
              "won't be called when binding");
count0 = std::count_if(str_values.begin(), str_values.end(),
        std::bind2nd(std::less<std::string>(), boost::cref(s)));
count1 = std::count_if(str_values.begin(), str_values.end(),
        boost::bind(std::less<std::string>(), _1, boost::cref(s)));
assert(count0 == count1);
```

Just one more example to show you how `boost::ref` can be used to concatenate strings:

```
void wierd_appender(std::string& to, const std::string& from) {
    to += from;
};

std::string result;
std::for_each(str_values.cbegin(), str_values.cend(),
boost::bind(&wierd_appender, boost::ref(result), _1));
assert(result == "We are the champions!");
```

The functions `ref` and `cref` (and `bind`) are accepted to the C++11 standard and defined in the `<functional>` header in the `std::` namespace. None of these functions dynamically allocate memory in the heap and they do not use virtual functions. The objects returned by them are easy to optimize and they do not apply any optimization barriers for good compilers.

STL implementations of those functions may have additional optimizations to reduce compilation time or just compiler-specific optimizations, but unfortunately, some STL implementations miss the functionality of Boost versions. You may use the STL version of those functions with any Boost library, or even mix Boost and STL versions.

See also

▶ The `Boost.Bind` library is used widely across this book; see *Chapter 6, Manipulating Tasks*, and *Chapter 5, Multithreading*, for more examples

▶ The official documentation contains many more examples and a description of advanced features at `http://www.boost.org/doc/libs/1_53_0/libs/bind/bind.html`

Using the C++11 move emulation

One of the greatest features of the C++11 standard is rvalue references. This feature allows us to modify temporary objects, "stealing" resources from them. As you can guess, the C++03 standard has no rvalue references, but using the `Boost.Move` library you can write some portable code that uses them, and even more, you actually get started with the emulation of move semantics.

Getting ready

It is highly recommended to at least know the basics of C++11 rvalue references.

How to do it...

Now, let's take a look at the following examples:

1. Imagine that you have a class with multiple fields, some of which are STL containers.

```
namespace other {
    // Its default construction is cheap/fast
    class characteristics{};
} // namespace other

struct person_info {
    // Fields declared here
    // ...
    bool is_male_;
    std::string name_;
    std::string second_name_;
    other::characteristics characteristic_;
};
```

2. It is time to add the move assignment and move constructors to it! Just remember that in C++03, STL containers have neither move operators nor move constructors.

3. The correct implementation of the move assignment is the same as `swap` and `clear` (if an empty state is allowed). The correct implementation of the move constructor is close to the default construct and `swap`. So, let's start with the `swap` member function:

```cpp
#include <boost/swap.hpp>

    void swap(person_info& rhs) {
        std::swap(is_male_, rhs.is_male_);
        name_.swap(rhs.name_);
        second_name_.swap(rhs.second_name_);
        boost::swap(characteristic_, rhs.characteristic_);
    }
```

4. Now put the following macro in the `private` section:

```cpp
BOOST_COPYABLE_AND_MOVABLE(classname)
```

5. Write a copy constructor.

6. Write a copy assignment, taking the parameter as BOOST_COPY_ASSIGN_REF(classname).

7. Write a move constructor and a move assignment, taking the parameter as BOOST_RV_REF(classname):

```cpp
struct person_info {
    // Fields declared here
    // ...
private:
    BOOST_COPYABLE_AND_MOVABLE(person_info)
public:
    // For the simplicity of example we will assume that
    // person_info default constructor and swap are very
    // fast/cheap to call
    person_info() {}

    person_info(const person_info& p)
        : is_male_(p.is_male_)
        , name_(p.name_)
        , second_name_(p.second_name_)
        , characteristic_(p.characteristic_)
    {}

    person_info(BOOST_RV_REF(person_info) person) {
        swap(person);
    }

    person_info& operator=(BOOST_COPY_ASSIGN_REF(person_info)
person) {
        if (this != &person) {
```

```
                person_info tmp(person);
                swap(tmp);
            }
        return *this;
    }

    person_info& operator=(BOOST_RV_REF(person_info) person) {
        if (this != &person) {
            swap(person);
            person_info tmp;
            tmp.swap(person);
        }
        return *this;
    }

    void swap(person_info& rhs) {
    // …
    }

};
```

8. Now we have a portable, fast implementation of the move assignment and move construction operators of the `person_info` class.

How it works...

Here is an example of how the move assignment can be used:

```
    person_info vasya;
    vasya.name_ = "Vasya";
    vasya.second_name_ = "Snow";
    vasya.is_male_ = true;

    person_info new_vasya(boost::move(vasya));
    assert(new_vasya.name_ == "Vasya");
    assert(new_vasya.second_name_ == "Snow");
    assert(vasya.name_.empty());
    assert(vasya.second_name_.empty());

    vasya = boost::move(new_vasya);
    assert(vasya.name_ == "Vasya");
    assert(vasya.second_name_ == "Snow");
    assert(new_vasya.name_.empty());
    assert(new_vasya.second_name_.empty());
```

The `Boost.Move` library is implemented in a very efficient way. When the C++11 compiler is used, all the macros for rvalues emulation will be expanded to C++11-specific features, otherwise (on C++03 compilers) rvalues will be emulated using specific datatypes and functions that never copy passed values nor called any dynamic memory allocations or virtual functions.

There's more...

Have you noticed the `boost::swap` call? It is a really helpful utility function, which will first search for a `swap` function in the namespace of a variable (the namespace `other::`), and if there is no swap function for the `characteristics` class, it will use the STL implementation of swap.

See also

▸ More information about emulation implementation can be found on the Boost website and in the sources of the `Boost.Move` library at `http://www.boost.org/doc/libs/1_53_0/doc/html/move.html`.

▸ The `Boost.Utility` library is the one that contains `boost::utility`, and it has many useful functions and classes. Refer to its documentation at `http://www.boost.org/doc/libs/1_53_0/libs/utility/utility.htm`.

▸ The *Initializing the base class by the member of the derived* recipe in *Chapter 3, Managing Resources*.

▸ The *Making a noncopyable class* recipe.

▸ In the *Making a noncopyable but movable class* recipe, there is more info about `Boost.Move` and some examples on how we can use the movable objects in containers in a portable and efficient way.

Making a noncopyable class

You must have almost certainly encountered situations where providing a copy constructor and move assignment operator for a class will require too much work, or where a class owns some resources that must not be copied for technical reasons:

```
class descriptor_owner {
    void* descriptor_;

public:
    explicit descriptor_owner(const char* params);

    ~descriptor_owner() {
        system_api_free_descriptor(descriptor_);
    }
};
```

The C++ compiler, in the case of the previous example, will generate a copy constructor and an assignment operator, so the potential user of the `descriptor_owner` class will be able to create the following awful things:

```
descriptor_owner d1("O_o");
descriptor_owner d2("^_^");

// Descriptor of d2 was not correctly freed
d2 = d1;

// destructor of d2 will free the descriptor
// destructor of d1 will try to free already freed descriptor
```

Getting ready

Only very basic knowledge of C++ is required for this recipe.

How to do it...

To avoid such situations, the `boost::noncopyable` class was invented. If you derive your own class from it, the copy constructor and assignment operator won't be generated by the C++ compiler:

```
#include <boost/noncopyable.hpp>

class descriptor_owner_fixed : private boost::noncopyable {
    ...
```

Now the user won't be able to do bad things:

```
descriptor_owner_fixed d1("O_o");
descriptor_owner_fixed d2("^_^");
// Won't compile
d2 = d1;
// Won't compile either
descriptor_owner_fixed d3(d1);
```

How it works...

A sophisticated reader will tell me that we can achieve exactly the same result by making a copy constructor and an assignment operator of `descriptor_owning_fixed` private, or just by defining them without actual implementation. Yes, you are correct. Moreover, this is the current implementation of the `boost::noncopyable` class. But `boost::noncopyable` also serves as good documentation for your class. It never raises questions such as "Is the copy constructor body defined elsewhere?" or "Does it have a nonstandard copy constructor (with a nonconst referenced parameter)?".

▸ The *Making a noncopyable but movable class* recipe will give you ideas on how to allow unique ownership of a resource in C++03 by moving it

▸ You may find a lot of helpful functions and classes in the `Boost.Utility` library's official documentation at `http://www.boost.org/doc/libs/1_53_0/libs/utility/utility.htm`

▸ The *Initializing the base class by the member of the derived* recipe in *Chapter 3, Managing Resources*

▸ The *Using the C++11 move emulation* recipe

Making a noncopyable but movable class

Now imagine the following situation: we have a resource that cannot be copied, which should be correctly freed in a destructor, and we want to return it from a function:

```
descriptor_owner construct_descriptor() {
    return descriptor_owner("Construct using this string");
}
```

Actually, you can work around such situations using the `swap` method:

```
void construct_descriptor1(descriptor_owner& ret) {
    descriptor_owner("Construct using this string").swap(ret);
}
```

But such a workaround won't allow us to use `descriptor_owner` in STL or Boost containers. And by the way, it looks awful!

Getting ready

It is highly recommended to know at least the basics of C++11 rvalue references. Reading the *Using the C++11 move emulation* recipe is also recommended.

How to do it...

Those readers who use C++11 already know about the move-only classes (like `std::unique_ptr` or `std::thread`). Using such an approach, we can make a move-only `descriptor_owner` class:

```
class descriptor_owner1 {
    void* descriptor_;
```

```cpp
public:
    descriptor_owner1()
        : descriptor_(NULL)
    {}

    explicit descriptor_owner1(const char* param)
        : descriptor_(strdup(param))
    {}

    descriptor_owner1(descriptor_owner1&& param)
        : descriptor_(param.descriptor_)
    {
        param.descriptor_ = NULL;
    }

    descriptor_owner1& operator=(descriptor_owner1&& param) {
        clear();
        std::swap(descriptor_, param.descriptor_);
        return *this;
    }

    void clear() {
        free(descriptor_);
        descriptor_ = NULL;
    }

    bool empty() const {
        return !descriptor_;
    }

    ~descriptor_owner1() {
        clear();
    }
};

// GCC compiles the following in with -std=c++0x
descriptor_owner1 construct_descriptor2() {
    return descriptor_owner1("Construct using this string");
}

void foo_rv() {
    std::cout << "C++11\n";
    descriptor_owner1 desc;
    desc = construct_descriptor2();
    assert(!desc.empty());
}
```

This will work only on C++11 compatible compilers. That is the right moment for `Boost.Move`! Let's modify our example so it can be used on C++03 compilers.

According to the documentation, to write a movable but noncopyable type in portable syntax, we need to follow these simple steps:

1. Put the `BOOST_MOVABLE_BUT_NOT_COPYABLE(classname)` macro in the `private` section:

```
class descriptor_owner_movable {
    void* descriptor_;
    BOOST_MOVABLE_BUT_NOT_COPYABLE(descriptor_owner_movable)
```

2. Write a move constructor and a move assignment, taking the parameter as `BOOST_RV_REF(classname)`:

```
#include <boost/move/move.hpp>

public:
    descriptor_owner_movable()
        : descriptor_(NULL)
    {}

    explicit descriptor_owner_movable(const char* param)
        : descriptor_(strdup(param))
    {}

    descriptor_owner_movable(
      BOOST_RV_REF(descriptor_owner_movable) param)
        : descriptor_(param.descriptor_)
    {
    param.descriptor_ = NULL;
    }

    descriptor_owner_movable& operator=(
      BOOST_RV_REF(descriptor_owner_movable) param)
    {
      clear();
      std::swap(descriptor_, param.descriptor_);
      return *this;
    }
    // ...
};

descriptor_owner_movable construct_descriptor3() {
    return descriptor_owner_movable("Construct using this
string");
}
```

How it works...

Now we have a movable but noncopyable class that can be used even on C++03 compilers and in `Boost.Containers`:

```cpp
#include <boost/container/vector.hpp>
...
    // Following code will work on C++11 and C++03 compilers
    descriptor_owner_movable movable;
    movable = construct_descriptor3();
    boost::container::vector<descriptor_owner_movable> vec;
    vec.resize(10);
    vec.push_back(construct_descriptor3());

    vec.back() = boost::move(vec.front());
```

But unfortunately, C++03 STL containers still won't be able to use it (that is why we used a vector from `Boost.Containers` in the previous example).

There's more...

If you want to use `Boost.Containers` on C++03 compilers and STL containers, on C++11 compilers you can use the following simple trick. Add the header file to your project with the following content:

```cpp
// your_project/vector.hpp
// Copyright and other stuff goes here

// include guards
#ifndef YOUR_PROJECT_VECTOR_HPP
#define YOUR_PROJECT_VECTOR_HPP

#include <boost/config.hpp>

// Those macro declared in boost/config.hpp header
// This is portable and can be used with any version of boost
// libraries
#if !defined(BOOST_NO_RVALUE_REFERENCES) && !defined(BOOST_NO_CXX11_RVALUE_REFERENCES)
// We do have rvalues
#include <vector>
```

```
namespace your_project_namespace {
  using std::vector;
} // your_project_namespace

#else
// We do NOT have rvalues
#include <boost/container/vector.hpp>

namespace your_project_namespace {
  using boost::container::vector;
} // your_project_namespace

#endif // !defined(BOOST_NO_RVALUE_REFERENCES) && !defined(BOOST_NO_
CXX11_RVALUE_REFERENCES)
#endif // YOUR_PROJECT_VECTOR_HPP
```

Now you can include `<your_project/vector.hpp>` and use a vector from the namespace `your_project_namespace`:

```
your_project_namespace::vector<descriptor_owner_movable> v;
v.resize(10);
v.push_back(construct_descriptor3());
v.back() = boost::move(v.front());
```

But beware of compiler- and STL-implementation-specific issues! For example, this code will compile on GCC 4.7 in C++11 mode only if you mark the move constructor, destructor, and move assignment operators with `noexcept`.

See also

> ▸ The *Reducing code size and increasing performance of user-defined types (UDTs) in C++11* recipe in *Chapter 10, Gathering Platform and Compiler Information*, for more info on `noexcept`

> ▸ More information about `Boost.Move` can be found on Boost's website `http://www.boost.org/doc/libs/1_53_0/doc/html/move.html`

2
Converting Data

In this chapter we will cover:

- ▸ Converting strings to numbers
- ▸ Converting numbers to strings
- ▸ Converting numbers to numbers
- ▸ Converting user-defined types to/from strings
- ▸ Casting polymorphic objects
- ▸ Parsing simple input
- ▸ Parsing input

Introduction

Now that we know some of the basic Boost types, it is time to get to know some data-converting functions. In this chapter we'll see how to convert strings, numbers, and user-defined types to each other, how to safely cast polymorphic types, and how to write small and large parsers right inside the C++ source files.

Converting strings to numbers

Converting strings to numbers in C++ makes a lot of people depressed because of its inefficiency and user unfriendliness. Let's see how string `100` can be converted to `int`:

```
#include <sstream>

    std::istringstream iss ("100");
    int i;
    iss >> i;
    // And now, 'iss' variable will get in the way all the time,
    // till end of the scope
    // It is better not to think, how many unnecessary operations,
    // virtual function calls and memory allocations occurred
    // during those operations
```

C methods are not much better:

```
#include <cstdlib>
    char * end;
    int i = std::strtol ("100", &end, 10);
    // Did it converted all the value to int, or stopped somewhere
    // in the middle?
    // And now we have 'end' variable will getting in the way
    // By the way, we want an integer, but strtol returns long
    // int... Did the converted value fit in int?
```

Getting ready

Only basic knowledge of C++ and STL is required for this recipe.

How to do it...

There is a library in Boost which will help you cope with the depressing difficulty of string to number conversions. It is called `Boost.LexicalCast` and consists of a `boost::bad_lexical_cast` exception class and a few `boost::lexical_cast` functions:

```
#include <boost/lexical_cast.hpp>

int i = boost::lexical_cast<int>("100");
```

It can even be used for non-zero-terminated strings:

```
char chars[] = {'1', '0', '0' };
int i = boost::lexical_cast<int>(chars, 3);
assert(i == 100);
```

How it works...

The `boost::lexical_cast` function accepts string as input and converts it to the type specified in triangular brackets. The `boost::lexical_cast` function will even check bounds for you:

```
try {
// on x86 short usually may not store values greater than 32767
    short s = boost::lexical_cast<short>("1000000");
    assert(false); // Must not reach this
} catch (const boost::bad_lexical_cast& /*e*/) {}
```

And also check for the correct syntax of input:

```
try {
    int i = boost::lexical_cast<int>("This is not a number!");
    assert(false); // Must not reach this
    (void)i; // Suppressing warning about unused variable
} catch (const boost::bad_lexical_cast& /*e*/) {}
```

There's-more...

Lexical cast just like all of the `std::stringstreams` classes uses `std::locale` and can convert localized numbers, but also has an impressive set of optimizations for C locale and for locales without number groupings:

```
#include <locale>

    std::locale::global(std::locale("ru_RU.UTF8"));
    // In Russia coma sign is used as a decimal separator
    float f = boost::lexical_cast<float>("1,0");
    assert(f < 1.01 && f > 0.99);
```

And that isn't all! You can even simply create template functions for conversions to numbers. Let's make a function that converts a container of some `string` values to a vector of `long int` values:

```
#include <algorithm>
#include <vector>
```

```
#include <iterator>
#include <boost/lexical_cast.hpp>

template <class ContainerT>
std::vector<long int> container_to_longs(const ContainerT& container)
{
    typedef typename ContainerT::value_type value_type;
    std::vector<long int> ret;
    typedef long int (*func_t)(const value_type&);
    func_t f = &boost::lexical_cast<long int, value_type>;
    std::transform(container.begin(), container.end(),
            std::back_inserter(ret), f);
    return ret;
}


    // Somewhere in source file...
    std::set<std::string> str_set;
    str_set.insert("1");
    assert(container_to_longs(str_set).front() == 1);
    std::deque<const char*> char_deque;
    char_deque.push_front("1");
    char_deque.push_back("2");
    assert(container_to_longs(char_deque).front() == 1);
    assert(container_to_longs(char_deque).back() == 2);

    // Obfuscating people with curly braces is fun!
    typedef boost::array<unsigned char, 2> element_t;
    boost::array<element_t, 2> arrays = {{ {{'1', '0'}}, {{'2', '0'}}
}};
    assert(container_to_longs(arrays).front() == 10);
    assert(container_to_longs(arrays).back() == 20);
```

See also

▶ Refer to the *Converting numbers to strings* recipe for information about `boost::lexical_cast` performance.

▶ The official documentation for `Boost.LexicalCast` contains some examples, performance measures, and answers to frequently asked questions. It is available at the following location:

```
http://www.boost.org/doc/libs/1_53_0/doc/html/boost_lexical_
cast.html
```

Converting numbers to strings

In this recipe we will continue discussing lexical conversions, but now we will be converting numbers to strings using `Boost.LexicalCast`. And as usual, `boost::lexical_cast` will provide a very simple way to convert the data.

Getting ready

Only basic knowledge of C++ and STL is required for this recipe.

How to do it...

1. Let's convert integer `100` to `std::string` using `boost::lexical_cast`:

   ```
   #include <boost/lexical_cast.hpp>

       std::string s = boost::lexical_cast<std::string>(100);
       assert(s == "100");
   ```

2. Compare this to the traditional C++ conversion method:

   ```
   #include <sstream>

       // C++ way of converting to strings
       std::stringstream ss;
       ss << 100;
       std::string s;
       ss >> s;
       // Variable 'ss' will dangle all the way, till the end
       // of scope
       // Multiple virtual methods were called during
       // conversion
       assert(s == "100");
   ```

   And against the C conversion method:

   ```
   #include <cstdlib>

       // C way of converting to strings
       char buffer[100];
       std::sprintf(buffer, "%i", 100);
       // You will need an unsigned long long int type to
       // count how many times errors were made in 'printf'
       // like functions all around the world. 'printf'
       // functions are a constant security threat!
       // But wait, we still need to construct a std::string
       std::string s(buffer);
   ```

```
// And now we have an buffer variable that won't be
// used
assert(s, == "100");
```

How it works...

The `boost::lexical_cast` function may also accept numbers as input and convert them to the string type specified in triangular brackets. Pretty close to what we did in the previous recipe.

There's more...

A careful reader will note that in the case of `lexical_cast` we have an additional call to string copy the constructor and that such a call will be a hit on the performance. It is true, but only for old or bad compilers. Modern compilers implement a **named return value optimization** (**NRVO**), which will eliminate the unnecessary call to copy the constructor and destructor. Even if the C++11-compatible compilers don't detect NRVO, they will use a move copy constructor of `std::string`, which is fast and efficient. The *Performance* section of the `Boost.LexicalCast` documentation shows the conversion speed on different compilers for different types, and in most cases `lexical_cast` is faster than the `std::stringstream` and `printf` functions.

If `boost::array` or `std::array` is passed to `boost::lexical_cast` as the output parameter type, less dynamic memory allocations will occur (or there will be no memory allocations at all; it depends on the `std::locale` implementation).

See also

▸ Boost's official documentation contains tables that compare the `lexical_cast` performance against other conversion approaches. And in most cases it wins. `http://www.boost.org/doc/libs/1_53_0/doc/html/boost_lexical_cast.html`. It also has some more examples and a frequently asked questions section.

▸ The *Converting strings to numbers* recipe.

▸ The *Converting user-defined types to/from strings* recipe.

Converting numbers to numbers

You might remember situations where you wrote something like the following code:

```
void some_function(unsigned short param);

int foo();
    // Somewhere in code
    // Some compilers may warn that int is being converted to
    // unsigned short and that there is a possibility of losing
    // data
    some_function(foo());
```

Usually, programmers just ignore such warnings by implicitly casting to unsigned short datatype, as demonstrated in the following code snippet:

```
    // Warning suppressed. Looks like a correct code
    some_function(
        static_cast<unsigned short>(foo())
    );
```

But this may make it extremely hard to detect errors. Such errors may exist in code for years before they get caught:

```
// Returns -1 if error occurred
int foo() {
    if (some_extremely_rare_condition()) {
        return -1;
    } else if (another_extremely_rare_condition()) {
        return 1000000;
    }
    return 65535;
}
```

Getting ready

Only basic knowledge of C++ is required for this recipe.

How to do it...

1. The library `Boost.NumericConversion` provides a solution for such cases. And it is easy to modify the existing code to use safe casts, just replace `static_cast` with `boost::numeric_cast`. It will throw an exception when the source value cannot be stored in the target. Let's take a look at the following example:

```cpp
#include <boost/numeric/conversion/cast.hpp>

void correct_implementation() {
    // 100% correct
    some_function(
        boost::numeric_cast<unsigned short>(foo())
    );
}

void test_function() {
    for (unsigned int i = 0; i < 100; ++i) {
        try {
            correct_implementation();
        } catch (const boost::numeric::bad_numeric_cast& e) {
            std::cout << '#' << i << ' ' << e.what() << std::endl;
        }
    }
}
```

2. Now if we run `test_function()` it will output the following:

```
#47 bad numeric conversion: negative overflow
#58 bad numeric conversion: positive overflow
```

3. We can even detect specific overflow types:

```cpp
void test_function1() {
    for (unsigned int i = 0; i < 100; ++i) {
        try {
            correct_implementation();
        } catch (const boost::numeric::positive_overflow& e) {
            // Do something specific for positive overflow
            std::cout << "POS OVERFLOW in #" << i << ' ' <<
            e.what() << std::endl;
        } catch (const boost::numeric::negative_overflow& e) {
            // Do something specific for negative overwlow
            std::cout <<"NEG OVERFLOW in #" << i << ' ' << e.what()
            << std::endl;
        }
    }
}
```

The `test_function1()` function will output the following:

```
NEG OVERFLOW in #47 bad numeric conversion: negative overflow
POS OVERFLOW in #59 bad numeric conversion: positive overflow
```

How it works...

It checks if the value of the input parameter fits into the new type without losing data and throws an exception if something is lost during conversion.

The `Boost.NumericConversion` library has a very fast implementation; it can do a lot of work at compile time. For example, when converting to types of a wider range, the source will just call the `static_cast` method.

There's more...

The `boost::numeric_cast` function is implemented via `boost::numeric::converter`, which can be tuned to use different overflow, range checking, and rounding policies. But usually, `numeric_cast` is just what you need.

Here is a small example that demonstrates how to make our own `mythrow_overflow_handler` overflow handler for `boost::numeric::cast`:

```
template <class SourceT, class TargetT>
struct mythrow_overflow_handler {
    void operator() (boost::numeric::range_check_result r) {
        if (r != boost::numeric::cInRange) {
            throw std::logic_error("Not in range!");
        }
    }
};

template <class TargetT, class SourceT>
TargetT my_numeric_cast(const SourceT& in) {
    using namespace boost;
    typedef numeric::conversion_traits<TargetT, SourceT>
        conv_traits;
    typedef numeric::numeric_cast_traits<TargetT, SourceT>
        cast_traits;
    typedef boost::numeric::converter
        <
            TargetT,
            SourceT,
            conv_traits,
```

```
                    mythrow_overflow_handler<SourceT, TargetT> // !!!
                > converter;
            return converter::convert(in);
    }


            // Somewhere in code
            try {
                my_numeric_cast<short>(100000);
            } catch (const std::logic_error& e) {
                std::cout << "It works! " << e.what() << std::endl;
            }
```

And this will output the following:

```
It works! Not in range!
```

See also

► Boost's official documentation contains detailed descriptions of all of the template parameters of the numeric converter; it is available at the following link:

```
http://www.boost.org/doc/libs/1_53_0/libs/numeric/conversion/
doc/html/index.html
```

Converting user-defined types to/from strings

There is a feature in `Boost.LexicalCast` that allows users to use their own types in `lexical_cast`. This feature just requires the user to write the correct `std::ostream` and `std::istream` operators for their types.

How to do it...

1. All you need is to provide an `operator<<` and `operator>>` stream operators. If your class is already streamable, nothing needs to be done:

```
#include <iosfwd>
#include <stdexcept>

// Somewhere in header file
// Negative number, that does not store minus sign
class negative_number {
    unsigned short number_;
public:
```

```
        explicit negative_number(unsigned short number)
            : number_(number)
        {}
        // operators and functions defined lower
        // ...
        unsigned short value_without_sign() const {
            return number_;
        }
    };

    std::ostream& operator<<(std::ostream& os,
        const negative_number& num)
    {
        os << '-' << num.value_without_sign();
        return os;
    }

    std::istream& operator>>(std::istream& is, negative_number& num) {
        char ch;
        is >> ch;
        if (ch != '-') {
            throw std::logic_error("negative_number class designed "
                        "to store ONLY negative values");
        }
        unsigned short s;
        is >> s;
        num = negative_number(s);
        return os;
    }
```

2. Now we may use `boost::lexical_cast` for conversions to and from the `negative_number` class. Here's an example:

```
#include <boost/lexical_cast.hpp>
#include <assert.h>
int main() {
    negative_number n
      = boost::lexical_cast<negative_number>("-100");
    assert(n.value_without_sign() == 100);
    int i = boost::lexical_cast<int>(n);
    assert(i == -100);

    typedef boost::array<char, 10> arr_t;
    arr_t arr = boost::lexical_cast<arr_t>(n);
    assert(arr[0] == '-');
```

```
        assert(arr[1] == '1');
        assert(arr[2] == '0');
        assert(arr[3] == '0');
        assert(arr[4] == '\0');
    }
```

How it works...

The `boost::lexical_cast` function can detect and use stream operators for converting user-defined types.

The `Boost.LexicalCast` library has many optimizations for basic types and they will be triggered when a user-defined type is being cast to basic type or when a basic type is being cast to a user-defined type.

There's more...

The `boost::lexical_cast` function may also convert to wide character strings, but the correct `basic_istream` and `basic_ostream` operator overloads are required for that:

```cpp
template <class CharT>
std::basic_ostream<CharT>& operator<<(std::basic_ostream<CharT>& os,
    const negative_number& num)
{
    os << static_cast<CharT>('-') << num.value_without_sign();
    return os;
}

template <class CharT>
std::basic_istream<CharT>& operator>>(std::basic_istream<CharT>& is,
negative_number& num) {
    CharT ch;
    is >> ch;
    if (ch != static_cast<CharT>('-')) {
        throw std::logic_error("negative_number class designed to "
                    "store ONLY negative values");
    }
    unsigned short s;
    is >> s;
    num = negative_number(s);
    return is;
}
```

```
int main() {
    negative_number n = boost::lexical_cast<negative_number>(L"-1");
    assert(n.value_without_sign() == 1);
    typedef boost::array<wchar_t, 10> warr_t;
    warr_t arr = boost::lexical_cast<warr_t>(n);
    assert(arr[0] == L'-');
    assert(arr[1] == L'1');
    assert(arr[4] == L'\0');
}
```

The `Boost.LexicalCast` library is not a part of C++11, but there is a proposal to add it to C++ standard. A lot of Boost libraries use it and I hope that it will make your life easier as well.

See also

▸ The `Boost.LexicalCast` documentation contains some examples, performance measures, and answers to frequently asked questions; it is available at `http://www.boost.org/doc/libs/1_53_0/doc/html/boost_lexical_cast.html`

▸ The *Converting strings to numbers* recipe

▸ The *Converting numbers to strings* recipe

Casting polymorphic objects

Imagine that some programmer designed an awful interface as follows (this is a good example of how interfaces should not be written):

```
struct object {
    virtual ~object() {}
};

struct banana: public object {
    void eat() const {}
    virtual ~banana(){}
};

struct pidgin: public object {
    void fly() const {}
    virtual ~pidgin(){}
};

object* try_produce_banana();
```

And our task is to make a function that eats bananas, and throws exceptions if something instead of banana came along (eating pidgins gross!). If we dereference a value returned by the `try_produce_banana()` function, we are getting in danger of dereferencing a null pointer.

Getting ready

Basic knowledge of C++ is required for this recipe.

How to do it...

So we need to write the following code:

```
void try_eat_banana_impl1() {
    const object* obj = try_produce_banana();
    if (!obj) {
        throw std::bad_cast();
    }
    dynamic_cast<const banana&>(*obj).eat();
}
```

Ugly, isn't it? `Boost.Conversion` provides a slightly better solution:

```
#include <boost/cast.hpp>
void try_eat_banana_impl2() {
    const object* obj = try_produce_banana();
    boost::polymorphic_cast<const banana*>(obj)->eat();
}
```

How it works...

The `boost::polymorphic_cast` function just wraps around code from the first example, and that is all. It checks input for null and then tries to do a dynamic cast. Any error during those operations will throw a `std::bad_cast` exception.

There's more...

The `Boost.Conversion` library also has a `polymorphic_downcast` function, which should be used only for downcasts that will always succeed. In debug mode (when NDEBUG is not defined) it will check for the correct downcast using `dynamic_cast`. When NDEBUG is defined, the `polymorphic_downcast` function will just do a `static_cast` operation. It is a good function to use in performance-critical sections, while still leaving the ability to detect errors in debug compilations.

- Initially, the `polymorphic_cast` idea was proposed in the book *The C++ Programming Language, Bjarne Stroustrup*. Refer to this book for more information and some good ideas on different topics.

- The official documentation may also be helpful; it is available at `http://www.boost.org/doc/libs/1_53_0/libs/conversion/cast.htm`.

Parsing simple input

It is a common task to parse a small text. And such situations are always a dilemma: shall we use some third-party professional tools for parsing such as Bison or ANTLR, or shall we try to write it by hand using only C++ and STL? The third-party tools are good for handling the parsing of complex texts and it is easy to write parsers using them, but they require additional tools for creating C++ or C code from their grammar, and add more dependencies to your project. Handwritten parsers are usually hard to maintain, but they require nothing except C++ compiler.

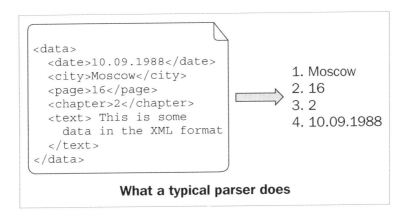

What a typical parser does

Let's start with a very simple task to parse a date in ISO format as follows:

    YYYY-MM-DD

The following are the examples of possible input:

    2013-03-01
    2012-12-31 // (woo-hoo, it almost a new year!)

Let's take a look at the parser's grammar from the following link `http://www.ietf.org/rfc/rfc3339.txt`:

```
date-fullyear   = 4DIGIT
date-month      = 2DIGIT   ; 01-12
date-mday       = 2DIGIT   ; 01-28, 01-29, 01-30, 01-31 based on
                           ; month/year
full-date       = date-fullyear "-" date-month "-" date-mday
```

Getting ready

Make sure that you are familiar with the placeholders concept or read the *Reordering the parameters of function* and *Binding a value as a function parameter* recipes in *Chapter 1, Starting to Write Your Application*. Basic knowledge of parsing tools would be good.

How to do it...

Let me introduce you to a `Boost.Spirit` library. It allows writing parsers (and lexers and generators) directly in C++ code format, which are immediately executable (that is, do not require additional tools for C++ code generation). The grammar of `Boost.Spirit` is very close to **Extended Backus-Naur Form** (**EBNF**), which is used for expressing grammar by many standards and understood by other popular parsers. The grammar at the beginning of this chapter is in EBNF.

1. We need to include the following headers:

```cpp
#include <boost/spirit/include/qi.hpp>
#include <boost/spirit/include/phoenix_core.hpp>
#include <boost/spirit/include/phoenix_operator.hpp>
#include <assert.h>
```

2. Now it's time to make a `date` structure to hold the parsed data:

```cpp
struct date {
    unsigned short year;
    unsigned short month;
    unsigned short day;
};
```

3. Now let's look at the parser (a step-by-step description of how it works can be found in the next section):

```cpp
// See recipe "Using a reference to string type" in Chapter 7,
// Manipulating Strings for a better type
// than std::string for parameter 's'
date parse_date_time1(const std::string& s) {
    using boost::spirit::qi::_1;
    using boost::spirit::qi::ushort_;
```

```
using boost::spirit::qi::char_;
using boost::phoenix::ref;

date res;
const char* first = s.data();
const char* const end = first + s.size();
bool success = boost::spirit::qi::parse(first, end,
    ushort_[ ref(res.year) = 1 ] >> char('-')
    >> ushort_[ ref(res.month) = 1 ] >> char('-')
    >> ushort_[ ref(res.day) = _1 ]
);

if (!success || first != end) {
    throw std::logic_error("Parsing failed");
}
return res;
}
```

4. Now we may use this parser wherever we want:

```
int main() {
    date d = parse_date_time1("2012-12-31");
    assert(d.year == 2012);
    assert(d.month == 12);
    assert(d.day == 31);
}
```

How it works...

This is a very simple implementation; it does not check the digit count for numbers. Parsing occurs in the `boost::spirit::qi::parse` function. Let's simplify it a little bit, removing the actions on successful parsing:

```
bool success = boost::spirit::qi::parse(first, end,
    ushort_ >> char_('-') >> ushort_ >> char_('-') >> ushort_
);
```

The `first` argument points to the beginning of the data to parse; it must be a modifiable (non-constant) variable because the `parse` function will use it to show the end of the parsed sequence. The `end` argument points to the element beyond the last one. `first` and `end` shall be iterators.

The third argument to the function is a parsing rule. And it does exactly what is written in the EBNF rule:

```
date-fullyear "-" date-month "-" date-md
```

We just replaced white spaces with the `>>` operator.

The `parse` function returns true on success. If we want to make sure that the whole string was successfully parsed, we need to check for the parser's return value and equality of the input iterators.

Now we need to deal with the actions on successful parse and this recipe will be over. Semantic actions in `Boost.Spirit` are written inside `[]` and they can be written using function pointers, function objects, `boost::bind`, `std::bind` (or the other `bind()` implementations), or C++11 lambda functions.

So, you could also write a rule for YYYY using C++11 lambda:

```
ushort_ [ [&res](unsigned short s) {res.year = s;} ]
```

Now, let's take a look at the month's semantic action closer:

```
ushort_ [ ref(res.month) = _1 ]
```

For those who have read the book from the beginning, this would remind you about `boost::bind` and placeholders. `ref(res.month)` means pass `res.month` as a modifiable reference and `_1` means the first input parameter, which would be a number (the result of `ushort_` parsing).

There's more...

Now let's modify our parser, so it can take care of the digits count. For that purpose, we will take the `unit_parser` template class and just set up the correct parameters:

```
date parse_date_time2(const std::string& s) {
    using boost::spirit::qi::_1;
    using boost::spirit::qi::uint_parser;
    using boost::spirit::qi::char_;
    using boost::phoenix::ref;

    // Use unsigned short as output type, require Radix 10, and from 2
    // to 2 digits
    uint_parser<unsigned short, 10, 2, 2> u2_;

    // Use unsigned short as output type, require Radix 10, and from 4
    // to 4 digits
    uint_parser<unsigned short, 10, 4, 4> u4_;

    date res;
    const char* first = s.data();
    const char* const end = first + s.size();
```

```
bool success = boost::spirit::qi::parse(first, end,
    u4_ [ ref(res.year) = _1 ] >> char_('-')
    >> u2_ [ ref(res.month) = _1 ] >> char_('-')
    >> u2_ [ ref(res.day) = _1 ]
);

if (!success || first != end) {
    throw std::logic_error("Parsing failed");
}
return res;
}
```

Don't worry if those examples seem complicated. The first time I was also frightened by `Boost.Spirit`, but now it really simplifies my life. You are extremely brave, if this code does not scare you.

If you want to avoid code bloat, try to write parsers in source files and not in headers. Also take care of iterator types passed to the `boost::spirit::parse` function, the fewer different types of iterators you use, the smaller binary you'll get. Writing parsers in source files has one more advantage: it does not slow down the project compilation (as you may notice, the `Spirit` parsers are slow to compile, so it is better to compile them once in the source file, than define them in the header files and use this file all around the project).

If you are now thinking that parsing dates was simpler to implement by hand using STL… you are right! But only for now. Take a look at the next recipe; it will give you more examples on `Boost.Spirit` usage and extend this example for a situation when writing the parser by hand is harder than using `Boost.Spirit`.

The `Boost.Spirit` library is not a part of C++11 and as far as I know, it is not proposed for inclusion in the closest upcoming C++ standard.

See also

- The *Reordering the parameters of function* recipe in *Chapter 1, Starting to Write Your Application*.
- The *Binding a value as a function parameter* recipe.
- `Boost.Spirit` is a huge header-only library. A separate book may be written about it, so feel free to use its documentation `http://www.boost.org/doc/libs/1_53_0/libs/spirit/doc/html/index.html`. You may also find information on how to write lexers and generators directly in C++11 code using Boost.

Parsing input

In the previous recipe we were writing a simple parser for dates. Imagine that some time has passed and the task has changed. Now we need to write a date-time parser that will support multiple input formats plus zone offsets. So now our parser should understand the following inputs:

```
2012-10-20T10:00:00Z         // date time with zero zone offset
2012-10-20T10:00:00          // date time with unspecified zone
                                offset
2012-10-20T10:00:00+09:15 // date time with zone offset
2012-10-20-09:15             // date time with zone offset
10:00:09+09:15               // time with zone offset
```

Getting ready

We'll be using the `Spirit` library, which was described in the *Parsing simple input* recipe. Read it before getting hands on with this recipe.

How to do it...

1. Let's start with writing a date-time structure that will hold a parsed result:

```cpp
struct datetime {
    enum zone_offsets_t {
        OFFSET_NOT_SET,
        OFFSET_Z,
        OFFSET_UTC_PLUS,
        OFFSET_UTC_MINUS
    };

private:
    unsigned short year_;
    unsigned short month_;
    unsigned short day_;
    unsigned short hours_;
    unsigned short minutes_;
    unsigned short seconds_;
    zone_offsets_t zone_offset_type_;
    unsigned int zone_offset_in_min_;

    static void dt_assert(bool v, const char* msg) {
        if (!v) {
```

```
            throw std::logic_error("Assertion failed: "
                + std::string(msg));
        }
    }

public:
    datetime()
        : year_(0), month_(0), day_(0)
        , hours_(0), minutes_(0), seconds_(0)
        , zone_offset_type_(OFFSET_NOT_SET), zone_offset_in_min_(0)
    {}
    // Getters: year(), month(), day(), hours(), minutes(),
    // seconds(), zone_offset_type(), zone_offset_in_min()
    // ...

    // Setters
    // void set_*(unsigned short val)
    { /*some assert and setting the *_ to val */ }
    // ...

};
```

2. Now let's write a function for setting the zone offset:

```
void set_zone_offset(datetime& dt, char sign, unsigned short
hours, unsigned short minutes) {
    dt.set_zone_offset_type(sign == '+' ?
        datetime::OFFSET_UTC_PLUS : datetime::OFFSET_UTC_MINUS);
    dt.set_zone_offset_in_min(hours * 60 + minutes);
}
```

3. Writing a parser can be split into writing a few simple parsers, so we start with writing a zone-offset parser.

```
//Default includes for Boost.Spirit
#include <boost/spirit/include/qi.hpp>
#include <boost/spirit/include/phoenix_core.hpp>
#include <boost/spirit/include/phoenix_operator.hpp>

// We'll use bind() function from Boost.Spirit,
// because it iterates better with parsers
#include <boost/spirit/include/phoenix_bind.hpp>

datetime parse_datetime(const std::string& s) {
    using boost::spirit::qi::_1;
    using boost::spirit::qi::_2;
```

```
        using boost::spirit::qi::_3;
        using boost::spirit::qi::uint_parser;
        using boost::spirit::qi::char_;
        using boost::phoenix::bind;
        using boost::phoenix::ref;

        datetime ret;

        // Use unsigned short as output type, require Radix 10, and
        // from 2 to 2 digits
        uint_parser<unsigned short, 10, 2, 2> u2_;

        // Use unsigned short as output type, require Radix 10, and
        // from 4 to 4 digits
        uint_parser<unsigned short, 10, 4, 4> u4_;

        boost::spirit::qi::rule<const char*, void()> timezone_parser
            = -(    // unary minus means optional rule
                    // Zero offset
                    char_('Z') [ bind(&datetime::set_zone_offset_type,
                                  &ret, datetime::OFFSET_Z) ]
                    |   // OR
                    // Specific zone offset
                    ((char_('+')|char_('-')) >> u2_ >> ':' >> u2_) [
                        bind(&set_zone_offset, ref(ret), _1, _2, _3) ]
            );
        // ...
        return ret;
    }
```

4. Let's finish our example by writing the remaining parsers:

```
    boost::spirit::qi::rule<const char*, void()> date_parser =
      u4_ [ bind(&datetime::set_year, &ret, _1) ]  >> char_('-')
      >> u2_ [ bind(&datetime::set_month, &ret, _1) ] >> char_('-')
      >> u2_ [ bind(&datetime::set_day, &ret, _1) ];

    boost::spirit::qi::rule<const char*, void()> time_parser =
      u2_ [ bind(&datetime::set_hours, &ret, _1) ] >> char_(':')
      >> u2_ [ bind(&datetime::set_minutes, &ret, _1) ] >> char_(':')
      >> u2_ [ bind(&datetime::set_seconds, &ret, _1) ];

    const char* first = s.data();
    const char* const end = first + s.size();
```

```
    bool success = boost::spirit::qi::parse(first, end,
        ((date_parser >> char_('T') >> time_parser) | date_parser
          | time_parser)
        >> timezone_parser
    );

    if (!success || first != end) {
        throw std::logic_error("Parsing of '" + s + "' failed");
    }
    return ret;
} // end of parse_datetime() function
```

How it works...

A very interesting method here is `boost::spirit::qi::rule<const char*, void()>`. It erases the type and allows you to write parsers in source files and export them to headers. For example:

```
// Somewhere in header file
class example_1 {
    boost::spirit::qi::rule<const char*, void()> some_rule_;
public:
    example_1();
};

// In source file
example_1::example_1() {
    some_rule_ = /* ... */;
}
```

But remember that this class implies an optimization barrier for compilers, so do not use it when it is not required.

There's more...

We can make our example slightly faster by removing the `rule<>` objects that do type erasure. For our example in C++11, we can just replace them with the `auto` keyword.

The `Boost.Spirit` library generates very fast parsers; there are some performance measures at the official site. There are also some recommendations for working with the `Boost.Spirit` library; one of them is to generate a parser only once, and then just re-use it (in our example this is not shown).

The rule that parses specific zone offset in `timezone_parser` uses the `boost::phoenix::bind` call, which is not mandatory. However, without it we'll be dealing with `boost::fusion::vector<char, unsigned short, unsigned short>`, which is not as user friendly as `bind(&set_zone_offset, ref(ret), _1, _2, _3)`.

When parsing large files, consider reading the *The fastest way to read files* recipe in *Chapter 11, Working with the System*, because incorrect work with files may slow down your program much more than parsing.

Compiling the code that uses the library `Boost.Spirit` (or `Boost.Fusion`) may take a lot of time, because of a huge number of template instantiations. When experimenting with the `Boost.Spirit` library use modern compilers, they provide better compilation times.

See also

▶ The `Boost.Spirit` library is worth writing a separate book on. It's impossible to describe all of its features in a few recipes, so referring to the documentation will help you to get more information about it. It is available at `http://www.boost.org/doc/libs/1_53_0/libs/spirit/doc/html/index.html`. There you'll find many more examples, ready parsers, and information on how to write lexers and generators directly in C++11 code using Boost.

3
Managing Resources

In this chapter we will cover:

- ▸ Managing pointers to classes that do not leave scope
- ▸ Reference counting of pointers to classes used across methods
- ▸ Managing pointers to arrays that do not leave scope
- ▸ Reference counting pointers to arrays used across methods
- ▸ Storing any functional objects in a variable
- ▸ Passing a function pointer in a variable
- ▸ Passing C++11 lambda functions in a variable
- ▸ Containers of pointers
- ▸ Doing something at scope exit
- ▸ Initializing the base class by a member of the derived class

Introduction

In this chapter, we'll continue to deal with datatypes, introduced by the Boost libraries, mostly focusing on working with pointers. We'll see how to easily manage resources, and how to use a datatype capable of storing any functional objects, functions, and lambda expressions. After reading this chapter, your code will become more reliable, and memory leaks will become history.

Managing pointers to classes that do not leave scope

There are situations where we are required to dynamically allocate memory and construct a class in that memory. And, that's where the troubles start. Have a look at the following code:

```
void foo1() {
    foo_class* p = new foo_class("Some initialization data");
    bool something_else_happened = some_function1(p);

    if (something_else_happened) {
        delete p;
        return false;
    }

    some_function2(p);

    delete p;
    return true;
}
```

This code looks correct at first glance. But, what if some_function1() or some_function2() throws an exception? In that case, p won't be deleted. Let's fix it in the following way:

```
void foo2() {
    foo_class* p = new foo_class("Some initialization data");
    try {
        bool something_else_happened = some_function1(p);
        if (something_else_happened) {
            delete p;
            return false;
        }
        some_function2(p);
    } catch (...) {
        delete p;
        throw;
    }
    delete p;
    return true;
}
```

Now the code is ugly and hard to read but is correct. Maybe we can do better than this.

Getting ready

Basic knowledge of C++ and code behavior during exceptions is required.

How to do it...

Let's take a look at the `Boost.SmartPtr` library. There is a `boost::scoped_ptr` class that may help you out:

```
#include <boost/scoped_ptr.hpp>

bool foo3() {
    boost::scoped_ptr<foo_class> p(new foo_class(
        "Some initialization data"));
    bool something_else_happened = some_function1(p.get());
    if (something_else_happened) {
        return false;
    }
    some_function2(p.get());
    return true;
}
```

Now, there is no chance that the resource will leak, and the source code is much clearer.

> If you have control over `some_function1()` and `some_function2()`, you may wish to rewrite them so they will take a reference to `scoped_ptr<foo_class>` (or just a reference) instead of a pointer to `foo_class`. Such an interface will be more intuitive.

How it works...

In the destructor, `boost::scoped_ptr<T>` will call `delete` for a pointer that it stores. When an exception is thrown, the stack is unwound, and the destructor of `scoped_ptr` is called.

The `scoped_ptr<T>` class template is not copyable; it stores only a pointer to the class and does not require `T` to be of a complete type (it can be forward declared). Some compilers do not warn when an incomplete type is being deleted, which may lead to errors that are hard to detect, but `scoped_ptr` (and all the classes in `Boost.SmartPtr`) has a specific compile-time assert for such cases. That makes `scoped_ptr` perfect for implementing the `Pimpl` idiom.

The `boost::scoped_ptr<T>` function is equal to `const std::auto_ptr<T>`, but it also has the `reset()` function.

There's more...

This class is extremely fast. In most cases, the compiler will optimize the code that uses `scoped_ptr` to the machine code, which is close to our handwritten version (and sometimes even better if the compiler detects that some functions do not throw exceptions).

See also

▶ The documentation of the `Boost.SmartPtr` library contains lots of examples and other useful information about all the smart pointers' classes. You can read about it at `http://www.boost.org/doc/libs/1_53_0/libs/smart_ptr/smart_ptr.htm`.

Reference counting of pointers to classes used across methods

Imagine that you have some dynamically allocated structure containing data, and you want to process it in different execution threads. The code to do this is as follows:

```cpp
#include <boost/thread.hpp>
#include <boost/bind.hpp>

void process1(const foo_class* p);
void process2(const foo_class* p);
void process3(const foo_class* p);

void foo1() {
    while (foo_class* p = get_data()) // C way
    {
        // There will be too many threads soon, see
        // recipe 'Executing different tasks in parallel'
        // for a good way to avoid uncontrolled growth of threads
        boost::thread(boost::bind(&process1, p))
            .detach();
        boost::thread(boost::bind(&process2, p))
            .detach();
        boost::thread(boost::bind(&process3, p))
            .detach();
        // delete p; Oops!!!!
    }
}
```

We cannot deallocate p at the end of the `while` loop because it can still be used by threads that run process functions. Process functions cannot delete p because they do not know that other threads are not using it anymore.

Getting ready

This recipe uses the `Boost.Thread` library, which is not a header-only library, so your program will need to link against the `libboost_thread` and `libboost_system` libraries. Make sure that you understand the concept of threads before reading further. Refer to the *See also* section for references on recipes that use threads.

You'll also need some basic knowledge on `boost::bind` or `std::bind`, which is almost the same.

How to do it...

As you may have guessed, there is a class in Boost (and C++11) that will help you to deal with it. It is called `boost::shared_ptr`, and it can be used as:

```cpp
#include <boost/shared_ptr.hpp>

void process_sp1(const boost::shared_ptr<foo_class>& p);
void process_sp2(const boost::shared_ptr<foo_class>& p);
void process_sp3(const boost::shared_ptr<foo_class>& p);

void foo2() {
    typedef boost::shared_ptr<foo_class> ptr_t;
    ptr_t p;
    while (p = ptr_t(get_data())) // C way
    {
        boost::thread(boost::bind(&process_sp1, p))
            .detach();
        boost::thread(boost::bind(&process_sp2, p))
            .detach();
        boost::thread(boost::bind(&process_sp3, p))
            .detach();
        // no need to anything
    }
}
```

Another example of this is as follows:

```
#include <string>
#include <boost/smart_ptr/make_shared.hpp>

void process_str1(boost::shared_ptr<std::string> p);
void process_str2(const boost::shared_ptr<std::string>& p);

void foo3() {
    boost::shared_ptr<std::string> ps =
      boost::make_shared<std::string>(
        "Guess why make_shared<std::string> "
        "is faster than shared_ptr<std::string> "
        "ps(new std::string('this string'))"
    );
    boost::thread(boost::bind(&process_str1, ps))
            .detach();
    boost::thread(boost::bind(&process_str2, ps))
            .detach();
}
```

How it works...

The `shared_ptr` class has an atomic reference counter inside. When you copy it, the reference counter is incremented, and when its destructor is called, the reference counter is decremented. When the reference counter equals zero, `delete` is called for the object pointed by `shared_ptr`.

Now, let's find out what's happening in the case of `boost::thread` `(boost::bind(&process_sp1, p))`. The function `process_sp1` takes a parameter as a reference, so why is it not deallocated when we get out of the `while` loop? The answer is simple. The functional object returned by `bind()` contains a copy of the shared pointer, and that means that the data pointed by `p` won't be deallocated until the functional object is destroyed.

Getting back to `boost::make_shared`, let's take a look at `shared_ptr<std::string>` `ps(new int(0))`. In this case, we have two calls to `new`: firstly while constructing a pointer to an integer, and secondly when constructing a `shared_ptr` class (it allocates an atomic counter on heap using call `new`). But, when we construct `shared_ptr` using `make_shared`, only one call to `new` will be made. It will allocate a single piece of memory and will construct an atomic counter and the `int` object in that piece.

There's more...

The atomic reference counter guarantees the correct behavior of `shared_ptr` across the threads, but you must remember that atomic operations are not as fast as nonatomic. On C++11 compatible compilers, you may reduce the atomic operations' count using `std::move` (move the constructor of the shared pointer in such a way that the atomic counter is neither incremented nor decremented).

The `shared_ptr` and `make_shared` classes are part of C++11, and they are declared in the header `<memory>` in `std::` namespace.

See also

- Refer to *Chapter 5*, *Multithreading*, for more information about `Boost.Thread` and atomic operations.

- Refer to the *Reordering the parameters of function* recipe in *Chapter 1*, *Starting to Write Your Application*, for more information about `Boost.Bind`.

- Refer to the *Binding a value as a function parameter* recipe in *Chapter 1*, *Starting to Write Your Application*, for more information about `Boost.Bind`.

- The documentation of the `Boost.SmartPtr` library contains lots of examples and other useful information about all the smart pointers' classes. You can read about it at `http://www.boost.org/doc/libs/1_53_0/libs/smart_ptr/smart_ptr.htm`.

Managing pointers to arrays that do not leave scope

We already saw how to manage pointers to a resource in the *Managing pointers to classes that do not leave scope* recipe. But, when we deal with arrays, we need to call `delete[]` instead of a simple `delete`, otherwise there will be a memory leak. Have a look at the following code:

```
void may_throw1(const char* buffer);
void may_throw2(const char* buffer);

void foo() {
    // we cannot allocate 10MB of memory on stack,
    // so we allocate it on heap
    char* buffer = new char[1024 * 1024 * 10];
    // Here comes some code, that may throw
    may_throw1(buffer);
    may_throw2(buffer);
    delete[] buffer;
}
```

Getting ready

Knowledge of C++ exceptions and templates are required for this recipe.

How to do it...

The `Boost.SmartPointer` library has not only the `scoped_ptr<>` class but also a `scoped_array<>` class.

```
#include <boost/scoped_array.hpp>

void foo_fixed() {
    // so we allocate it on heap
    boost::scoped_array<char> buffer(new char[1024 * 1024 * 10]);

    // Here comes some code, that may throw,
    // but now exception won't cause a memory leak
    may_throw1(buffer.get());
    may_throw2(buffer.get());

    // destructor of 'buffer' variable will call delete[]
}
```

How it works...

It works just like a `scoped_ptr<>` class but calls `delete[]` instead of `delete` in the destructor.

There's more...

The `scoped_array<>` class has the same guarantees and design as `scoped_ptr<>`. It has neither additional memory allocations nor virtual functions' call. It cannot be copied and is not a part of C++11.

See also

> ▸ The documentation of the `Boost.SmartPtr` library contains lots of examples and other useful information about all the smart pointers' classes. You can read about it at `http://www.boost.org/doc/libs/1_53_0/libs/smart_ptr/smart_ptr.htm`.

Reference counting pointers to arrays used across methods

We continue coping with pointers, and our next task is to reference count an array. Let's take a look at a program that gets some data from the stream and processes it in different threads. The code to do this is as follows:

```cpp
#include <cstring>
#include <boost/thread.hpp>
#include <boost/bind.hpp>

void do_process(const char* data, std::size_t size);

void do_process_in_background(const char* data, std::size_t size)
{
    // We need to copy data, because we do not know,
    // when it will be deallocated by the caller
    char* data_cpy = new char[size];
    std::memcpy(data_cpy, data, size);

    // Starting thread of execution to process data
    boost::thread(boost::bind(&do_process, data_cpy, size))
            .detach();

    // We cannot delete[] data_cpy, because
    // do_process1 or do_process2 may still work with it
}
```

Just the same problem that occurred in the *Reference counting of pointers to classes used across methods* recipe.

Getting ready

This recipe uses the `Boost.Thread` library, which is not a header-only library, so your program will need to link against the `libboost_thread` and `libboost_system` libraries. Make sure that you understand the concept of threads before reading further.

You'll also need some basic knowledge on `boost::bind` or `std::bind`, which is almost the same.

How to do it...

There are three solutions. The main difference between them is of type and construction of the `data_cpy` variable. Each of these solutions does exactly the same things that are described in the beginning of this recipe but without memory leaks. The solutions are:

▶ The first solution:

```cpp
#include <boost/shared_array.hpp>

void do_process(const boost::shared_array<char>& data,
    std::size_t size) {
    do_process(data.get(), size);
}

void do_process_in_background_v1(const char* data,
    std::size_t size) {
    // We need to copy data, because we do not know, when
    // it will be deallocated by the caller
    boost::shared_array<char> data_cpy(new char[size]);
    std::memcpy(data_cpy.get(), data, size);

    // Starting threads of execution to process data
    boost::thread(boost::bind(&do_process1, data_cpy))
        .detach();

    // no need to call delete[] for data_cpy, because
    // data_cpy destructor will deallocate data when
    // reference count will be zero
}
```

▶ The second solution:

Since Boost 1.53 `shared_ptr` itself can take care of arrays:

```cpp
#include <boost/shared_ptr.hpp>
#include <boost/make_shared.hpp>

void do_process_shared_ptr(
        const boost::shared_ptr<char[]>& data,
        std::size_t size)
{
    do_process(data.get(), size);
}
```

```
void do_process_in_background_v2(const char* data,
  std::size_t size) {
    // Faster than 'First solution'
    boost::shared_ptr<char[]> data_cpy =
      boost::make_shared<char[]>(size);
    std::memcpy(data_cpy.get(), data, size);

    // Starting thread of execution to process data
    boost::thread(boost::bind(
       &do_process_shared_ptr, data_cpy, size
    )).detach();

    // data_cpy destructor will deallocate data when
    // reference count will be zero
}
```

► The third solution:

```
void do_process_shared_ptr2(
        const boost::shared_ptr<char>& data,
        std::size_t size)
{
    do_process(data.get(), size);
}
void do_process_in_background_v3(const char* data,
  std::size_t size) {
    // Same speed as in First solution
    boost::shared_ptr<char> data_cpy(
                new char[size],
                boost::checked_array_deleter<char>()
    );
    std::memcpy(data_cpy.get(), data, size);

    // Starting threads of execution to process data
    boost::thread(boost::bind(
       &do_process_shared_ptr2, data_cpy, size
    )).detach();

    // data_cpy destructor will deallocate data when
    // reference count will be zero
}
```

How it works...

In each of these examples, shared classes count references and call `delete[]` for a pointer when the reference count becomes equal to zero. The first and second examples are trivial. In the third example, we provide a `deleter` object for a shared pointer. The `deleter` object will be called instead of the default call to `delete`. This `deleter` is the same as used in C++11 in `std::unique_ptr` and `std::shared_ptr`.

There's more...

The first solution is traditional to Boost; prior to Boost 1.53, the functionality of the second solution was not implemented in `shared_ptr`.

The second solution is the fastest one (it uses fewer calls to `new`), but it can be used only with Boost 1.53 and higher.

The third solution is the most portable one. It can be used with older versions of Boost and with C++11 STL's `shared_ptr<>` (just don't forget to change `boost::checked_array_deleter<T>()` to `std::default_delete<T[]>()`).

See also

> ▸ The documentation of the `Boost.SmartPtr` library contains lots of examples and other useful information about all the smart pointers' classes. You can read about it at `http://www.boost.org/doc/libs/1_53_0/libs/smart_ptr/smart_ptr.htm`.

Storing any functional objects in a variable

C++ has a syntax to work with pointers to functions and member functions' pointers. And, that is good! However, this mechanism is hard to use with functional objects. Consider the situation when you are developing a library that has its API declared in the header files and implementation in the source files. This library shall have a function that accepts any functional objects. How would you pass a functional object to it? Have a look at the following code:

```
// Required for std::unary_function<> template
#include <functional>

// making a typedef for function pointer accepting int
// and returning nothing
typedef void (*func_t)(int);
```

```
// Function that accepts pointer to function and
// calls accepted function for each integer that it has
// It cannot work with functional objects :(
void process_integers(func_t f);

// Functional object
class int_processor: public std::unary_function<int, void> {
    const int min_;
    const int max_;
    bool& triggered_;

public:
    int_processor(int min, int max, bool& triggered)
        : min_(min)
        , max_(max)
        , triggered_(triggered)
    {}

    void operator()(int i) const {
        if (i < min_ || i > max_) {
            triggered_ = true;
        }
    }
};
```

Getting ready

Reading the *Storing any value in a container/variable* recipe in *Chapter 1, Starting to Write Your Application*, is recommended before starting this recipe.

You'll also need some basic knowledge on `boost::bind` or `std::bind`, which is almost the same.

How to do it...

Let's see how to fix the example and make `process_integers` accept functional objects:

1. There is a solution, and it is called a `Boost.Function` library. It allows you to store any function, a member function, or a functional object if its signature is a match to the one described in a template argument:

    ```
    #include <boost/function.hpp>
    ```

```
typedef boost::function<void(int)> fobject_t;

// Now this function may accept functional objects
void process_integers(const fobject_t& f);

int main() {
    bool is_triggered = false;
    int_processor fo(0, 200, is_triggered);
    process_integers(fo);
    assert(is_triggered);
}
```

The `boost::function` class has a default constructor and has an empty state.

2. Checking for an empty/default constructed state can be done like this:

```
void foo(const fobject_t& f) {
    // boost::function is convertible to bool
    if (f) {
        // we have value in 'f'
        // ...
    } else {
        // 'f' is empty
        // ...
    }
}
```

How it works...

The `fobject_t` method stores in itself data from functional objects and erases their exact type. It is safe to use the `boost::function` objects such as the following code:

```
bool g_is_triggered = false;
void set_functional_object(fobject_t& f) {
    int_processor fo( 100, 200, g_is_triggered);
    f = fo;
    // fo leavs scope and will be destroyed,
    // but 'f' will be usable eve inouter scope
}
```

Does it remind you of the `boost::any` class? It uses the same technique—type erasure for storing any function objects.

There's more...

The `Boost.Function` library has an insane amount of optimizations; it may store small functional objects without additional memory allocations and has optimized move assignment operators. It is accepted as a part of C++11 STL library and is defined in the `<functional>` header in the `std::` namespace.

But, remember that `boost::function` implies an optimization barrier for the compiler. It means that:

```
std::for_each(v.begin(), v.end(),
    boost::bind(std::plus<int>(), 10, _1));
```

will be better optimized by the compiler than

```
fobject_t f(boost::bind(std::plus<int>(), 10, _1));
std::for_each(v.begin(), v.end(), f);
```

This is why you should try to avoid using `Boost.Function` when its usage is not really required. In some cases, the C++11 `auto` keyword can be handy instead:

```
auto f = boost::bind(std::plus<int>(), 10, _1);
std::for_each(v.begin(), v.end(), f);
```

See also

▶ The official documentation of `Boost.Function` contains more examples, performance measures, and class reference documentation. You can read about it at `http://www.boost.org/doc/libs/1_53_0/doc/html/function.html`.

▶ The *Passing a function pointer in a variable* recipe.

▶ The *Passing C++11 lambda functions in a variable* recipe.

Passing a function pointer in a variable

We are continuing with the previous example, and now we want to pass a pointer to a function in our `process_integeres()` method. Shall we add an overload for just function pointers, or is there a more elegant way?

Getting ready

This recipe is continuing the previous one. You must read the previous recipe first.

How to do it...

Nothing needs to be done as `boost::function<>` is also constructible from the function pointers:

```
void my_ints_function(int i);

int main() {
    process_integeres(&my_ints_function);
}
```

How it works...

A pointer to `my_ints_function` will be stored inside the `boost::function` class, and calls to `boost::function` will be forwarded to the stored pointer.

There's more...

The `Boost.Function` library provides good performance for pointers to functions, and it will not allocate memory on heap. However, whatever you store in `boost::function`, it will use an RTTI. If you disable RTTI, it will continue to work but will dramatically increase the size of a compiled binary.

See also

> ▶ The official documentation of `Boost.Function` contains more examples, performance measures, and class reference documentation. You can read about it at `http://www.boost.org/doc/libs/1_53_0/doc/html/function.html`.

> ▶ The *Passing C++11 lambda functions in a variable* recipe.

Passing C++11 lambda functions in a variable

We are continuing with the previous example, and now we want to use a lambda function with our `process_integers()` method.

Getting ready

This recipe is continuing the series of the previous two. You must read them first. You will also need a C++11 compatible compiler or at least a compiler with C++11 lambda support.

How to do it...

Nothing needs to be done as `boost::function<>` is also usable with lambda functions of any difficulty:

```
// lambda function with no parameters that does nothing
process_integeres([](int /*i*/){});

// lambda function that stores a reference
std::deque<int> ints;
process_integeres([&ints](int i){
    ints.push_back(i);
});

// lambda function that modifies its content
std::size_t match_count = 0;
process_integeres([ints, &match_count](int i) mutable {
    if (ints.front() == i) {
        ++ match_count;
    }
    ints.pop_front();
});
```

There's more...

Performance of the lambda function storage in `Boost.Functional` is the same as in other cases. While the functional object produced by the lambda expression is small enough to fit in an instance of `boost::function`, no dynamic memory allocation will be performed. Calling an object stored in `boost::function` is close to the speed of calling a function by a pointer. Copying of an object is close to the speed of constructing `boost::function` and will exactly use a dynamic memory allocation in similar cases. Moving objects won't allocate and deallocate memory.

See also

▶ Additional information about performance and `Boost.Function` can be found on the official documentation page at `http://www.boost.org/doc/libs/1_53_0/doc/html/function.html`

Containers of pointers

There are such cases when we need to store pointers in the container. The examples are: storing polymorphic data in containers, forcing fast copy of data in containers, and strict exception requirements for operations with data in containers. In such cases, the C++ programmer has the following choices:

▸ Store pointers in containers and take care of their destructions using the operator delete:

```cpp
#include <set>
#include <algorithm>
#include <boost/bind.hpp>
#include <boost/type_traits/remove_pointer.hpp>
#include <cassert>

template <class T>
struct ptr_cmp: public std::binary_function<T, T, bool> {
    template <class T1>
    bool operator()(const T1& v1, const T1& v2) const {
        return operator ()(*v1, *v2);
    }

    bool operator()(const T& v1, const T& v2) const {
        return std::less<T>()(v1, v2);
    }
};

void example1() {
    std::set<int*, ptr_cmp<int> > s;
    s.insert(new int(1));
    s.insert(new int(0));
    // ...
    assert(**s.begin() == 0);
    // ...
    // Deallocating resources
    // Any exception in this code will lead to
    // memory leak
    std::for_each(s.begin(), s.end(),
        boost::bind(::operator delete, _1));
}
```

Such an approach is error prone and requires a lot of writing

▶ Store smart pointers in containers:

For the C++03 version:

```
    void example2_a() {
    typedef std::auto_ptr<int> int_aptr_t;
    std::set<int_aptr_t, ptr_cmp<int> > s;
    s.insert(int_aptr_t(new int(1)));
    s.insert(int_aptr_t(new int(0)));
    // ...
    assert(**s.begin() == 0);
    // ...
    // resources will be deallocated by auto_ptr<>
}
```

The `std::auto_ptr` method is deprecated, and it is not recommended to use it in containers. Moreover, this example will not compile with C++11.

For the C++11 version:

```
void example2_b() {
    typedef std::unique_ptr<int> int_uptr_t;
    std::set<int_uptr_t, ptr_cmp<int> > s;
    s.insert(int_uptr_t(new int(1)));
    s.insert(int_uptr_t(new int(0)));
    // ...
    assert(**s.begin() == 0);
    // ...
    // resources will be deallocated by unique_ptr<>
}
```

This solution is a good one, but it cannot be used in C++03, and you still need to write a comparator functional object

▶ Use `Boost.SmartPtr` in the container:

```
#include <boost/shared_ptr.hpp>
void example3() {
    typedef boost::shared_ptr<int> int_sptr_t;
    std::set<int_sptr_t, ptr_cmp<int> > s;
    s.insert(int_sptr_t(new int(1)));
    s.insert(int_sptr_t(new int(0)));
    // ...
    assert(**s.begin() == 0);
    // ...
    // resources will be deallocated by shared_ptr<>
}
```

This solution is portable, but you still need to write comparators, and it adds performance penalties (an atomic counter requires additional memory, and its increments/decrements are not as fast as nonatomic operations)

Getting ready

Knowledge of STL containers is required for better understanding of this recipe.

How to do it...

The `Boost.PointerContainer` library provides a good and portable solution:

```
#include <boost/ptr_container/ptr_set.hpp>
void correct_impl() {
    boost::ptr_set<int> s;
    s.insert(new int(1));
    s.insert(new int(0));
    // ...
    assert(*s.begin() == 0);
    // ...
    // resources will be deallocated by container itself
}
```

How it works...

The `Boost.PointerContainer` library has classes `ptr_array`, `ptr_vector`, `ptr_set`, `ptr_multimap`, and others. All these containers simplify your life. When dealing with pointers, they will be deallocating pointers in destructors and simplifying access to data pointed by the pointer (no need for additional dereference in `assert(*s.begin() == 0);`).

There's more...

Previous examples were not cloning pointer data, but when we want to clone some data, all we need to do is to just define a freestanding function such as `new_clone()` in the namespace of the object to be cloned. Moreover, you may use the default `T* new_clone( const T& r )` implementation if you include the header file `<boost/ptr_container/clone_allocator.hpp>` as shown in the following code:

```
#include <boost/ptr_container/clone_allocator.hpp>
#include <boost/ptr_container/ptr_vector.hpp>
```

```
// Creating vector of 10 elements with values 100
boost::ptr_vector<int> v;
v.resize(10, new int(100));
assert(v.size() == 10);
assert(v.back() == 100);
```

See also

▸ The official documentation contains detailed reference for each class, and you may read about it at `http://www.boost.org/doc/libs/1_53_0/libs/ptr_container/doc/ptr_container.html`

▸ The first four recipes of this chapter will give you some examples of smart pointers' usage

Doing something at scope exit

If you were dealing with languages such as Java, C#, or Delphi, you were obviously using the `try{} finally{}` construction or `scope(exit)` in the D programming language. Let me briefly describe to you what do these language constructions do.

When a program leaves the current scope via return or exception, code in the `finally` or `scope(exit)` blocks is executed. This mechanism is perfect for implementing the **RAII** pattern as shown in the following code snippet:

```
// Some pseudo code (suspiciously similar to Java code)
try {
    FileWriter f = new FileWriter("example_file.txt");
    // Some code that may trow or return
    // …
} finally {
    // Whatever happened in scope, this code will be executed
    // and file will be correctly closed
    if (f != null) {
        f.close()
    }
}
```

Is there a way to do such a thing in C++?

Getting ready

Basic C++ knowledge is required for this recipe. Knowledge of code behavior during thrown exceptions will be useful.

How to do it...

The `Boost.ScopeExit` library was designed to solve such problems:

```
#include <boost/scope_exit.hpp>
#include <cstdlib>
#include <cstdio>
#include <cassert>
int main() {
    std::FILE* f = std::fopen("example_file.txt", "w");
    assert(f);
    BOOST_SCOPE_EXIT(f) {
      // Whatever happened in scope, this code will be
      // executed and file will be correctly closed.
        std::fclose(f);
    } BOOST_SCOPE_EXIT_END
    // Some code that may throw or return.
    // ...
}
```

How it works...

The variable `f` is passed by value via `BOOST_SCOPE_EXIT(f)`. When the program leaves the scope of execution, the code between `BOOST_SCOPE_EXIT(f) {` and `} BOOST_SCOPE_EXIT_END` will be executed. If we wish to pass the value by reference, use the `&` symbol in the `BOOST_SCOPE_EXIT` macro. If we wish to pass multiple values, just separate them using a comma.

 Passing references to a pointer does not work well on some compilers. The `BOOST_SCOPE_EXIT(&f)` macro cannot be compiled there, which is why we do not capture it by reference in the example.

There's more...

To capture this inside a member function, we use a special symbol `this_`:

```
class theres_more_example {
public:
    void close(std::FILE*);
    void theres_more_example_func() {
        std::FILE* f = 0;
```

```
        BOOST_SCOPE_EXIT(f, this_) { // Capture object `this_`.
            this_->close(f);
        } BOOST_SCOPE_EXIT_END
    }
};
```

The `Boost.ScopeExit` library allocates no additional memory on heap and does not use virtual functions. Use the default syntax and do not define `BOOST_SCOPE_EXIT_CONFIG_USE_LAMBDAS` because otherwise scope exit will be implemented using `boost::function`, which may allocate additional memory and imply the optimization barrier.

See also

▶ The official documentation contains more examples and use cases. You can read about it at `http://www.boost.org/doc/libs/1_53_0/libs/scope_exit/doc/html/index.html`.

Initializing the base class by a member of the derived class

Let's take a look at the following example. We have some base class that has virtual functions and must be initialized with reference to the `std::ostream` object:

```cpp
#include <boost/noncopyable.hpp>
#include <sstream>

class tasks_processor: boost::noncopyable {
    std::ostream& log_;

protected:
    virtual void do_process() = 0;

public:
    explicit tasks_processor(std::ostream& log)
        : log_(log)
    {}

    void process() {
        log_ << "Starting data processing";
        do_process();
    }
};
```

We also have a derived class that has a `std::ostream` object and implements the `do_process()` function:

```
class fake_tasks_processor: public tasks_processor {
    std::ostringstream logger_;

    virtual void do_process() {
        logger_ << "Fake processor processed!";
    }

public:
    fake_tasks_processor()
        : tasks_processor(logger_) // Oops! logger_ does
                                   // not exist here
        , logger_()
    {}
};
```

This is not a very common case in programming, but when such mistakes happen, it is not always simple to get the idea of bypassing it. Some people try to bypass it by changing the order of `logger_` and the base type initialization:

```
    fake_tasks_processor()
        : logger_() // Oops! logger_ still will be constructed
                    // AFTER tasks_processor
        , tasks_processor(logger_)
    {}
```

It won't work as they expect because direct base classes are initialized before nonstatic data members, regardless of the order of the member initializers.

Getting ready

Basic knowledge of C++ is required for this recipe.

How to do it...

The `Boost.Utility` library provides a quick solution for such cases; it is called the `boost::base_from_member` template. To use it, you need to carry out the following steps:

1. Include the `base_from_member.hpp` header:

   ```
   #include <boost/utility/base_from_member.hpp>
   ```

2. Derive your class from `boost::base_from_member<T>` where `T` is a type that must be initialized before the base (take care about the order of the base classes; `boost::base_from_member<T>` must be placed before the class that uses `T`):

```
class fake_tasks_processor_fixed
    : boost::base_from_member<std::ostringstream>
    , public tasks_processor
```

3. Correctly write the constructor as follows:

```
{
    typedef boost::base_from_member<std::ostringstream>
      logger_t;
    // ...
public:
    fake_tasks_processor_fixed()
        : logger_t()
        , tasks_processor(logger_t::member)
    {}
};
```

How it works...

If direct base classes are initialized before nonstatic data members, and if direct base classes would be initialized in declaration order as they appear in the base-specifier-list, we need to somehow make a base class our nonstatic data member. Or make a base class that has a member field with the required member:

```
template < typename MemberType, int UniqueID = 0 >class
  base_from_member{protected:    MemberType  member;    //
    Constructors go there...};
```

There's more...

As you may see, `base_from_member` has an integer as a second template argument. This is done for cases when we need multiple `base_from_member` classes of the same type:

```
class fake_tasks_processor2
    : boost::base_from_member<std::ostringstream, 0>
    , boost::base_from_member<std::ostringstream, 1>
    , public tasks_processor
{
```

```
    typedef boost::base_from_member<std::ostringstream, 0>
      logger0_t;
    typedef boost::base_from_member<std::ostringstream, 1>
      logger1_t;

    virtual void do_process() {
        logger0_t::member << "0: Fake processor2 processed!";
        logger1_t::member << "1: Fake processor2 processed!";
    }
public:
    fake_tasks_processor2()
        : logger0_t()
        , logger1_t()
        , tasks_processor(logger0_t::member)
    {}
};
```

The `boost::base_from_member` class neither applies additional dynamic memory allocations nor has virtual functions. The current implementation does not support C++11 features (such as perfect forwarding and variadic templates), but in Boost's trunk branch, there is an implementation that can use all the benefits of C++11. It possibly will be merged to release a branch in the nearest future.

See also

► The `Boost.Utility` library contains many helpful classes and methods; documentation for getting more information about it is at `http://www.boost.org/doc/libs/1_53_0/libs/utility/utility.htm`

► The *Making a noncopyable class* recipe in *Chapter 1, Starting to Write Your Application*, contains more examples of classes from `Boost.Utility`

► Also, the *Using the C++11 move emulation* recipe in *Chapter 1, Starting to Write Your Application*, contains more examples of classes from `Boost.Utility`

4
Compile-time Tricks

In this chapter we will cover:

- ▶ Checking sizes at compile time
- ▶ Enabling the usage of templated functions for integral types
- ▶ Disabling templated functions' usage for real types
- ▶ Creating a type from number
- ▶ Implementing a type trait
- ▶ Selecting an optimal operator for a template parameter
- ▶ Getting a type of expression in C++03

Introduction

In this chapter we'll see some basic examples on how the Boost libraries can be used in compile-time checking, for tuning algorithms, and in other metaprogramming tasks.

Some readers may ask, "Why shall we care about compile-time things?". That's because the released version of the program is compiled once, and runs multiple times. The more we do at compile time, the less work remains for runtime, resulting in much faster and reliable programs. Runtime checks are executed only if a part of the code with check is executed. Compile-time checks won't give you to compile a program with error.

This chapter is possibly one of the most important. Understanding Boost sources and other Boost-like libraries is impossible without it.

Checking sizes at compile time

Let's imagine that we are writing some serialization function that stores values in buffer of a specified size:

```cpp
#include <cstring>
#include <boost/array.hpp>

template <class T, std::size_t BufSizeV>
void serialize(const T& value, boost::array<unsigned char,
  BufSizeV>& buffer) {
    // TODO: fixme
    std::memcpy(&buffer[0], &value, sizeof(value));
}
```

This code has the following troubles:

 ▸   The size of the buffer is not checked, so it may overflow

 ▸   This function can be used with non-plain old data (POD) types, which would lead to incorrect behavior

We may partially fix it by adding some asserts, for example:

```cpp
template <class T, std::size_t BufSizeV>
void serialize(const T& value, boost::array<unsigned char,
  BufSizeV>& buffer) {
    assert(BufSizeV >= sizeof(value));
    // TODO: fixme
    std::memcpy(&buffer[0], &value, sizeof(value));
}
```

But, this is a bad solution. The `BufSizeV` and `sizeof(value)` values are known at compile time, so we can potentially make this code to fail compilation if the buffer is too small, instead of having a runtime assert (which may not trigger during debug, if function was not called, and may even be optimized out in release mode, so very bad things may happen).

Getting ready

This recipe requires some knowledge of C++ templates and the `Boost.Array` library.

How to do it...

Let's use the `Boost.StaticAssert` and `Boost.TypeTraits` libraries to correct the solutions, and the output will be as follows:

```
#include <boost/static_assert.hpp>
#include <boost/type_traits/is_pod.hpp>

template <class T, std::size_t BufSizeV>
void serialize(const T& value, boost::array<unsigned char,
  BufSizeV>& buffer) {
    BOOST_STATIC_ASSERT(BufSizeV >= sizeof(value));
    BOOST_STATIC_ASSERT(boost::is_pod<T>::value);
    std::memcpy(&buffer[0], &value, sizeof(value));
}
```

How it works...

The `BOOST_STATIC_ASSERT` macro can be used only if an assert expression can be evaluated at compile time and implicitly convertible to `bool`. It means that you may only use `sizeof()`, static constants, and other constant expressions in it. If assert expression will evaluate to `false`, `BOOST_STATIC_ASSERT` will stop our program compilation. In case of `serialization()` function, if first static assertion fails, it means that someone used that function for a very small buffer and that code must be fixed by the programmer. The C++11 standard has a `static_assert` keyword that is equivalent to Boost's version.

Here are some more examples:

```
BOOST_STATIC_ASSERT(3 >= 1);

struct some_struct { enum enum_t { value = 1}; };
BOOST_STATIC_ASSERT(some_struct::value);

template <class T1, class T2>
struct some_templated_struct {
    enum enum_t { value = (sizeof(T1) == sizeof(T2))};
};
BOOST_STATIC_ASSERT((some_templated_struct<int, unsigned
  int>::value));
```

 If the `BOOST_STATIC_ASSERT` macro's assert expression has a comma sign in it, we must wrap the whole expression in additional brackets.

The last example is very close to what we can see on the second line of the `serialize()` function. So now it is time to know more about the `Boost.TypeTraits` library. This library provides a large number of compile-time metafunctions that allow us to get information about types and modify types. The metafunctions usages look like `boost::function_name<parameters>::value` or `boost::function_name<parameters>::type`. The metafunction `boost::is_pod<T>::value` will return `true`, only if `T` is a POD type.

Let's take a look at some more examples:

```
#include <iostream>
#include <boost/type_traits/is_unsigned.hpp>
#include <boost/type_traits/is_same.hpp>
#include <boost/type_traits/remove_const.hpp>

template <class T1, class T2>
void type_traits_examples(T1& /*v1*/, T2& /*v2*/) {
    // Returns true if T1 is an unsigned number
    std::cout << boost::is_unsigned<T1>::value;

    // Returns true if T1 has exactly the same type, as T2
    std::cout << boost::is_same<T1, T2>::value;

    // This line removes const modifier from type of T1.
    // Here is what will happen with T1 type if T1 is:
    // const int => int
    // int => int
    // int const volatile => int volatile
    // const int& => const int&
    typedef typename boost::remove_const<T1>::type t1_nonconst_t;
}
```

 Some compilers may compile this code even without the `typename` keyword, but such behavior violates the C++ standard, so it is highly recommended to write `typename`.

There's more...

The `BOOST_STATIC_ASSSERT` macro has a more verbose variant called `BOOST_STATIC_ASSSERT_MSG` that will output an error message in the compiler log (or in the IDE window) if assertion fails. Take a look at the following code:

```
template <class T, std::size_t BufSizeV>
void serialize2(const T& value, boost::array<unsigned char,
  BufSizeV>& buf) {
```

```
        BOOST_STATIC_ASSERT_MSG(boost::is_pod<T>::value,
            "This serialize2 function may be used only "
            "with POD types."
        );

        BOOST_STATIC_ASSERT_MSG(BufSizeV >= sizeof(value),
            "Can not fit value to buffer. "
            "Make buffer bigger."
        );

        std::memcpy(&buf[0], &value, sizeof(value));
    }

        // Somewhere in code:
        boost::array<unsigned char, 1> buf;
        serialize2(std::string("Hello word"), buf);
```

The preceding code will give the following result during compilation on the g++ compiler in the C++11 mode:

```
../../../BoostBook/Chapter4/static_assert/main.cpp: In instantiation
  of 'void serialize2(const T&, boost::array<unsigned char,
    BufSizeV>&) [with T = std::basic_string<char>; long unsigned int
      BufSizeV = 1ul]':
../../../BoostBook/Chapter4/static_assert/main.cpp:77:46: required
  from here
../../../BoostBook/Chapter4/static_assert/main.cpp:58:5: error:
  static assertion failed: This serialize2 function may be used only
    with POD types.
../../../BoostBook/Chapter4/static_assert/main.cpp:63:5: error:
  static assertion failed: Can not fit value to buffer. Make buffer
    bigger.
```

Neither BOOST_STATIC_ASSSERT, nor BOOST_STATIC_ASSSERT_MSG, nor any of the type traits library imply runtime penalty. All those functions are executed at compile time, and won't add a single assembly instruction in binary file.

The Boost.TypeTraits library was partially accepted into the C++11 standard; you may thus find traits in the <type_traits> header in the std:: namespace. C++11 <type_traits> has some functions that do not exist in Boost.TypeTraits, but some metafunctions exist only in Boost. When there is a similar function in Boost and STL, the STL version (in rare cases) may work slightly better because of compiler-specific intrinsics usage.

As we have already mentioned earlier, the BOOST_STATIC_ASSERT_MSG macro was also accepted into C++11 (and even into C11) as the keyword static_assert(expression, message).

Use the Boost version of those libraries if you need portability across compilers or metafunctions that does not exist in STLs `<type_traits>`.

See also

▸ The next recipes in this chapter will give you more examples and ideas on how static asserts and type traits may be used

▸ Read the official documentation of `Boost.StaticAssert` for more examples at `http://www.boost.org/doc/libs/1_53_0/doc/html/boost_staticassert.html`

Enabling the usage of templated functions for integral types

It's a common situation, when we have a templated class that implements some functionality. Have a look at the following code snippet:

```
// Generic implementation
template <class T>
class data_processor {
    double process(const T& v1, const T& v2, const T& v3);
};
```

After execution of the preceding code, we have additional two optimized versions of that class, one for integral, and another for real types:

```
// Integral types optimized version
template <class T>
class data_processor {
    typedef int fast_int_t;
    double process(fast_int_t v1, fast_int_t v2, fast_int_t v3);
};

// SSE optimized version for float types
template <class T>
class data_processor {
    double process(double v1, double v2, double v3);
};
```

Now the question, how to make the compiler to automatically choose the correct class for a specified type, arises.

Getting ready

This recipe requires the knowledge of C++ templates.

How to do it...

We'll be using `Boost.Utility` and `Boost.TypeTraits` to resolve this problem:

1. Let's start with including headers:

```
#include <boost/utility/enable_if.hpp>
#include <boost/type_traits/is_integral.hpp>
#include <boost/type_traits/is_float.hpp>
```

2. Let's add an additional template parameter with default value to our generic implementation:

```
// Generic implementation
template <class T, class Enable = void>
class data_processor {
    // ...
};
```

3. Modify optimized versions in the following way, so that now they will be treated by the compiler as template partial specializations:

```
// Integral types optimized version
template <class T>
class data_processor<T, typename boost::enable_if_c<
    boost::is_integral<T>::value
>::type> { /* ... */ };

// SSE optimized version for float types
template <class T>
class data_processor<T, typename boost::enable_if_c<
    boost::is_float<T>::value
>::type> { /* ... */ };
```

4. And, that's it! Now the compiler will automatically choose the correct class:

```
template <class T>
double example_func(T v1, T v2, T v3) {
    data_processor<T> proc;
    return proc.process(v1, v2, v3);
}
```

```
int main () {
    // Integral types optimized version
    // will be called
    example_func(1, 2, 3);
    short s = 0;
    example_func(s, s, s);

    // Real types version will be called
    example_func(1.0, 2.0, 3.0);
    example_func(1.0f, 2.0f, 3.0f);

    // Generic version will be called
    example_func("Hello", "word", "processing");
}
```

How it works...

The `boost::enable_if_c` template is a tricky one. It makes use of the **SFINAE** (**Substitution Failure Is Not An Error**) principle, which is used during template instantiation. Here is how the principle works: if an invalid argument or return type is formed during the instantiation of a function or class template, the instantiation is removed from the overload resolution set and does not cause a compilation error. Now let's get back to the solution, and we'll see how it works with different types passed to the `data_processor` class as the `T` parameter.

If we pass an `int` as `T` type, first the compiler will try to instantiate template partial specializations, before using our nonspecialized (generic) version. When it tries to instantiate a `float` version, the `boost::is_float<T>::value` metafunction will return `false`. The `boost::enable_if_c<false>::type` metafunction cannot be correctly instantiated (because `boost::enable_if_c<false>` has no `::type`), and that is the place where SFINAE will act. Because class template cannot be instantiated, and this must be interpreted as not an error, compiler will skip this template specialization. Next, partial specialization is the one that is optimized for integral types. The `boost::is_integral<T>::value` metafunction will return `true`, and `boost::enable_if_c<true>::type` can be instantiated, which makes it possible to instantiate the whole `data_processor` specialization. The compiler found a matching partial specialization, so it does not need to try to instantiate the nonspecialized method.

Now, let's try to pass some nonarithmetic type (for example, `const char *`), and let's see what the compiler will do. First the compiler will try to instantiate template partial specializations. The specializations with `is_float<T>::value` and `is_integral<T>::value` will fail to instantiate, so the compiler will try to instantiate our generic version, and will succeed.

Without `boost::enable_if_c<>`, all the partial specialized versions may be instantiated at the same time for any type, which leads to ambiguity and failed compilation.

 If you are using templates and compiler reports that cannot choose between two template classes of methods, you probably need `boost::enable_if_c<>`.

There's more...

Another version of this method is called `boost::enable_if` (without `_c` at the end). Difference between them is that `enable_if_c` accepts constant as a template parameter; however, the short version accepts an object that has a `value` static member. For example, `boost::enable_if_c<boost::is_integral<T>::value >::type` is equal to `boost::enable_if<boost::is_integral<T> >::type>`.

C++11 has an `std::enable_if` defined in the `<type_traits>` header, which behaves exactly like `boost::enable_if_c`. No difference between them exists, except that Boost's version will work on non C++11 compilers too, providing better portability.

All the enabling functions are executed only at compile time and do not add a performance overhead at runtime. However, adding an additional template parameter may produce a bigger class name in `typeid(T).name()`, and add an extremely tiny performance overhead when comparing two `typeid()` results on some platforms.

See also

- ▸ Next recipes will give you more examples on `enable_if` usage.
- ▸ You may also consult the official documentation of `Boost.Utility`. It contains many examples and a lot of useful classes (which are used widely in this book). Read about it at `http://www.boost.org/doc/libs/1_53_0/libs/utility/utility.htm`.
- ▸ You may also read some articles about template partial specializations at `http://msdn.microsoft.com/en-us/library/3967w96f%28v=vs.110%29.aspx`.

Disabling templated functions' usage for real types

We continue working with Boost metaprogramming libraries. In the previous recipe, we saw how to use `enable_if_c` with classes, now it is time to take a look at its usage in template functions. Consider the following example.

Initially, we had a template function that works with all the available types:

```
template <class T>
T process_data(const T& v1, const T& v2, const T& v3);
```

Now that we write code using `process_data` function, we use an optimized `process_data` version for types that do have an `operator +=` function:

```
template <class T>
T process_data_plus_assign(const T& v1, const T& v2, const T& v3);
```

But, we do not want to change the already written code; instead whenever it is possible, we want to force the compiler to automatically use optimized function in place of the default one.

Getting ready

Read the previous recipe to get an idea of what `boost::enable_if_c` does, and for understanding the concept of SFINAE. However, the knowledge of templates is still required.

How to do it...

Template magic can be done using the Boost libraries. Let's see how to do it:

1. We will need the `boost::has_plus_assign<T>` metafunction and the `<boost/enable_if.hpp>` header:

    ```
    #include <boost/utility/enable_if.hpp>
    #include <boost/type_traits/has_plus_assign.hpp>
    ```

2. Now we will disable default implementation for types with plus assign operator:

    ```
    // Modified generic version of process_data
    template <class T>
    typename boost::disable_if_c<boost::has_plus_assign<T>
      ::value,T>::type
        process_data(const T& v1, const T& v2, const T& v3);
    ```

3. Enable optimized version for types with plus assign operator:

```
// This process_data will call a process_data_plus_assign
template <class T>
typename boost::enable_if_c<boost::has_plus_assign<T>::value,
T>::type
    process_data(const T& v1, const T& v2, const T& v3)
{
    return process_data_plus_assign(v1, v2, v3);
}
```

4. Now, users won't feel the difference, but the optimized version will be used wherever possible:

```
int main() {
    int i = 1;
    // Optimized version
    process_data(i, i, i);

    // Default version
    // Explicitly specifing template parameter
    process_data<const char*>("Testing", "example", "function");
}
```

How it works...

The `boost::disable_if_c<bool_value>::type` metafunction disables method, if `bool_value` equals to `true` (works just like `boost::enable_if_c<!bool_value>::type`).

If we pass a class as the second parameter for `boost::enable_if_c` or `boost::disable_if_c`, it will be returned via `::type` in case of successful evaluation.

Let's go through the instantiation of templates step-by-step. If we pass `int` as `T` type, first the compiler will search for function overload with required signature. Because there is no such function, the next step will be to instantiate a template version of this function. For example, the compiler started from our second (optimized) version; in that case, it will successfully evaluate the `typename boost::enable_if_c<boost::has_plus_assign<T>::value, T>::type` expression, and will get the `T` return type. But, the compiler won't stop; it will continue instantiation attempts. It'll try to instantiate our first version of function, but will get a failure during evaluation of `typename boost::disable_if_c<boost::has_plus_assign<T>::value`. This failure won't be treated as an error (refer SFINAE). As you can see, without `enable_if_c` and `disable_if_c`, there will be ambiguity.

There's more...

As in case of `enable_if_c` and `enable_if`, there is a `disable_if` version of the disabling function:

```
// First version
template <class T>
typename boost::disable_if<boost::has_plus_assign<T>, T>::type
process_data2(const T& v1, const T& v2, const T& v3);

// process_data_plus_assign
template <class T>
typename boost::enable_if<boost::has_plus_assign<T>, T>::type
process_data2(const T& v1, const T& v2, const T& v3);
```

C++11 has neither `disable_if_c`, nor `disable_if` (you may use `std::enable_if<!bool_value>::type` instead).

As it was mentioned in the previous recipe, all the enabling and disabling functions are executed only at compile time, and do not add performance overhead at runtime.

See also

- ▶ Read this chapter from the beginning to get more examples of compile-time tricks.

- ▶ Consider reading the `Boost.TypeTraits` official documentation for more examples and full list of metafunctions at http://www.boost.org/doc/libs/1_53_0/libs/type_traits/doc/html/index.html.

- ▶ The `Boost.Utility` library may provide you more examples of `boost::enable_if` usage. Read about it at http://www.boost.org/doc/libs/1_53_0/libs/utility/utility.htm.

Creating a type from number

We have now seen examples of how we can choose between functions without `boost::enable_if_c` usage. Let's consider the following example, where we have a generic method for processing POD datatypes:

```
#include <boost/static_assert.hpp>
#include <boost/type_traits/is_pod.hpp>

// Generic implementation
template <class T>
T process(const T& val) {
    BOOST_STATIC_ASSERT((boost::is_pod<T>::value));
    // ...
}
```

And, we have the same function optimized for sizes 1, 4, and 8 bytes. How do we rewrite process function, so that it can dispatch calls to optimized versions?

Getting ready

Reading at least the first recipe from this chapter is highly recommended, so that you will not be confused by all the things that are happening here. Templates and metaprogramming shall not scare you (or just get ready to see a lot of them).

How to do it...

We are going to see how the size of a template type can be converted to a variable of some type, and how that variable can be used for deducing the right function overload.

1. Let's define our generic and optimized versions of `process_impl` function:

```cpp
#include <boost/mpl/int.hpp>

namespace detail {
    // Generic implementation
    template <class T, class Tag>
    T process_impl(const T& val, Tag /*ignore*/) {
        // ...
    }

    // 1 byte optimized implementation
    template <class T>
    T process_impl(const T& val, boost::mpl::int_<1> /*ignore*/) {
        // ...
    }

    // 4 bytes optimized implementation
    template <class T>
    T process_impl(const T& val, boost::mpl::int_<4> /*ignore*/) {
        // ...
    }

    // 8 bytes optimized implementation
    template <class T>
    T process_impl(const T& val, boost::mpl::int_<8> /*ignore*/) {
        // ...
    }
} // namespace detail
```

2. Now we are ready to write process function:

```
// will be only dispatching calls
template <class T>
T process(const T& val) {
    BOOST_STATIC_ASSERT((boost::is_pod<T>::value));
    return detail::process_impl(
        val, boost::mpl::int_<sizeof(T)>());
}
```

How it works...

The most interesting part here is `boost::mpl::int_<sizeof(T)>()`. `sizeof(T)` executes at compile time, so its output can be used as a template parameter. The class `boost::mpl::int_<>` is just an empty class that holds a compile-time value of integral type (in the `Boost.MPL` library, such classes are called Integral Constants). It can be implemented as shown in the following code:

```
template <int Value>
struct int_ {
    static const int value = Value;
    typedef int_<Value> type;
    typedef int value_type;
};
```

We need an instance of this class, that is why we have a round parentheses at the end of `boost::mpl::int_<sizeof(T)>()`.

Now, let's take a closer look at how the compiler will decide which `process_impl` function to use. First of all, the compiler will try to match functions that have a second parameter and not a template. If `sizeof(T)` is 4, the compiler will try to search the function with signatures like `process_impl(T, boost::mpl::int_<8>)`, and will find our 4 bytes optimized version from the `detail` namespace. If `sizeof(T)` is 34, compiler won't find the function with signature like `process_impl(T, boost::mpl::int_<34>)`, and will use a templated variant `process_impl(const T& val, Tag /*ignore*/)`.

There's more...

The `Boost.MPL` library has several data structures for metaprogramming. In this recipe, we only scratched a top of the iceberg. You may find the following Integral Constant classes from MPL useful:

- `bool_`
- `int_`

- ▸ long_
- ▸ size_t
- ▸ char_

All the `Boost.MPL` functions (except the `for_each` runtime function) are executed at compile time and won't add runtime overhead. The `Boost.MPL` library is not a part of C++11, but many STL libraries implement functions from it for their own needs.

See also

- ▸ The recipes from *Chapter 8*, *Metaprogramming*, will give you more examples of the `Boost.MPL` library usage. If you feel confident, you may also try to read its documentation at `http://www.boost.org/doc/libs/1_53_0/libs/mpl/doc/index.html`.
- ▸ Read more examples of tags usage at `http://www.boost.org/doc/libs/1_53_0/libs/type_traits/doc/html/boost_typetraits/examples/fill.html` and `http://www.boost.org/doc/libs/1_53_0/libs/type_traits/doc/html/boost_typetraits/examples/copy.html`.

Implementing a type trait

We need to implement a type trait that returns true if the `std::vector` type is passed to it as a template parameter.

Getting ready

Some basic knowledge of the `Boost.TypeTrait` or STL type traits is required.

How to do it...

Let's see how to implement a type trait:

```
#include <vector>
#include <boost/type_traits/integral_constant.hpp>

template <class T>
struct is_stdvector: boost::false_type {};

template <class T, class Allocator>
struct is_stdvector<std::vector<T, Allocator> >: boost::true_type
{};
```

How it works...

Almost all the work is done by the `boost::true_type` and `boost::false_type` classes. The `boost::true_type` class has a boolean `::value` static constant in it that equals to `true`, the `boost::false_type` class has a boolean `::value` static constant in it that equals to `false`. They also have some typedefs, and are usually derived from `boost::mpl::integral_c`, which makes it easy to use types derived from `true_type`/`false_type` with `Boost.MPL`.

Our first `is_stdvector` structure is a generic structure that will be used always when template specialized version of such structure is not found. Our second `is_stdvector` structure is a template specialization for the `std::vector` types (note that it is derived from `true_type`!). So, when we pass vector type to the `is_stdvector` structure, template specialized version will be used, otherwise generic version will be used, which is derived from `false_type`.

> 3 lines There is no public keyword before `boost::false_type` and `boost::true_type` in our trait because we use `struct` keyword, and by default it uses public inheritance.

There's more...

Those readers who use the C++11 compatible compilers may use the `true_type` and `false_type` types declared in the `<type_traits>` header from the `std::` namespace for creating their own type traits.

As usual, the Boost version is more portable because it can be used on C++03 compilers.

See also

► Almost all the recipes from this chapter use type traits. Refer to the `Boost.TypeTraits` documentation for more examples and information at `http://www.boost.org/doc/libs/1_53_0/libs/type_traits/doc/html/index.html`.

Selecting an optimal operator for a template parameter

Imagine that we are working with classes from different vendors that implement different amounts of arithmetic operations and have constructors from integers. And, we do want to make a function that increments by one when any class is passed to it. Also, we want this function to be effective! Take a look at the following code:

```
template <class T>
void inc(T& value) {
    // call ++value
    // or call value ++
    // or value += T(1);
    // or value = value + T(1);
}
```

Getting ready

Some basic knowledge of the C++ templates, and the `Boost.TypeTrait` or STL type traits is required.

How to do it...

All the selecting can be done at compile time. This can be achieved using the `Boost.TypeTraits` library, as shown in the following steps:

1. Let's start from making correct functional objects:

```
namespace detail {
    struct pre_inc_functor {
        template <class T>
        void operator()(T& value) const {
            ++ value;
        }
    };

    struct post_inc_functor {
        template <class T>
        void operator()(T& value) const {
            value++;
        }
    };
```

```
struct plus_assignable_functor {
    template <class T>
    void operator()(T& value) const {
        value += T(1);
    }
};

struct plus_functor {
    template <class T>
    void operator()(T& value) const {
        value = value + T(1);
    }
};
}
```

2. After that we will need a bunch of type traits:

```
#include <boost/type_traits/conditional.hpp>
#include <boost/type_traits/has_plus_assign.hpp>
#include <boost/type_traits/has_plus.hpp>
#include <boost/type_traits/has_post_increment.hpp>
#include <boost/type_traits/has_pre_increment.hpp>
```

3. And, we are ready to deduce correct functor and use it:

```
template <class T>
void inc(T& value) {
    typedef detail::plus_functor step_0_t;

    typedef typename boost::conditional<
      boost::has_plus_assign<T>::value,
      detail::plus_assignable_functor,
      step_0_t
    >::type step_1_t;

    typedef typename boost::conditional<
      boost::has_post_increment<T>::value,
      detail::post_inc_functor,
      step_1_t
    >::type step_2_t;

    typedef typename boost::conditional<
      boost::has_pre_increment<T>::value,
      detail::pre_inc_functor,
      step_2_t
```

```
>::type step_3_t;

    step_3_t() // default constructing functor
        (value); // calling operator() of a functor
}
```

How it works...

All the magic is done via the `conditional<bool Condition, class T1, class T2>` metafunction. When this metafunction accepts `true` as a first parameter, it returns `T1` via the `::type` typedef. When the `boost::conditional` metafunction accepts `false` as a first parameter, it returns `T2` via the `::type` typedef. It acts like some kind of compile-time `if` statement.

So, `step0_t` holds a `detail::plus_functor` metafunction and `step1_t` will hold `step0_t` or `detail::plus_assignable_functor`. The `step2_t` type will hold `step1_t` or `detail::post_inc_functor`. The `step3_t` type will hold `step2_t` or `detail::pre_inc_functor`. What each `step*_t` typedef holds is deduced using type trait.

There's more...

There is a C++11 version of this function, which can be found in the `<type_traits>` header in the `std::` namespace. Boost has multiple versions of this function in different libraries, for example, `Boost.MPL` has function `boost::mpl::if_c`, which acts exactly like `boost::conditional`. It also has a version `boost::mpl::if_` (without `c` at the end), which will call `::type` for its first template argument; and if it is derived from `boost::true_type` (or is a `boost::true_type` type), it will return its second argument during the `::type` call, otherwise it will return the last template parameter. We can rewrite our `inc()` function to use `Boost.MPL`, as shown in the following code:

```
#include <boost/mpl/if.hpp>

template <class T>
void inc_mpl(T& value) {
    typedef detail::plus_functor step_0_t;

    typedef typename boost::mpl::if_<
      boost::has_plus_assign<T>,
      detail::plus_assignable_functor,
      step_0_t
    >::type step_1_t;

    typedef typename boost::mpl::if_<
      boost::has_post_increment<T>,
```

```
       detail::post_inc_functor,
       step_1_t
   >::type step_2_t;

   typedef typename boost::mpl::if_<
       boost::has_pre_increment<T>,
       detail::pre_inc_functor,
       step_2_t
   >::type step_3_t;

   step_3_t() // default constructing functor
       (value); // calling operator() of a functor
}
```

See also

 ▸ The recipe *Enabling the usage of templated functions for integral types*

 ▸ The recipe *Disabling templated functions' usage for real types*

 ▸ The `Boost.TypeTraits` documentation has a full list of available metafunctions. Read about it at `http://www.boost.org/doc/libs/1_53_0/libs/type_traits/doc/html/index.html`.

 ▸ The recipes from *Chapter 8, Metaprogramming*, will give you more examples of the `Boost.MPL` library usage. If you feel confident, you may also try to read its documentation at `http://www.boost.org/doc/libs/1_53_0/libs/mpl/doc/index.html`.

 ▸ There is a proposal to add type switch to C++, and you may find it interesting. Read about it at `http://www.stroustrup.com/OOPSLA-typeswitch-draft.pdf`.

Getting a type of expression in C++03

In the previous recipes, we saw some examples on `boost::bind` usage. It is a good and useful tool with a small drawback; it is hard to store `boost::bind` metafunction's functor as a variable in C++03.

```
#include <functional>
#include <boost/bind.hpp>

const ??? var = boost::bind(std::plus<int>(), _1, _1);
```

In C++11, we can use `auto` keyword instead of `???`, and that will work. Is there a way to do it in C++03?

Getting ready

The knowledge of the C++11 `auto` and `decltype` keywords may help you to understand this recipe.

How to do it...

We will need a `Boost.Typeof` library for getting return type of expression:

```
#include <boost/typeof/typeof.hpp>
BOOST_AUTO(var, boost::bind(std::plus<int>(), _1, _1));
```

How it works...

It just creates a variable with the name `var`, and the value of the expression is passed as a second argument. Type of `var` is detected from the type of expression.

There's more...

An experienced C++11 reader will note that there are more keywords in the new standard for detecting the types of expression. Maybe `Boost.Typeof` has macro for them too. Let's take a look at the following C++11 code:

```
typedef decltype(0.5 + 0.5f) type;
```

Using `Boost.Typeof`, the preceding code can be written like the following code:

```
typedef BOOST_TYPEOF(0.5 + 0.5f) type;
```

C++11 version's `decltype(expr)` deduces and returns the type of `expr`.

```
template<class T1, class T2>
auto add(const T1& t1, const T2& t2) ->decltype(t1 + t2) {
    return t1 + t2;
};
```

Using `Boost.Typeof`, the preceding code can be written like the following code:

```
template<class T1, class T2>
BOOST_TYPEOF_TPL(T1() + T2()) add(const T1& t1, const T2& t2) {
    return t1 + t2;
};
```

C++11 has a special syntax for specifying return type at the end of the function declaration. Unfortunately, this cannot be emulated in C++03, so we cannot use `t1` and `t2` variables in macro.

You can freely use the results of the `BOOST_TYPEOF()` functions in templates and in any other compile-time expressions:

```
#include <boost/static_assert.hpp>
#include <boost/type_traits/is_same.hpp>
BOOST_STATIC_ASSERT((boost::is_same<BOOST_TYPEOF(add(1, 1)),
    int>::value));
```

But unfortunately, this magic does not always work without help. For example, user-defined classes are not always detected, so the following code may fail on some compilers:

```
namespace readers_project {
    template <class T1, class T2, class T3>
    struct readers_template_class{};
}

#include <boost/tuple/tuple.hpp>

typedef
    readers_project::readers_template_class<int, int, float>
readers_template_class_1;

typedef BOOST_TYPEOF(boost::get<0>(
    boost::make_tuple(readers_template_class_1(), 1)
)) readers_template_class_deduced;

BOOST_STATIC_ASSERT((
    boost::is_same<
        readers_template_class_1,
        readers_template_class_deduced
    >::value
));
```

In such situations, you may give `Boost.Typeof` a helping hand and register a template:

```
BOOST_TYPEOF_REGISTER_TEMPLATE(
        readers_project::readers_template_class /*class name*/,
        3 /*number of template classes*/
)
```

However, three most popular compilers correctly detected type even without `BOOST_TYPEOF_REGISTER_TEMPLATE` and without C++11.

See also

- The official documentation of `Boost.Typeof` has more examples. Read about it at `http://www.boost.org/doc/libs/1_53_0/doc/html/typeof.html`.

- *Bjarne Stroustrup* may introduce some of the C++11 features to you. Read about it at `http://www.stroustrup.com/C++11FAQ.html`.

5
Multithreading

In this chapter we will cover:

- ▶ Creating an execution thread
- ▶ Syncing access to a common resource
- ▶ Fast access to a common resource using atomics
- ▶ Creating a work_queue class
- ▶ Multiple-readers-single-writer lock
- ▶ Creating variables that are unique per thread
- ▶ Interrupting a thread
- ▶ Manipulating a group of threads

Introduction

In this chapter we'll take care of threads and all of the stuff connected with them. Basic knowledge of multithreading is encouraged.

Multithreading means that multiple execution threads exist within a single process. Threads may share process resources and have their own resources. Those execution threads may run independently on different CPUs, leading to faster and more responsive programs.

The `Boost.Thread` library provides uniformity across operating system interfaces for working with threads. It is not a header-only library, so all of the examples from this chapter will need to link against the `libboost_thread` and `libboost_system` libraries.

Creating an execution thread

On modern multi-core compilers, to achieve maximal performance (or just to provide a good user experience), programs usually must use multiple execution threads. Here is a motivating example in which we need to create and fill a big file in a thread that draws the user interface:

```
#include <algorithm>
#include <fstream>
#include <iterator>

void set_not_first_run();
bool is_first_run();

// Function, that executes for a long time
void fill_file_with_data(char fill_char, std::size_t size, const char*
filename){
  std::ofstream ofs(filename);
  std::fill_n(std::ostreambuf_iterator<char>(ofs), size, fill_char);
  set_not_first_run();
}

// ...
// Somewhere in thread that draws a user interface
if (is_first_run()) {
  // This will be executing for a long time during which
  // users interface will freeze..
  fill_file_with_data(0, 8 * 1024 * 1024, "save_file.txt");
}
```

Getting ready

This recipe will require knowledge of the boost::bind library.

How to do it...

Starting an execution thread was never so easy:

```
#include <boost/thread.hpp>

// ...
// Somewhere in thread that draws a user interface
if (is_first_run()) {
```

```
    boost::thread(boost::bind(
        &fill_file_with_data,
        0,
        8 * 1024 * 1024,
        "save_file.txt"
    )).detach();
}
```

How it works...

The `boost::thread` variable accepts a functional object that can be called without parameters (we provided one using `boost::bind`) and creates a separate execution thread. That functional object will be copied into a constructed execution thread and will be run there.

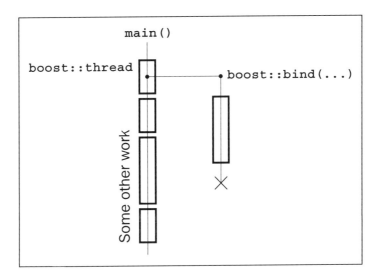

 In all of the recipes with the `Boost.Thread` library, we'll be using Version 4 (defined `BOOST_THREAD_VERSION` to `4`) of threads by default and pointing out some important differences between `Boost.Thread` versions.

After that, we call the `detach()` function, which will do the following:

▸ The execution thread will be detached from the `boost::thread` variable but will continue its execution

▸ The `boost::thread` variable will hold a `Not-A-Thread` state

Note that without a call to `detach()`, the destructor of `boost::thread` will notice that it still holds a thread and will call `std::terminate`, which will terminate our program.

Default constructed threads will also have a `Not-A-Thread` state, and they won't create a separate execution thread.

There's more...

What if we want to make sure that a file was created and written before doing some other job? In that case we need to join a thread using the following:

```
// ...
// Somewhere in thread that draws a user interface
if (is_first_run()) {
  boost::thread t(boost::bind(
      &fill_file_with_data,
      0,
      8 * 1024 * 1024,
      "save_file.txt"
  ));
  // Do some work
  // ...
  // Waiting for thread to finish
  t.join();
}
```

After the thread is joined, the `boost::thread` variable will hold a `Not-A-Thread` state and its destructor won't call `std::terminate`.

> Remember that the thread must be joined or detached before its destructor is called. Otherwise, your program will terminate!
>
> Beware that `std::terminate()` is called when any exception that is not of type `boost::thread_interrupted` leaves the boundary of the functional object and is passed to the `boost::thread` constructor.

The `boost::thread` class was accepted as a part of the C++11 standard and you can find it in the `<thread>` header in the `std::` namespace. By default, with `BOOST_THREAD_VERSION=2`, the destructor of `boost::thread` will call `detach()`, which won't lead to `std::terminate`. But doing so will break compatibility with `std::thread`, and some day, when your project is moving to the C++ standard library threads or when `BOOST_THREAD_VERSION=2` is no longer supported this will give you a lot of surprises. Version 4 of `Boost.Thread` is more explicit and strong, which is usually preferable in C++ language.

There is a very helpful wrapper that works as a RAII wrapper around the thread and allows you to emulate the `BOOST_THREAD_VERSION=2` behavior; it is called `boost::scoped_thread<T>`, where `T` can be one of the following classes:

- `boost::interrupt_and_join_if_joinable`: To interrupt and join thread at destruction
- `boost::join_if_joinable`: To join a thread at destruction
- `boost::detach`: To detach a thread at destruction

Here is a small example:

```
#include <boost/thread/scoped_thread.hpp>
void some_func();
void example_with_raii() {
  boost::scoped_thread<boost::join_if_joinable> t(
    (boost::thread(&some_func))
  );
  // 't' will be joined at scope exit
}
```

 We added additional parentheses around `(boost::thread(&some_func))` so that the compiler won't interpret it as a function declaration instead of a variable construction.

There is no big difference between the Boost and C++11 STL versions of the `thread` class; however, `boost::thread` is available on the C++03 compilers, so its usage is more versatile.

See also

- All of the recipes in this chapter will be using `Boost.Thread`; you may continue reading to get more information about them
- The official documentation has a full list of the `boost::thread` methods and remarks about their availability in the C++11 STL implementation; it can be found at `http://www.boost.org/doc/libs/1_53_0/doc/html/thread.html`
- The *Interrupting a thread* recipe will give you an idea of what the `boost::interrupt_and_join_if_joinable` class does

Syncing access to a common resource

Now that we know how to start execution threads, we want to have access to some common resources from different threads:

```cpp
#include <cassert>
#include <cstddef>

// In previous recipe we included
// <boost/thread.hpp>, which includes all
// the classes of Boost.Thread
#include <boost/thread/thread.hpp>

int shared_i = 0;

void do_inc() {
  for (std::size_t i = 0; i < 30000; ++i) {
    // do some work
    // ...

    const int i_snapshot = ++ shared_i;

    // do some work with i_snapshot
    // ...
  }
}

void do_dec() {
  for (std::size_t i = 0; i < 30000; ++i) {
    // do some work
    // ...

    const int i_snapshot = -- shared_i;

    // do some work with i_snapshot
    // ...
  }
}

void run() {
  boost::thread t1(&do_inc);
  boost::thread t2(&do_dec);
```

```
t1.join();
t2.join();

// assert(shared_i == 0); // Oops!
std::cout << "shared_i == " << shared_i;
}
```

This 'Oops!' is not written there accidentally. For some people it will be a surprise, but there is a big chance that shared_i won't be equal to 0:

```
shared_i == 19567
```

 Modern compilers and processors have a huge number of different, tricky optimizations that can break the preceding code. We won't discuss them here, but there is a useful link in the *See also* section to a document that briefly describes them.

And it will get even worse in cases when a common resource has some non-trivial classes; segmentation faults and memory leaks may (and will) occur.

We need to change the code so that only one thread modifies the shared_i variable at a single moment of time and so that all of the processor and compiler optimizations that inflict multithreaded code are bypassed.

Getting ready

Basic knowledge of threads is recommended for this recipe.

How to do it...

Let's see how we can fix the previous example and make shared_i equal at the end of the run:

1. First of all we'll need to create a mutex:

    ```
    #include <boost/thread/mutex.hpp>
    #include <boost/thread/locks.hpp>

    int shared_i = 0;
    boost::mutex i_mutex;
    ```

2. Put all the operations that modify or get data from the `shared_i` variable between the following:

```
{ // Critical section begin
  boost::lock_guard<boost::mutex> lock(i_mutex);
```

And the following:

```
} // Critical section end
```

This is what it will look like:

```
void do_inc() {
  for (std::size_t i = 0; i < 30000; ++i) {

    // do some work
    // ...

    int i_snapshot;
    { // Critical section begin
      boost::lock_guard<boost::mutex> lock(i_mutex);
      i_snapshot = ++ shared_i;
    } // Critical section end

    // do some work with i_snapshot
    // ...
  }
}

void do_dec() {
  for (std::size_t i = 0; i < 30000; ++i) {
    // do some work
    // ...

    int i_snapshot;
    { // Critical section begin
      boost::lock_guard<boost::mutex> lock(i_mutex);
      i_snapshot = -- shared_i;
    } // Critical section end

    // do some work with i_snapshot
    // ...
  }
}
```

How it works...

The `boost::mutex` class takes care of all of the synchronization stuff. When a thread tries to lock it via the `boost::lock_guard<boost::mutex>` variable and there is no other thread holding a lock, it will successfully acquire unique access to the section of code until the lock is unlocked or destroyed. If some other thread already holds a lock, the thread that tried to acquire the lock will wait until another thread unlocks the lock. All the locking/unlocking operations imply specific instructions so that the changes made in a **critical section** will be visible to all threads. Also, you no longer need to *make sure that modified values of resources are visible to all cores and are not just modified in the processor's register* and *force the processor and compiler to not reorder the instructions*.

The `boost::lock_guard` class is a very simple RAII class that stores a reference to the mutex and calls `lock()` in the single-parameter constructor and `unlock()` in the destructor. Note the curly bracket usage in the preceding example; the `lock` variable is constructed inside them so that, on reaching the `critical section` closing bracket, the destructor for the `lock` variable will be called and the mutex will be unlocked. Even if some exception occurs in the critical section, the mutex will be correctly unlocked.

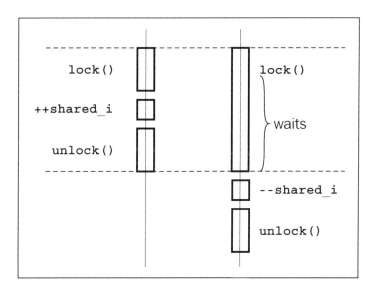

 If you have some resources that are used from different threads, usually all the code that uses them must be treated as a critical section and secured by a mutex.

There's more...

Locking a mutex is potentially a very slow operation, which may stop your code for a long time, until some other thread releases a lock. Try to make critical sections as small as possible and try to have less of them in your code.

Let's take a look at how some operating systems (OS) handle locking on a multicore CPU. When `thread` #1, running on CPU1, tries to lock a mutex that is already locked by another thread, `thread` #1 is stopped by the OS till the lock is released. The stopped thread does not *eat* processor resources, so the OS will still execute other threads on CPU1. Now we have some threads running on CPU1; some other thread releases the lock, and now the OS has to resume execution of a `thread` #1. So it will resume its execution on a currently free CPU, for example, CPU2. This will result in CPU cache misses, and code will be running slightly slower after the mutex is released. This is another reason to reduce the number of critical sections. However, things are not so bad because a good OS will try to resume the thread on the same CPU that it was using before.

Do not attempt to lock a `boost::mutex` variable twice in the same thread; it will lead to a **deadlock**. If locking a mutex multiple times from a single thread is required, use `boost::recursive_mutex` instead of the `<boost/thread/recursive_mutex.hpp>` header. Locking it multiple times won't lead to a deadlock. The `boost::recursive_mutex` will release the lock only after `unlock()` is called once for each `lock()` call. Avoid using `boost::recursive_mutex`; it is slower than `boost::mutex` and usually indicates bad code flow design.

The `boost::mutex`, `boost::recursive_mutex`, and `boost::lock_guard` classes were accepted to the C++11 standard, and you may find them in the `<mutex>` header in the `std::` namespace. No big difference between Boost and STL versions exists; a Boost version may have some extensions (which are marked in the official documentation as *EXTENSION*) and provide better portability because they can be used even on C++03 compilers.

See also

- ▶ The next recipe will give you some ideas on how to make this example much faster (and shorter).

- ▶ Read the first recipe from this chapter to get more information about the `boost::thread` class. The official documentation for Boost.Thread may help you too; it can be found at `http://www.boost.org/doc/libs/1_53_0/doc/html/thread.html`.

- ▶ For more information about why the first example will fail and how multiprocessors work with common resources, see *Memory Barriers: a Hardware View for Software Hackers* at `http://www.rdrop.com/users/paulmck/scalability/paper/whymb.2010.07.23a.pdf`.

Fast access to common resource using atomics

In the previous recipe, we saw how to safely access a common resource from different threads. But in that recipe, we were doing two system calls (in locking and unlocking the mutex) just to get the value from an integer:

```
{ // Critical section begin
  boost::lock_guard<boost::mutex> lock(i_mutex);
  i_snapshot = ++ shared_i;
} // Critical section end
```

This looks lame! And slow! Can we make the code from the previous recipe better?

Getting ready

Reading the first recipe is all you need to start with this. Or just some basic knowledge of multithreading.

How to do it...

Let's see how to improve our previous example:

1. We will need different headers:

    ```
    #include <cassert>
    #include <cstddef>

    #include <boost/thread/thread.hpp>
    #include <boost/atomic.hpp>
    ```

2. Changing the type of `shared_i` is required (as it is no longer needed in the mutex):

    ```
    boost::atomic<int> shared_i(0);
    ```

3. Remove all the `boost::lock_guard` variables:

    ```
    void do_inc() {
      for (std::size_t i = 0; i < 30000; ++i) {
        // do some work
        // ...
    ```

```
        const int i_snapshot = ++ shared_i;
        // do some work with i_snapshot
        // ...
    }
}

void do_dec() {
    for (std::size_t i = 0; i < 30000; ++i) {
        // do some work
        // ...
        const int i_snapshot = -- shared_i;
        // do some work with i_snapshot
        // ...
    }
}
```

And that's it! Now it works.

```
int main() {
    boost::thread t1(&do_inc);
    boost::thread t2(&do_dec);
    t1.join();
    t2.join();
    assert(shared_i == 0);
    std::cout << "shared_i == " << shared_i << std::endl;
}
```

How it works...

Processors provide specific atomic operations that cannot be interfered with by other processors or processor cores. These operations appear to occur instantaneously for a system. Boost.Atomic provides classes that wrap around system-specific atomic operations and provide a uniform and portable interface to work with them.

In other words, it is safe to use the boost::atomic<> variables from different threads simultaneously. Each operation on the atomic variable will be seen by the system as a single transaction. Series of operations on the atomic variables will be treated by the system as a series of transactions:

```
-- shared_i; // Transaction #1
// Some other thread may work here with shared_i and change its value
++shared_i; // Transaction #2
```

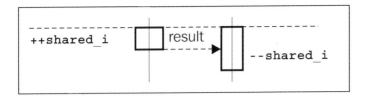

There's more...

The `Boost.Atomic` library can work only with POD types; otherwise, its behavior is undefined. Some platforms/processors do not provide atomic operations for some types, so `Boost.Atomic` will emulate atomic behavior using `boost::mutex`. The atomic type won't use `boost::mutex` if the type-specific macro is set to 2:

```
#include <boost/static_assert.hpp>
BOOST_STATIC_ASSERT(BOOST_ATOMIC_INT_LOCK_FREE == 2);
```

The `boost::atomic<T>::is_lock_free` member function depends on runtime, so it is not good for compile-time checks but may provide a more readable syntax when the runtime check is enough:

```
assert(shared_i.is_lock_free());
```

Atomics work much faster than mutexes. If we compare the execution time of a recipe that uses mutexes (0:00.08 seconds) and the execution time of the preceding example in this recipe (0:00.02 seconds), we'll see the difference (tested on 3,00,000 iterations).

The C++11 compilers should have all the atomic classes, typedefs, and macros in the `<atomic>` header in the `std::` namespace. Compiler-specific implementations of `std::atomic` may work faster than the Boost's version, if the compiler correctly supports the C++11 memory model and atomic operations are not a compiler barrier for it any more.

See also

▸ The official documentation may give you many more examples and some theoretical information on the topic; it can be found at `http://www.boost.org/doc/libs/1_53_0/doc/html/atomic.html`

▸ For more information about how atomics work, see *Memory Barriers: a Hardware View for Software Hackers* at `http://www.rdrop.com/users/paulmck/scalability/paper/whymb.2010.07.23a.pdf`

Creating a work_queue class

Let's call the functional object that takes no arguments (a task, in short).

```
typedef boost::function<void()> task_t;
```

And now, imagine a situation where we have threads that post tasks and threads that execute posted tasks. We need to design a class that can be safely used by both types of thread. This class must have methods for getting a task (or blocking and waiting for a task until it is posted by another thread), checking and getting a task if we have one (returning an empty task if no tasks remain), and a method to post tasks.

Getting ready

Make sure that you feel comfortable with `boost::thread` or `std::thread` and know some basics of mutexes.

How to do it...

The classes that we are going to implement will be close in functionality to `std::queue<task_t>` and will also have thread synchronization. Let's start:

1. We'll need the following headers and members:

    ```
    #include <deque>
    #include <boost/function.hpp>
    #include <boost/thread/mutex.hpp>
    #include <boost/thread/locks.hpp>
    #include <boost/thread/condition_variable.hpp>

    class work_queue {
    public:
        typedef boost::function<void()> task_type;

    private:
        std::deque<task_type>     tasks_;
        boost::mutex              tasks_mutex_;
        boost::condition_variable cond_;
    ```

2. A function for putting a task in the queue will look like this:

```
public:
  void push_task(const task_type& task) {
    boost::unique_lock<boost::mutex> lock(tasks_mutex_);
    tasks_.push_back(task);
    lock.unlock();
    cond_.notify_one();
  }
```

3. A non-blocking function for getting a pushed task or an empty task (if no tasks remain):

```
task_type try_pop_task() {
  task_type ret;
  boost::lock_guard<boost::mutex> lock(tasks_mutex_);
  if (!tasks_.empty()) {
    ret = tasks_.front();
    tasks_.pop_front();
  }
  return ret;
}
```

4. Blocking function for getting a pushed task or for blocking while the task is pushed by another thread:

```
task_type pop_task() {
  boost::unique_lock<boost::mutex> lock(tasks_mutex_);
  while (tasks_.empty()) {
    cond_.wait(lock);
  }
  task_type ret = tasks_.front();
  tasks_.pop_front();
  return ret;
}
};
```

And this is how a `work_queue` class may be used:

```
#include <boost/thread/thread.hpp>

work_queue g_queue;

void do_nothing(){}
```

```
const std::size_t tests_tasks_count = 3000;

void pusher() {
  for (std::size_t i = 0; i < tests_tasks_count; ++i) {
    // Adding task to do nothing
    g_queue.push_task(&do_nothing);
  }
}

void popper_sync() {
  for (std::size_t i = 0; i < tests_tasks_count; ++i) {
    g_queue.pop_task() // Getting task
    (); // Executing task
  }
}

int main() {
  boost::thread pop_sync1(&popper_sync);
  boost::thread pop_sync2(&popper_sync);
  boost::thread pop_sync3(&popper_sync);

  boost::thread push1(&pusher);
  boost::thread push2(&pusher);
  boost::thread push3(&pusher);

  // Waiting for all the tasks to pop
  pop_sync1.join();
  pop_sync2.join();
  pop_sync3.join();

  push1.join();
  push2.join();
  push3.join();

  // Asserting that no tasks remained,
  // and falling though without blocking
  assert(!g_queue.try_pop_task());

  g_queue.push_task(&do_nothing);
  // Asserting that there is a task,
  // and falling though without blocking
  assert(g_queue.try_pop_task());
}
```

```
struct user_info {
  std::string address;
  unsigned short age;

  // Other parameters
  // ...
};

class users_online {
  typedef boost::mutex               mutex_t;
  mutable mutex_t                    users_mutex_;
  std::map<std::string, user_info>   users_;

public:
  bool is_online(const std::string& username) const {
    boost::lock_guard<mutex_t> lock(mutex_);
    return users_.find(username) != users_.end();
  }

  unsigned short get_age(const std::string& username) const {
    boost::lock_guard<mutex_t> lock(mutex_);
    return users_.at(username).age;
  }

  void set_online(const std::string& username, const user_info& data)
  {
    boost::lock_guard<mutex_t> lock(mutex_);
    users_.insert(std::make_pair(username, data));
  }

  // Other methods
  // ...
};
```

But any operation will acquire a unique lock on the `mutex_` variable, so even getting resources will result in waiting on a locked mutex; therefore, this class will become a bottleneck very soon.

Can we fix it?

How to do it...

Replace `boost::unique_locks` with `boost::shared_lock` for methods that do not modify data:

```cpp
#include <boost/thread/shared_mutex.hpp>

class users_online {
    typedef boost::shared_mutex        mutex_t;
    mutable mutex_t                    users_mutex_;
    std::map<std::string, user_info>   users_;

public:
    bool is_online(const std::string& username) const {
        boost::shared_lock<mutex_t> lock(users_mutex_);
        return users_.find(username) != users_.end();
    }

    unsigned short get_age(const std::string& username) const {
        boost::shared_lock<mutex_t> lock(users_mutex_);
        return users_.at(username).age;
    }

    void set_online(const std::string& username, const user_info& data)
    {
        boost::lock_guard<mutex_t> lock(users_mutex_);
        users_.insert(std::make_pair(username, data));
    }

    // Other methods
    // ...
};
```

How it works...

We can allow getting the data from multiple threads simultaneously if those threads do not modify it. We need to uniquely own the mutex only if we are going to modify the data in it; in all other situations simultaneous access to it is allowed. And that is what `boost::shared_mutex` was designed for. It allows shared locking (read locking), which allows multiple simultaneous access to resources.

When we do try to unique lock a resource that is shared locked, operations will be blocked until there are no read locks remaining and only after that resource is unique locked, forcing new shared locks to wait until the unique lock is released.

Some readers may be seeing the mutable keyword for the first time. This keyword can be applied to non-static and non-constant class members. The mutable data member can be modified in the constant member functions.

There's more...

When you do need only unique locks, do not use `boost::shared_mutex` because it is slightly slower than a usual `boost::mutex` class. However, in other cases, it may give a big performance gain. For example, with four reading threads, shared mutex will work almost four times faster than `boost::mutex`.
Unfortunately, shared mutexes are not the part of the C++11 standard.

See also

▸ There is also a `boost::upgrade_mutex` class, which may be useful for cases when a shared lock needs promotion to unique lock. See the `Boost.Thread` documentation at `http://www.boost.org/doc/libs/1_53_0/doc/html/thread.html` for more information.

▸ For more information about the mutable keyword see `http://herbsutter.com/2013/01/01/video-you-dont-know-const-and-mutable/`.

Creating variables that are unique per thread

Let's take a glance at the recipe *Creating a work_queue class*. Each task there can be executed in one of many threads and we do not know which one. Imagine that we want to send the results of an executed task using some connection.

```
#include <boost/noncopyable.hpp>

class connection: boost::noncopyable {
public:
  // Opening a connection is a slow operation
  void open();

  void send_result(int result);

  // Other methods
  // ...
};
```

We have the following solutions:

- ▶ Open a new connection when we need to send the data (which is slow)

- ▶ Have a single connection for all the threads and wrap them in mutex (which is also slow)

- ▶ Have a pool of connections, get a connection from it in a thread-safe manner and use it (a lot of coding is required, but this solution is fast)

- ▶ Have a single connection per thread (fast and simple to implement)

So, how can we implement the last solution?

Getting ready

Basic knowledge of threads is required.

How to do it...

It is time to make a thread local variable:

```cpp
// In header file
#include <boost/thread/tss.hpp>

connection& get_connection();

// In source file
boost::thread_specific_ptr<connection> connection_ptr;

connection& get_connection() {
  connection* p = connection_ptr.get();
  if (!p) {
    connection_ptr.reset(new connection);
    p = connection_ptr.get();
    p->open();
  }
  return *p;
}
```

Using a thread-specific resource was never so easy:

```cpp
void task() {
  int result;
  // Some computations go there
  // ...

  // Sending result
  get_connection().send_result(result);
}
```

How it works...

The `boost::thread_specific_ptr` variable holds a separate pointer for each thread. Initially, this pointer is equal to `NULL`; that is why we check for `!p` and open a connection if it is `NULL`.

So, when we enter `get_connection()` from the thread that has already initiated the pointer, `!p` will return the value `false` and we'll return the already opened connection. `delete` for the pointer will be called when the thread is exiting, so we do not need to worry about memory leaks.

There's more...

You may provide your own cleanup function that will be called instead of `delete` at thread exit. A cleanup function must have the `void (*cleanup_function)(T*)` signature and will be passed during the `boost::thread_specific_ptr` construction.

C++11 has a special keyword, `thread_local`, to declare variables with thread local storage duration. C++11 has no `thread_specific_ptr` class, but you may use `thread_local boost::scoped_ptr<T>` or `thread_local std::unique_ptr<T>` to achieve the same behavior on compilers that support `thread_local`.

See also

► The `Boost.Thread` documentation gives a lot of good examples on different cases; it can be found at `http://www.boost.org/doc/libs/1_53_0/doc/html/thread.html`

► Reading this topic at `http://stackoverflow.com/questions/13106049/c11-gcc-4-8-thread-local-performance-penalty.html` and about the GCC `__thread` keyword at `http://gcc.gnu.org/onlinedocs/gcc-3.3.1/gcc/Thread-Local.html` may give you some ideas about how `thread_local` is implemented in compilers and how fast it is

Interrupting a thread

Sometimes, we need to kill a thread that ate too many resources or that is just executing for too long. For example, some parser works in a thread (and actively uses `Boost.Thread`), but we already have the required amount of data from it, so parsing can be stopped. All we have is:

```
boost::thread parser_thread(&do_parse);
  // Some code goes here
  // ...
  if (stop_parsing) {
    // no more parsing required
    // TODO: stop parser
  }
```

How can we do it?

Getting ready

Almost nothing is required for this recipe. You only need to have at least basic knowledge of threads.

How to do it...

We can stop a thread by interrupting it:

```
if (stop_parsing) {
  // no more parsing required
  parser_thread.interrupt();
}
```

How it works...

`Boost.Thread` provides some predefined interruption points in which the thread is checked for being interrupted via the `interrupt()` call. If the thread was interrupted, the exception `boost::thread_interrupted` is thrown.

`boost::thread_interrupted` is not derived from `std::exception`!

There's more...

As we know from the first recipe, if a function passed into a thread won't catch an exception and the exception will leave function bounds, the application will terminate. `boost::thread_interrupted` is the only exception to that rule; it may leave function bounds and does not `std::terminate()` application; instead, it stops the execution thread.

We may also add interruption points at any point. All we need is to call `boost::this_thread::interruption_point()`:

```
void do_parse() {
  while (not_end_of_parsing) {
    boost::this_thread::interruption_point();
    // Some parsing goes here
  }
}
```

If interruptions are not required for a project, defining `BOOST_THREAD_DONT_PROVIDE_INTERRUPTIONS` gives a small performance boost and totally disables thread interruptions.

C++11 has no thread interruptions but you can partially emulate them using atomic operations:

- ▶ Create an atomic Boolean variable

- ▶ Check the atomic variable in the thread and throw some exception if it has changed

- ▶ Do not forget to catch that exception in the function passed to the thread (otherwise your application will terminate)

However, this won't help you if the code is waiting somewhere in a conditional variable or in a sleep method.

See also

- ▶ The official documentation for `Boost.Thread` provides a list of predefined interruption points at `http://www.boost.org/doc/libs/1_53_0/doc/html/thread/thread_management.html#thread.thread_management.tutorial.interruption.html`

- ▶ As an exercise, see the other recipes from this chapter and think of where additional interruption points would improve the code

- ▶ Reading other parts of the `Boost.Thread` documentation may be useful; go to `http://www.boost.org/doc/libs/1_53_0/doc/html/thread.html`

Manipulating a group of threads

Those readers who were trying to repeat all the examples by themselves or those who were experimenting with threads must already be bored with writing the following code to launch threads:

```
boost::thread t1(&some_function);
boost::thread t2(&some_function);
boost::thread t3(&some_function);
// ...
t1.join();
t2.join();
t3.join();
```

Maybe there is a better way to do this?

Getting ready

Basic knowledge of threads will be more than enough for this recipe.

How to do it...

We may manipulate a group of threads using the `boost::thread_group` class.

1. Construct a `boost::thread_group` variable:

   ```
   boost::thread_group threads;
   ```

2. Create threads into the preceding variable:

   ```
   // Launching 10 threads
   for (unsigned i = 0; i < 10; ++i) {
     threads.create_thread(&some_function);
   }
   ```

3. Now you may call functions for all the threads inside `boost::thread_group`:

   ```
   // Joining all threads
   threads.join_all();

   // We can also interrupt all of them
   // by calling threads.interrupt_all();
   ```

How it works...

The `boost::thread_group` variable just holds all the threads constructed or moved to it and may send some calls to all the threads.

There's more...

C++11 has no `thread_group` class; it's Boost specific.

See also

▸ The official documentation of `Boost.Thread` may surprise you with a lot of other useful classes that were not described in this chapter; go to `http://www.boost.org/doc/libs/1_53_0/doc/html/thread.html`

6
Manipulating Tasks

In this chapter we will cover:

- ▶ Registering a task for processing an arbitrary datatype
- ▶ Making timers and processing timer events as tasks
- ▶ Network communication as a task
- ▶ Accepting incoming connections
- ▶ Executing different tasks in parallel
- ▶ Conveyor tasks processing
- ▶ Making a nonblocking barrier
- ▶ Storing an exception and making a task from it
- ▶ Getting and processing system signals as tasks

Introduction

This chapter is all about tasks. We'll be calling the functional object a task (because it is shorter and better reflects what it shall do). The main idea of this chapter is that we can split all the processing, computations, and interactions into **functors** (tasks) and process each of those tasks almost independently. Moreover, we may not block on some slow operations (such as receiving data from a socket or waiting for a time-out), but instead provide a callback task and continue working with other tasks. Once the OS finishes the slow operation, our callback will be executed.

Before you start

This chapter requires at least a basic knowledge of the first, third, and fifth chapters.

Registering a task for processing an arbitrary datatype

First of all, let's take care of the class that will hold all the tasks and provide methods for their execution. We were already doing something like this in the *Creating a work_queue class* recipe, but some of the following problems were not addressed:

- ▸ A task may throw an exception that leads a call to `std::terminate`
- ▸ An interrupted thread may not notice interruption but will finish its task and interrupt only during the next task (which is not what we wanted; we wanted to interrupt the previous task)
- ▸ Our `work_queue` class was only storing and returning tasks, but we need to add methods for executing existing tasks
- ▸ We need a way to stop processing the tasks

Getting ready

This recipe requires linking with the `libboost_system` library. Knowledge of `Boost.Bind` and basic knowledge of `Boost.Thread` is also required.

How to do it...

We'll be using `boost::io_service` instead of `work_queue` from the previous chapter. There is a reason for doing this, and we'll see it in the following recipes.

1. Let's start with the structure that wraps around a user task:

```
#include <boost/thread/thread.hpp>

namespace detail {

  template <class T>
  struct task_wrapped {
  private:
    T task_unwrapped_;

  public:
    explicit task_wrapped(const T& task_unwrapped)
      : task_unwrapped_(task_unwrapped)
    {}

    void operator()() const {
      // resetting interruption
```

```
    try {
      boost::this_thread::interruption_point();
    } catch(const boost::thread_interrupted&){}

    try {
      // Executing task
      task_unwrapped_();
    } catch (const std::exception& e) {
      std::cerr<< "Exception: " << e.what() << '\n';
    } catch (const boost::thread_interrupted&) {
      std::cerr<< "Thread interrupted\n";
    } catch (...) {
      std::cerr<< "Unknown exception\n";
    }
  }
};
```

2. For ease of use, we'll create a function that produces `task_wrapped` from the user's functor:

```
template <class T>
task_wrapped<T> make_task_wrapped(const T& task_unwrapped)
{
    return task_wrapped<T>(task_unwrapped);
}

} // namespace detail
```

3. Now we are ready to write the `tasks_processor` class:

```
#include <boost/asio/io_service.hpp>
class tasks_processor: private boost::noncopyable {
  boost::asio::io_service          ios_;
  boost::asio::io_service::work    work_;
  tasks_processor()
    : ios_()
    , work_(ios_)
  {}
public:
  static tasks_processor& get();
```

4. Now we will add the `push_task` method:

```
template <class T>
inline void push_task(const T& task_unwrapped) {
    ios_.post(detail::make_task_wrapped(task_unwrapped));
}
```

5. Let's finish this class by adding the member functions for starting and stopping a task's execution loop:

```
void start() {
   ios_.run();
}
void stop() {
   ios_.stop();
}
}; // tasks_processor
```

It is time to test our class. For that, we'll create a testing function:

```
int g_val = 0;
void func_test() {
  ++ g_val;
  if (g_val == 3) {
     throw std::logic_error("Just checking");
  }

  boost::this_thread::interruption_point();
  if (g_val == 10) {
     // Emulation of thread interruption.
     // Will be caught and won't stop execution.
     throw boost::thread_interrupted();
  }
  if (g_val == 90) {
     tasks_processor::get().stop();
  }
}
```

The main function might look like this:

```
int main () {
   static const std::size_t tasks_count = 100;
   // stop() is called at 90
   BOOST_STATIC_ASSERT(tasks_count > 90);
   for (std::size_t i =0; i < tasks_count; ++i) {
      tasks_processor::get().push_task(&func_test);
   }

   // We can also use result of boost::bind call
   // as a task
   tasks_processor::get().push_task(
      boost::bind(std::plus<int>(), 2, 2) // counting 2 + 2
   );
```

```
    // Processing was not started.
    assert(g_val == 0);

    // Will not throw, but blocks till
    // one of the tasks it is owning
    // calls stop().
    tasks_processor::get().start();
    assert(g_val== 90);
}
```

How it works...

The `boost::io_service` variable can store and execute tasks posted to it. But we may not post a user's tasks to it directly because they may throw or receive an interruption addressed to other tasks. That is why we wrap a user's task in the `detail::task_wrapped` structure. It resets all the previous interruptions by calling:

```
try {
  boost::this_thread::interruption_point();
} catch(const boost::thread_interrupted&){}
```

And this executes the task within the `try{}catch()` block making sure that no exception will leave the `operator()` bounds.

The `boost::io_service::run()` method will be getting ready tasks from the queue and executing them one by one. This loop is stopped via a call to `boost::io_service::stop()`. The `boost::io_service` class will return from the `run()` function if there are no more tasks left, so we force it to continue execution using an instance of `boost::asio::io_service::work`.

> The **iostream** classes and variables such as `std::cerr` and `std::cout` are not thread safe. In real projects, additional synchronization must be used to get readable output. For simplicity, we do not do that here.

There's more...

The C++11 STL library has no `io_service`; however, it (and a large part of the `Boost.Asio` library) is proposed as a **Technical Report** (**TR**) as an addition to C++.

See also

► The following recipes will show you why we chose `boost::io_service` instead of our handwritten code

▶ You may consider the `Boost.Asio` documentation to get some examples, tutorials, and class references at `http://www.boost.org/doc/libs/1_53_0/doc/html/boost_asio.html`

▶ You may also read the *Boost.Asio C++ Network Programming* book, which gives a smoother introduction to `Boost.Asio` and covers some details that are not covered in this book

Making timers and processing timer events as tasks

It is a common task to check something at specified intervals; for example, we need to check some session for an activity once every 5 seconds. There are two popular solutions to such a problem: creating a thread or sleeping for 5 seconds. This is a very lame solution that consumes a lot of system resources and scales badly. We could instead use system specific APIs for manipulating timers asynchronously. This is a better solution, but it requires a lot of work and is not very portable (until you write many wrappers for different platforms). It also makes you work with OS APIs that are not always very nice.

Getting ready

You must know how to use `Boost.Bind` and `Boost.SmartPtr`. See the first recipe of this chapter to get information about the `boost::asio::io_service` and `task_queue` classes. Link this recipe with the `libboost_system` library.

This recipe is a tricky one, so get ready!

How to do it...

This recipe is based on the code from the previous recipe. We just modify the `tasks_processor` class by adding new methods to run a task at some specified time.

1. Let's add a method to our `tasks_processor` class for running a task at some time:

```
typedef boost::asio::deadline_timer::time_type time_type;

template <class Functor>
void run_at(time_type time, const Functor& f) {
  detail::make_timer_task(ios_, time, f)
    .push_task();
}
```

2. We add a method to our `task_queue` class for running a task after the required time duration passes:

```
typedef boost::asio::deadline_timer::duration_type
  duration_type;

template <class Functor>
void run_after(duration_type duration, const Functor& f) {
  detail::make_timer_task(ios_, duration, f)
    .push_task();
}
```

3. It's time to take care of the `detail::make_timer_task` function:

```
namespace detail {
  template <class Time, class Functor>
  inline timer_task<Functor> make_timer_task(
    boost::asio::io_service& ios,
    const Time& duration_or_time,
    const Functor& task_unwrapped)
  {
    return timer_task<Functor>(ios, duration_or_time,
      task_unwrapped);
  }
}
```

4. And the final step will be writing a `timer_task` structure:

```
#include <boost/asio/io_service.hpp>
#include <boost/asio/deadline_timer.hpp>
#include <boost/system/error_code.hpp>
#include <boost/make_shared.hpp>
#include <iostream>

namespace detail {

  typedef boost::asio::deadline_timer::duration_type
    duration_type;

  template <class Functor>
  struct timer_task: public task_wrapped<Functor> {
  private:
    typedef task_wrapped<Functor> base_t;
    boost::shared_ptr<boost::asio::deadline_timer> timer_;

  public:
    template <class Time>
    explicit timer_task(
      boost::asio::io_service& ios,
      const Time& duration_or_time,
      const Functor& task_unwrapped)
```

```
          : base_t(task_unwrapped)
          , timer_(boost::make_shared<boost::asio::deadline_timer>(
            boost::ref(ios), duration_or_time
        ))
    {}

    void push_task() const {
      timer_->async_wait(*this);
    }

    void operator()(const boost::system::error_code& error) const
    {
      if (!error) {
        base_t::operator()();
      } else {
        std::cerr << error << '\n';
      }
    }
  };
} // namespace detail
```

How it works...

That's how it all works; the user provides a timeout and a functor to the `run_after` function. In it, a `detail::timer_task` object is constructed that stores a user provided functor and creates a shared pointer to `boost::asio::deadline_timer`. The constructed `detail::timer_task` object is pushed as a functor that must be called when the timer is triggered. The `detail::timer_task::operator()` method accepts `boost::system::error_code`, which will contain the description of any error that occurred while waiting. If no error is occurred, we call the user's functor that is wrapped to catch exceptions (we re-use the `detail::task_wrapped` structure from the first recipe). The following diagram illustrates this:

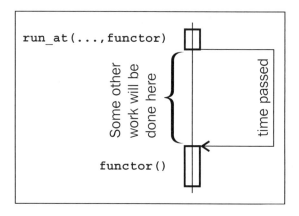

Note that we wrapped `boost::asio::deadline_timer` in `boost::shared_ptr` and passed the whole `timer_task` functor (including `shared_ptr`) in `timer_->async_wait(*this)`. This is done because `boost::asio::deadline_timer` must not be destroyed until it is triggered, and storing the `timer_task` functor in `io_service` guarantees this.

 In short, when a specified amount of time has passed, `boost::asio::deadline_timer` will push the user's task to the `boost::asio::io_service` queue class for execution.

There's more...

Some platforms have no APIs to implement timers in a good way, so the `Boost.Asio` library emulates the behavior of the asynchronous timer using an additional execution thread per `io_service`. Anyways, `Boost.Asio` is one of the most portable and effective libraries to deal with timers.

See also

▶ Reading the first recipe from this chapter will teach you the basics of `boost::asio::io_service`. The following recipes will provide you with more examples of `io_service` usage and will show you how to deal with network communications, signals, and other features using `Boost.Asio`.

▶ You may consider the `Boost.Asio` documentation to get some examples, tutorials, and class references at `http://www.boost.org/doc/libs/1_53_0/doc/html/boost_asio.html`.

Network communication as a task

Receiving or sending data by network is a slow operation. While packets are received by the machine, and while the OS verifies them and copies the data to the user-specified buffer, multiple seconds may pass. And we may be able to do a lot of work instead of waiting. Let's modify our `tasks_processor` class so that it will be capable of sending and receiving data in an asynchronous manner. In nontechnical terms, we ask it to "receive at least N bytes from the remote host and after that is done, call our functor. And by the way, do not block on this call". Those readers who know about `libev`, `libevent`, or `Node.js` will find a lot of familiar things in this recipe.

Getting ready

The previous and first recipes from this chapter are required to adopt this material more easily. Knowledge of `boost::bind`, `boost::shared_ptr`, and placeholders are required to get through it. Also, information on linking this recipe with the `libboost_system` library is required.

How to do it...

Let's extend the code from the previous recipe by adding methods to create connections. A connection would be represented by a `tcp_connection_ptr` class, which must be constructed using only `tasks_processor` (As an analogy, `tasks_processor` is a factory for constructing such connections).

1. We need a method in `tasks_processor` to create sockets to endpoints (we will be calling them connections):

```
tcp_connection_ptr create_connection(const char* addr,
  unsigned short port_num)
{
  return tcp_connection_ptr(
    ios_,
    boost::asio::ip::tcp::endpoint(
      boost::asio::ip::address_v4::from_string(addr), port_num
    )
  );
}
```

2. We'll need a lot of header files included as follows:

```
#include <boost/asio/ip/tcp.hpp>
#include <boost/asio/placeholders.hpp>
#include <boost/asio/write.hpp>
#include <boost/asio/read.hpp>
#include <boost/shared_ptr.hpp>
#include <boost/function.hpp>
#include <boost/enable_shared_from_this.hpp>
```

3. The class `tcp_connection_ptr` is required to manage connections. It owns the socket and manages its lifetime. It's just a thin wrapper around `boost::shared_ptr<boost::asio::ip::tcp::socket>` that hides `Boost.Asio` from the user.

```
class tcp_connection_ptr {
  boost::shared_ptr<boost::asio::ip::tcp::socket> socket_;

public:
  explicit tcp_connection_ptr(
    boost::shared_ptr<boost::asio::ip::tcp::socket> socket)
    : socket_(socket)
  {}
```

```
    explicit tcp_connection_ptr(
      boost::asio::io_service& ios,
      const boost::asio::ip::tcp::endpoint& endpoint)
      : socket_(boost::make_shared<boost::asio::ip::tcp::socket>(
        boost::ref(ios)
      ))
    {
      socket_->connect(endpoint);
    }
```

4. The `tcp_connection_ptr` class will need methods for reading data:

```
    template <class Functor>
    void async_read(
      const boost::asio::mutable_buffers_1& buf,
      const Functor& f,
      std::size_t at_least_bytes) const
    {
      boost::asio::async_read(
        *socket_, buf, boost::asio::transfer_at_least(
          at_least_bytes
        ), f
      );
    }
```

5. Methods for writing data are also required:

```
    template <class Functor>
    void async_write(
      const boost::asio::const_buffers_1& buf,
      const Functor& f) const
    {
      boost::asio::async_write(*socket_, buf, f);
    }

    template <class Functor>
    void async_write(
      const boost::asio::mutable_buffers_1& buf,
      const Functor& f) const
    {
      boost::asio::async_write(*socket_, buf, f);
    }
```

6. We will also add a method to shutdown the connection:

```
    void shutdown() const {
      socket_->shutdown(boost::asio::ip::tcp::socket::shutdown_both);
      socket_->close();
    }
};
```

Now the library user can use the preceding class like this to send the data:

```cpp
const unsigned short g_port_num = 65001;

void send_auth_task() {
  tcp_connection_ptr soc = tasks_processor::get()
    .create_connection("127.0.0.1", g_port_num);

  boost::shared_ptr<std::string> data
    = boost::make_shared<std::string>("auth_name");

  soc.async_write(
    boost::asio::buffer(*data),
    boost::bind(
      &recieve_auth_task,
      boost::asio::placeholders::error,
      soc,
      data
    )
  );
}
```

Users may also use it like this to receive data:

```cpp
void recieve_auth_task(
    const boost::system::error_code& err,
    const tcp_connection_ptr& soc,
    const boost::shared_ptr<std::string>& data)
{
    if (err) {
      std::cerr << "recieve_auth_task: Client error on recieve: "
              << err.message() << '\n';
      assert(false);
    }

  soc.async_read(
    boost::asio::buffer(&(*data)[0], data->size()),
    boost::bind(
      &finsh_socket_auth_task,
      boost::asio::placeholders::error,
      boost::asio::placeholders::bytes_transferred,
      soc,
      data
    ),
    1
  );
}
```

And this is how a library user may handle the received data:

```cpp
bool g_authed = false;

void finsh_socket_auth_task(
    const boost::system::error_code& err,
    std::size_t bytes_transfered,
    const tcp_connection_ptr& soc,
    const boost::shared_ptr<std::string>& data)
{
  if (err && err != boost::asio::error::eof) {
    std::cerr << "finsh_socket_auth_task: Client error "
            << "on recieve: " << err.message() << '\n';
    assert(false);
  }

  if (bytes_transfered != 2) {
    std::cerr << "finsh_socket_auth_task: wrong bytes count\n";
    assert(false);
  }

  data->resize(bytes_transfered);
  if (*data != "OK") {
    std::cerr << "finsh_socket_auth_task: wrong response: "
      << *data << '\n';
    assert(false);
  }

  g_authed = true;
  soc.shutdown();
  tasks_processor::get().stop();
}
```

How it works...

All the interesting things happen in the `async_*` function's call. Just as in the case of
timers, asynchronous calls return immediately without executing a function. They only tell
the `boost::asio::io_service` class to execute the callback task after some operation
(for example, reading data from the socket) finishes. `io_service` will execute our function
in one of the threads that called the `io_service::run()` method.

The following diagram illustrates this:

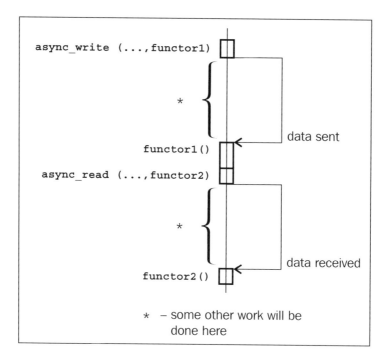

Now, let's examine this step-by-step.

The `tcp_connection_ptr` class holds a shared pointer to `boost::asio::ip::tcp::socket`, which is a `Boost.Asio` wrapper around native sockets. We do not want to give a user the ability to use this wrapper directly because it has synchronous methods whose usage we are trying to avoid.

The first constructor accepts a pointer to the socket (and will be used in our next recipe). This constructor won't be used by the user because the `boost::asio::ip::tcp::socket` constructor requires a reference to `boost::asio::io_service`, which is hidden inside `tasks_processor`.

> Of course, some users of our library could be smart enough to create an instance of `boost::asio::io_service`, initialize sockets, and push tasks to that instance. Moving the `Boost.Asio` library's contents into the source file and implementing the **Pimpl idiom** will help you to protect users from shooting their own feet, but we won't implement it here for simplicity. Another way to do things is to declare the `tasks_processor` class as a friend to `tcp_connection_ptr` and make the `tcp_connection_ptr` constructors private.

The second constructor accepts a remote endpoint and a reference to `io_service`. There you may see how the socket is connected to an endpoint using the `socket_->connect(endpoint)` method. Also, this constructor should not be used by the user; the user should use `tasks_processor::create_connection` instead.

Special care should be taken while using the `async_write` and `async_read` functions. Socket and buffer must not be destructed until the asynchronous operation is completed; that is why we bind `shared_ptr` to the functional object when calling the `async_*` functions:

```
tcp_connection_ptr soc = tasks_processor::get()
    .create_connection("127.0.0.1", g_port_num);

boost::shared_ptr<std::string> data
    = boost::make_shared<std::string>("auth_name");

soc.async_write(
  boost::asio::buffer(*data),
  boost::bind(
    &recieve_auth_task,
    boost::asio::placeholders::error,
    soc,
    data
  )
);
```

Binding the shared pointer to the functional object, which will be called at the end of the asynchronous operation, guarantees that at least one instance of `boost::shared_ptr` to the connection and data exists. This means that both connection and data won't be destroyed until the functional object destructor is called.

 `Boost.Asio` may copy functors and that is why we used a `boost::shared_ptr<std::string>` class instead of passing the `std::string` class by value (which would invalidate `boost::asio::buffer(*data)` and lead to a segmentation fault).

There's more...

Take a closer look at the `finsh_socket_auth_task` function. It checks for `err != boost::asio::error::eof`. This is done because the end of a data input is treated as an error; however, this may also mean that the end host closed the socket, which is not always bad (in our example, we treat it as a nonerror behavior).

`Boost.Asio` is not a part of C++11, but it is proposed for inclusion in C++, and we may see it (or at least some parts of it) included in the next TR.

See also

▶ See the official documentation to `Boost.Asio` for more examples, tutorials, and full references at `http://www.boost.org/doc/libs/1_53_0/doc/html/boost_asio.html`, as well as an example of how to use the UDP and ICMP protocols. For readers familiar with the BSD socket API, the `http://www.boost.org/doc/libs/1_53_0/doc/html/boost_asio/overview/networking/bsd_sockets.html` page provides information about what a BSD call looks like in `Boost.Asio`.

▶ Read the *Recording the parameters of function* and *Binding a value as a function parameter* recipes from *Chapter 1, Starting to Write Your Application*, for more information about `Boost.Bind`. The *Reference counting of pointers to classes used across methods* recipe from *Chapter 3, Managing Resources*, will give you more information about what the `boost::shared_ptr` class does.

▶ You may also read the book *Boost.Asio C++ Network Programming, Packt Publishing*, which describes `Boost.Asio` in more detail.

Accepting incoming connections

A server side working with a network usually looks like a sequence where we first get data, then process it, and then send the result. Imagine that we are creating some kind of authorization server that will process a huge number of requests per second. In that case, we will need to receive and send data asynchronously and process tasks in multiple threads.

In this recipe, we'll see how to extend our `tasks_processor` class to accept and process incoming connections, and in the next recipe, we'll see how to make it multithreaded.

Getting ready

This recipe requires a good knowledge of `boost::asio::io_service` basics as described in the first and third recipes of this chapter. Some knowledge of network communications will be of help to you. Knowledge of `boost::bind, boost::function, boost::shared_ptr`, and information from at least the two previous recipes is also required. Don't forget to link this example with `libboost_system`.

How to do it...

Just as in the previous recipes, we'll be adding new methods to our `tasks_processor` class.

1. First of all, we need to add a function that starts listening on a specified port:

```
template <class Functor>
void add_listener(unsigned short port_num, const Functor& f) {
  listeners_map_t::const_iterator it = listeners_.find(port_num);
```

```
                if (it != listeners_.end()) {
                    throw std::logic_error(
                        "Such listener for port '"
                        + boost::lexical_cast<std::string>(port_num)
                        + "' already created"
                    );
                }

            listeners_[port_num]
                = boost::make_shared<detail::tcp_listener>(
                    boost::ref(ios_), port_num, f
                );
            listeners_[port_num]->push_task(); // Start accepting
        }
```

2. We will also add a `std::map` variable that holds all the listeners:

```
        typedef std::map<
            unsigned short,
            boost::shared_ptr<detail::tcp_listener>
        > listeners_map_t;

        listeners_map_t listeners_;
```

3. And a function to stop the listener:

```
        void remove_listener(unsigned short port_num) {
            listeners_map_t::iterator it = listeners_.find(port_num);
            if (it == listeners_.end()) {
                throw std::logic_error(
                    "No listener for port '"
                    + boost::lexical_cast<std::string>(port_num)
                    + "' created"
                );
            }

            (*it).second->stop();
            listeners_.erase(it);
        }
```

4. Now we need to take care of the `detail::tcp_listener` class itself. It must have an acceptor:

```
namespace detail {
  class tcp_listener
      : public boost::enable_shared_from_this<tcp_listener>
  {
      typedef boost::asio::ip::tcp::acceptor acceptor_t;
      acceptor_t acceptor_;
```

5. And a function that will be called on a successful accept:

```
        boost::function<void(tcp_connection_ptr)> func_;
    public:
      template <class Functor>
      tcp_listener(
        boost::asio::io_service& io_service,
        unsigned short port,
        const Functor& task_unwrapped)
      : acceptor_(io_service,boost::asio::ip::tcp::endpoint(
        boost::asio::ip::tcp::v4(), port
      ))
      , func_(task_unwrapped)
      {}
```

6. This is what a function for starting an accept will look like:

```
      void push_task() {
        if (!acceptor_.is_open()) {
          return;
        }

        typedef boost::asio::ip::tcp::socket socket_t;
        boost::shared_ptr<socket_t> socket
          = boost::make_shared<socket_t>(
            boost::ref(acceptor_.get_io_service())
          );

        acceptor_.async_accept(*socket, boost::bind(
          &tcp_listener::handle_accept,
          this->shared_from_this(),
          tcp_connection_ptr(socket),
          boost::asio::placeholders::error
        ));
      }
```

7. A function to stop accepting is written like this:

```
      void stop() {
        acceptor_.close();
      }
```

8. And that is our wrapper function that will be called on a successful accept:

```
    private:
      void handle_accept(
        const tcp_connection_ptr& new_connection,
        const boost::system::error_code& error)
```

```
    {
      push_task();

      if (!error) {
        make_task_wrapped(boost::bind(func_, new_connection))
        (); // Run the task
      } else {
        std::cerr << error << '\n';
      }
    }
  }; // class tcp_listener
} // namespace detail
```

How it works...

The function `add_listener` just checks that we have no listeners on the specified port already, constructs a new `detail::tcp_listener`, and adds it to the `listeners_` list.

When we construct `boost::asio::ip::tcp::acceptor` specifying the endpoint (see step 5), it opens a socket at the specified address.

Calling `async_accept(socket, handler)` for `boost::asio::ip::tcp::acceptor` makes a call to our handler when the incoming connection is accepted. When a new connection comes in, `acceptor_` binds this connection to a socket and pushes the ready task to execute the handler in `task_queue` (in `boost::asio::io_service`). As we understood from the previous recipe, all the `async_*` calls return immediately and `async_accept` is not a special case, so it won't call the handler directly. Let's take a closer look at our handler:

```
boost::bind(
   &tcp_listener::handle_accept,
   this->shared_from_this(),
   tcp_connection_ptr(socket),
   boost::asio::placeholders::error
)
```

We need an instance of the current class to be alive when an accepting operation occurs, so we provide a `boost::shared_ptr` variable as a second parameter for `boost::bind` (we do it via `this->shared_from_this()` call). We also need to keep the socket alive, so we provide it as a third parameter. The last parameter is a placeholder (such as `_1` and `_2` for `boost::bind`) that says where the `async_accept` function should put the `error` variable into your method.

Now let's take a closer look at our `handle_accept` method. Calling the `push_task()` method is required to restart accepting our `acceptor_`. After that, we will check for errors and if there are no errors, we will bind the user-provided handler to `tcp_connection_ptr`, make an instance of `task_wrapped` from it (required for correctly handling exceptions and interruption points), and execute it.

Now let's take a look at the `remove_listener()` method. On call, it will find a listener in the list and call `stop()` for it. Inside `stop()`, we will call `close()` for an acceptor, return to the `remove_listener` method, and erase the shared pointer to `tcp_listener` from the map of listeners. After that, shared pointers to `tcp_listener` remain only in one accept task.

When we call `stop()` for an acceptor, all of its asynchronous operations will be canceled and handlers will be called. If we take a look at the `handle_accept` method in the last step, we'll see that in case of an error (or stopped acceptor), no more accepting tasks will be added.

After all the handlers are called, no shared pointer to the acceptor remains and a destructor for `tcp_connection` will be called.

There's more...

We did not use all the features of the `boost::asio::ip::tcp::acceptor` class. It can bind to a specific IPv6 or IPv4 address, if we provide a specific `boost::asio::ip::tcp::endpoint`. You may also get a native socket via the `native_handle()` method and use some OS-specific calls to tune the behavior. You may set up some options for `acceptor_` by calling `set_option`. For example, this is how you may force an acceptor to reuse the address:

```
boost::asio::socket_base::reuse_address option(true);
acceptor_.set_option(option);
```

> Reusing the address provides an ability to restart the server quickly after it was terminated without correct shutdown. After the server was terminated, a socket may be opened for some time and you won't be able to start the server on the same address without the `reuse_address` option.

See also

- Starting this chapter from the beginning is a good idea to get much more information about `Boost.Asio`.

- See the official documentation of `Boost.Asio` for more examples, tutorials, and a complete reference at `http://www.boost.org/doc/libs/1_53_0/doc/html/boost_asio.html`.

- Read the *Reordering the parameters of function* and *Binding a value as a function parameter* recipes from *Chapter 1, Starting to Write Your Application*, for more information about `Boost.Bind`.

- The *Reference counting of pointers to classes used across methods* recipe in *Chapter 3, Managing Resources*, will give you more information about what `boost::shared_ptr` does.

Executing different tasks in parallel

Now it is time to make our `tasks_queue` process tasks in multiple threads. How hard could this be?

Getting ready

You will need to read the first recipe from this chapter. Some knowledge of multithreading is also required, especially reading the *Manipulating a group of threads* recipe in *Chapter 5, Multithreading*.

How to do it...

All we need to do is to add the `start_multiple` method to our `tasks_queue` class:

```cpp
#include <boost/thread/thread.hpp>

// Default value will attempt to guess optimal count of threads
void start_multiple(std::size_t threads_count = 0) {
  if (!threads_count) {
    threads_count = (std::max)(static_cast<int>(
      boost::thread::hardware_concurrency()), 1
    );
  }

  // one thread is the current thread
  -- threads_count;
  boost::thread_group tg;
  for (std::size_t i = 0; i < threads_count; ++i) {
    tg.create_thread(boost::bind(
      &boost::asio::io_service::run, boost::ref(ios_)
    ));
  }

  ios_.run();
  tg.join_all();
}
```

And now we are able to do much more work, as illustrated in the following diagram:

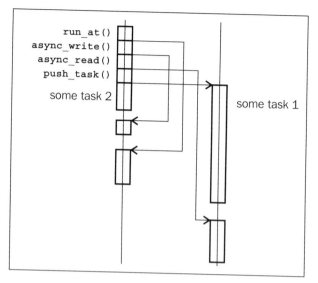

How it works...

The `boost::asio::io_service::run` method is thread safe. Almost all the methods of `Boost.Asio` are thread safe, so all we need to do is run the `boost::asio::io_service::run` method from different threads.

 If you are executing tasks that modify a common resource, you will need to add mutexes around that resource.

See the call to `boost::thread::hardware_concurrency()`? It returns the number of threads that can be run concurrently. But it is just a hint and may sometimes return a `0` value, which is why we are calling the `std::max` function for it. This ensures that `threads_count` will store at least the value `1`.

 We wrapped `std::max` in parenthesis because some popular compilers define the `min()` and `max()` macros, so we need additional tricks to work-around this.

There's more...

The `boost::thread::hardware_concurrency()` function is a part of C++11; you will find it in the `<thread>` header of the `std::` namespace. However, not all the `boost::asio` classes are part of C++11 (but they are proposed for inclusion, so we may see them in the next Technical Report (TR) for C++).

See also

- See the `Boost.Asio` documentation for more examples and information about different classes at `http://www.boost.org/doc/libs/1_53_0/doc/html/boost_asio.html`

- See the `Boost.Thread` documentation for information about `boost::thread_group` and `boost::threads` at `http://www.boost.org/doc/libs/1_53_0/doc/html/thread.html`

- Recipes from *Chapter 5, Multithreading*, (especially the last recipe called *Manipulating a group of threads*) will give you information about `Boost.Thread` usage

- The *Binding a value as a function parameter* recipe will help you to understand the `boost::bind` function better

Conveyor tasks processing

Sometimes there is a requirement to process tasks within a specified time interval. Compared to previous recipes, where we were trying to process tasks in the order of their appearance in the queue, this is a big difference.

Consider an example where we are writing a program that connects two subsystems, one of which produces data packets and the other writes modified data to the disk (something like this can be seen in video cameras, sound recorders, and other devices). We need to process data packets one by one, smoothly with the least jitter, and in multiple threads.

Our previous `tasks_queue` was bad at processing tasks in a specified order:

```
// global variables
tasks_queue queue;
subsystem1 subs1;
subsystem2 subs2;

tasks_queue& operator<< (tasks_queue&, data_packet& data) {
  decoded_data d_decoded = decode_data(data);
  compressed_data c_data = compress_data(d_decoded);
  subs2.send_data(c_data);
}

void start_data_accepting() {
  while (!subs1.is_stopped()) {
    queue << subs1.get_data();
  }
}

#include <boost/thread/thread.hpp>
```

```
int main() {
  // Getting data packets from first device
  // and putting them to queue
  boost::thread t(&start_data_accepting);
  // Which data packet will be processed first in
  // multi-threaded environment?
  // packet #2 may be processed before packet #1,
  // no guarantee that packets will be processed in
  // order of their appearance
  queue.run_multiple();
  t.join();
}
```

So how can we solve this?

Getting ready

Basic knowledge of `boost::asio::io_service` is required for this recipe; read at least the first recipe from this chapter. The *Creating a work_queue class* recipe from *Chapter 5, Multithreading*, is required for understanding this example. Code must be linked against the `boost_thread` library.

How to do it...

This recipe is based on the code of the `work_queue` class from the *Creating a work_queue class* recipe of *Chapter 5, Multithreading*. We'll make some modifications and will be using a few instances of that class.

1. Let's start by creating separate queues for data decoding, data compressing, and data sending:

   ```
   workqueue decoding_queue, compressing_queue, sending_queue;
   ```

2. Now it is time to refactor the operator `<<` and split it into multiple functions:

   ```
   #include <boost/bind.hpp>

   void do_decode(const data_packet& packet);
   void start_data_accepting() {
     while (!subs1.is_stopped()) {
       decoding_queue.push_task(boost::bind(
         &do_decode, subs1.get_data()
       ));
     }
   }
   ```

```
void do_compress(const decoded_data& packet);
void do_decode(const data_packet& packet) {
  compressing_queue.push_task(boost::bind(
    &do_compress, decode_data(packet)
  ));
}

void do_compress(const decoded_data& packet) {
  sending_queue.push_task(boost::bind(
    &subsystem2::send_data,
    boost::ref(subs2),
    compress_data(packet)
  ));
}
```

3. Our `work_queue` class from *Chapter 5*, *Multithreading*, had no `stop()` function. Let's add it:

```
// class work_queue from chapter 5
#include <deque>
#include <boost/function.hpp>
#include <boost/thread/mutex.hpp>
#include <boost/thread/locks.hpp>
#include <boost/thread/condition_variable.hpp>

class work_queue {
public:
  typedef boost::function<void()> task_type;

private:
  std::deque<task_type>   tasks_;
  boost::mutex            mutex_;
  boost::condition_variable cond_;
  bool                   is_stopped_;

public:
  work_queue()
    : is_stopped_(false)
  {}

  void stop() {
    boost::unique_lock<boost::mutex> lock(mutex_);
    is_stopped_ = true;
    lock.unlock();
    cond_.notify_all();
```

```
    }

    void push_task(const task_type& task) {
      boost::unique_lock<boost::mutex> lock(mutex_);
      if (is_stopped_) {
        return;
      }
      tasks_.push_back(task);
      lock.unlock();
      cond_.notify_one();
    }

    task_type pop_task() {
      boost::unique_lock<boost::mutex> lock(mutex_);
      while (tasks_.empty()) {
        if (is_stopped_) {
          return task_type();
        }
        cond_.wait(lock);
      }

      task_type ret = tasks_.front();
      tasks_.pop_front();
      return ret;
    }
};
```

Now the `work_queue` class can be stopped. The `pop_task()` method will return empty tasks if `work_queue` is stopped and no further tasks remain in the `tasks_` variable.

4. After doing all that is shown in step 3, we can write the code like this:

```
void run_while_not_stopped(work_queue& queue) {
  work_queue::task_type task;
  while (task = queue.pop_task()) {
    task();
  }
}
```

5. That is all! Now we only need to start the conveyor:

```
#include <boost/thread/thread.hpp>
int main() {
  // Getting data packets from first device and putting them
  // to queue
```

```
boost::thread t_data_accepting(&start_data_accepting);

boost::thread t_data_decoding(boost::bind(
   &run_while_not_stopped, boost::ref(decoding_queue)
));

boost::thread t_data_compressing(boost::bind(
   &run_while_not_stopped, boost::ref(compressing_queue)
));

boost::thread t_data_sending(boost::bind(
   &run_while_not_stopped, boost::ref(sending_queue)
));
```

6. The conveyor can be stopped like this:

```
t_data_accepting.join();
decoding_queue.stop();
t_data_decoding.join();
compressing_queue.stop();
t_data_compressing.join();
sending_queue.stop();
t_data_sending.join();
```

How it works...

The trick is to split the processing of a single data packet into some equally small subtasks and process them one by one in different `work_queues`. In this example, we can split the data process into data decoding, data compression, and data send.

The processing of six packets, ideally, would look like this:

Time	Receiving	Decoding	Compressing	Sending
Tick 1:	packet #1			
Tick 2:	packet #2	packet #1		
Tick 3:	packet #3	packet #2	packet #1	
Tick 4:	packet #4	packet #3	packet #2	packet #1
Tick 5:	packet #5	packet #4	packet #3	packet #2
Tick 6:	packet #6	packet #5	packet #4	packet #3
Tick 7:		packet #6	packet #5	packet #4
Tick 8:			packet #6	packet #5
Tick 9:				packet #6

However, our world is not ideal, so some tasks may finish faster than others. For example, receiving may go faster than decoding and in that case, the decoding queue will be holding a set of tasks to be done. We did not use `io_service` in our example because it does not guarantee that posted tasks will be executed in order of their posting.

There's more...

All the tools used to create a conveyor in this example are available in C++11, so nothing would stop you creating the same things without Boost on a C++11 compatible compiler. However, Boost will make your code more portable, and usable on C++03 compilers.

See also

- This technique is well known and used by processor developers. See `http://en.wikipedia.org/wiki/Instruction_pipeline`. Here you will find a brief description of all the characteristics of the conveyor.

- The *Creating a work_queue class* recipe from *Chapter 5, Multithreading*, and the *Binding a value as a function parameter* recipe from *Chapter 1, Starting to Write Your Application*, will give you more information about methods used in this recipe.

Making a nonblocking barrier

In multithreaded programming, there is an abstraction called **barrier**. It stops execution threads that reach it until the requested number of threads are not blocked on it. After that, all the threads are released and they continue with their execution. Consider the following example of where it can be used.

We want to process different parts of the data in different threads and then send the data:

```
#include <cstddef>
static const std::size_t data_length = 10000;

#include <boost/array.hpp>
struct vector_type : public boost::array<std::size_t, data_length> {
  void* alignment;
};
```

```
typedef boost::array<vector_type, 4> data_t;
void fill_data(vector_type& data);
void compute_send_data(data_t& data);

#include <boost/thread/barrier.hpp>
void runner(std::size_t thread_index, boost::barrier& data_barrier,
data_t& data) {
  for (std::size_t i = 0; i < 1000; ++i) {
    fill_data(data.at(thread_index));
    data_barrier.wait();
    if (!thread_index) {
      compute_send_data(data);
    }
    data_barrier.wait();
  }
}

#include <boost/thread/thread.hpp>
int main() {
  // Initing barriers
  boost::barrier data_barrier(data_t::static_size);

  // Initing data
  data_t data;

  // Run on 4 threads
  boost::thread_group tg;
  for (std::size_t i = 0; i < data_t::static_size; ++i) {
    tg.create_thread(boost::bind(
      &runner,
      i,
      boost::ref(data_barrier),
      boost::ref(data)
    ));
  }

  tg.join_all();
}
```

The `data_barrier.wait()` method blocks until all the threads fill the data. After that, all the threads are released; the thread with the index `0` will compute data to be sent using `compute_send_data(data)`, while others are again waiting at the barrier as shown in the following diagram:

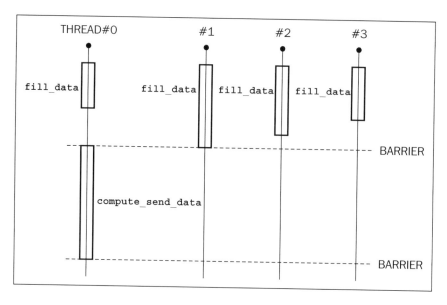

Looks lame, isn't it?

Getting ready

This recipe requires knowledge of the first recipe of this chapter. Knowledge of `Boost.Bind` and `Boost.Thread` is also required. Code from this recipe requires linking against the `boost_thread` and `boost_system` libraries.

How to do it...

We do not need to block at all! Let's take a closer look at the example. All we need to do is to post four `fill_data` tasks and make the last finished task call `compute_send_data(data)`.

1. We'll need the `tasks_processor` class from the first recipe; no changes to it are needed.

2. Instead of a barrier, we'll be using the atomic variable:

   ```
   #include <boost/atomic.hpp>
   typedef boost::atomic<unsigned int> atomic_count_t;
   ```

3. Our new runner function will look like this:

```
void clever_runner(
  std::size_t thread_index,
  std::size_t iteration,
  atomic_count_t& counter,
  data_t& data)
{
  fill_data(data.at(thread_index));

  if (++counter == data_t::static_size) {
    compute_send_data(data);
    ++ iteration;

    if (iteration == 1000) {
      // exiting, because 1000 iterations are done
      tasks_processor::get().stop();
      return;
    }

    counter = 0;
    for (std::size_t i = 0; i < data_t::static_size; ++ i) {
      tasks_processor::get().push_task(boost::bind(
        clever_runner,
        i,
        iteration,
        boost::ref(counter),
        boost::ref(data)
      ));
    }

  }
}
```

4. Only the main function will change slightly, as follows:

```
// Initing counter
atomic_count_t counter(0);

// Initing data
data_t data;

// Run on 4 threads
tasks_processor& tp = tasks_processor::get();
for (std::size_t i = 0; i < data_t::static_size; ++i) {
```

```
tp.push_task(boost::bind(
  &clever_runner,
  i,
  0, // first run
  boost::ref(counter),
  boost::ref(data)
));
}

tp.start();
```

How it works...

We don't block as no threads will be waiting for resources. Instead of blocking, we count the tasks that finished filling the data. This is done by the `counter atomic` variable. The last remaining task will have a `counter` variable equal to `data_t::static_size`. It will only need to compute and send the data.

After that, we check for the exit condition (1000 iterations are done), and post the new data by filling tasks to the queue.

There's more...

Is this solution better? Well, first of all, it scales better:

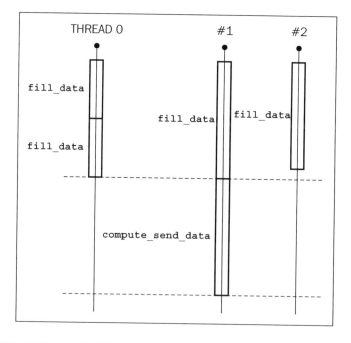

This method can also be more effective for situations where a program does a lot of different work. Because no threads are waiting in barriers, free threads may do other work while one of the threads computes and sends the data.

All the tools used for this example are available in C++11 (you'll only need to replace `io_service` inside `tasks_processor` with `work_queue` from *Chapter 5, Multithreading*).

See also

- The official documentation for `Boost.Asio` may give you more information about `io_service` usage at `http://www.boost.org/doc/libs/1_53_0/doc/html/boost_asio.html`

- See all the `Boost.Function` related recipes from *Chapter 3, Managing Resources*, and the official documentation at `http://www.boost.org/doc/libs/1_53_0/doc/html/function.html` for getting an idea of how tasks work

- See the recipes from *Chapter 1, Starting to Write Your Application*, related to `Boost.Bind` to get more information about what the `boost::bind` function does, or see the official documentation at `http://www.boost.org/doc/libs/1_53_0/libs/bind/bind.html`

Storing an exception and making a task from it

Processing exceptions is not always trivial and may take a lot of time. Consider the situation where an exception must be serialized and sent by the network. This may take milliseconds and a few thousand lines of code. After the exception is caught is not always the best time and place to process it.

So, can we store exceptions and delay their processing?

Getting ready

This recipe requires knowledge of `boost::asio::io_service`, which was described in the first recipe of this chapter. Knowledge of `Boost.Bind` is also required.

How to do it...

All we need is to have the ability to store exceptions and pass them between threads just like a normal variable.

1. Let's start with the function that processes exceptions. In our case, it will only be outputting the exception information to the console:

```cpp
#include <boost/exception_ptr.hpp>
#include <boost/lexical_cast.hpp>
void func_test2(); // Forward declaration

void process_exception(const boost::exception_ptr& exc) {
  try {
    boost::rethrow_exception(exc);
  } catch (const boost::bad_lexical_cast& /*e*/) {
    std::cout << "Lexical cast exception detected\n" << std::endl;

    // Pushing another task to execute
    tasks_processor::get().push_task(&func_test2);
  } catch (...) {
    std::cout << "Can not handle such exceptions:\n"
      << boost::current_exception_diagnostic_information()
      << std::endl;

    // Stopping
    tasks_processor::get().stop();
  }
}
```

2. Now we will write some functions to demonstrate how exceptions work:

```cpp
void func_test1() {
  try {
    boost::lexical_cast<int>("oops!");
  } catch (...) {
    tasks_processor::get().push_task(boost::bind(
      &process_exception, boost::current_exception()
    ));
  }
}

#include <stdexcept>
void func_test2() {
  try {
    // Some code goes here
```

```
      BOOST_THROW_EXCEPTION(std::logic_error(
        "Some fatal logic error"
      ));
      // Some code goes here
    } catch (...) {
      tasks_processor::get().push_task(boost::bind(
        &process_exception, boost::current_exception()
      ));
    }
  }
}
```

3. Now, if we run the example like this:

```
    tasks_processor::get().push_task(&func_test1);
    tasks_processor::get().start();
```

We'll get the following output:

```
Lexical cast exception detected

Can not handle such exceptions:
../../../BoostBook/Chapter6/exception_ptr/main.cpp(109): Throw in
function void func_test2()
Dynamic exception type: boost::exception_detail::clone_
impl<boost::exception_detail::error_info_injector<std::logic_
error> >
std::exception::what: Some fatal logic error
```

How it works...

The `Boost.Exception` library provides an ability to store and rethrow exceptions. The `boost::current_exception()` method must be called from inside the `catch()` block, and it returns an object of the type `boost::exception_ptr`. So in `func_test1()`, the `boost::bad_lexical_cast` exception will be thrown, which will be returned by `boost::current_exception()`, and a task (a functional object) will be created from that exception and the `process_exception` function's pointer.

The `process_exception` function will re-throw the exception (the only way to restore the exception type from `boost::exception_ptr` is to rethrow it using `boost::rethrow_exception(exc)` and then catch it by specifying the exception type).

In `func_test2`, we are throwing a `std::logic_error` exception using the BOOST_THROW_EXCEPTION macro. This macro does a lot of useful work: it checks that our exception is derived from `std::exception` and adds information to our exception about the source filename, function name, and the number of the line of code where the exception was thrown. So when an exception is re-thrown and caught by `catch(...)`, `boost::current_exception_diagnostic_information()`, we will be able to output much more information about it.

There's more...

Usually, `exception_ptr` is used to pass exceptions between threads. For example:

```cpp
void run_throw(boost::exception_ptr& ptr) {
  try {
    // A lot of code goes here
  } catch (...) {
    ptr = boost::current_exception();
  }
}

int main () {
  boost::exception_ptr ptr;
  // Do some work in parallel
  boost::thread t(boost::bind(
    &run_throw,
    boost::ref(ptr)
  ));

  // Some code goes here
  // ...

  t.join();

  // Checking for exception
  if (ptr) {
    // Exception occured in thread
    boost::rethrow_exception(ptr);
  }
}
```

The `boost::exception_ptr` class may allocate memory through heap multiple times, uses atomics, and implements some of the operations by rethrowing and catching exceptions. Try not to use it without an actual need.

C++11 has adopted `boost::current_exception`, `boost::rethrow_exception`, and `boost::exception_ptr`. You will find them in the `<exception>` header of the `std::` namespace. However, the `BOOST_THROW_EXCEPTION` and `boost::current_exception_diagnostic_information()` methods are not in C++11, so you'll need to realize them on your own (or just use the Boost versions).

See also

▶ The official documentation for `Boost.Exception` contains a lot of useful information about implementation and restrictions at `http://www.boost.org/doc/libs/1_53_0/libs/exception/doc/boost-exception.html`. You may also find some information that is not covered in this recipe (for example, how to add additional information to an already thrown exception).

▶ The first recipe from this chapter will give you information about the `tasks_processor` class. Recipes *Binding a value as a function parameter* from *Chapter 1, Starting to Write Your Application*, and *Converting strings to numbers* from *Chapter 2, Converting Data*, will help you with `Boost.Bind` and `Boost.LexicalCast`.

Getting and processing system signals as tasks

When writing some server applications (especially for Linux OS), catching and processing signals is required. Usually, all the signal handlers are set up at server start and do not change during the application's execution.

The goal of this recipe is to make our `tasks_processor` class capable of processing signals.

Getting ready

We will need code from the first recipe of this chapter. Good knowledge of `Boost.Bind` and `Boost.Function` is also required.

How to do it...

This recipe is similar to previous ones; we have some signal handlers, functions to register them, and some support code.

1. Let's start with including the following headers:

```
#include <boost/asio/signal_set.hpp>
#include <boost/function.hpp>
```

2. Now we add a member for signals processing to the `tasks_processor` class:

```
private:
    boost::asio::signal_set signals_;
    boost::function<void(int)>   users_signal_handler_;
```

3. The function that will be called upon signal capture is as follows:

```cpp
// private
void handle_signals(
        const boost::system::error_code& error,
        int signal_number)
{
  if (error) {
    std::cerr << "Error in signal handling: "
      << error << '\n';
  } else {
      // If signals occurs while there is no
      // waiting handlers, signal notification
      // is queued, so it won't be missed
      // while we are running
      // the users_signal_handler_
      detail::make_task_wrapped(boost::bind(
        boost::ref(users_signal_handler_),
        signal_number
      ))(); // make and run task_wrapped
  }

    signals_.async_wait(boost::bind(
        &tasks_processor::handle_signals, this, _1, _2
    ));
}
```

4. Do not forget to initialize the `signals_` member in the `tasks_processor` constructor:

```cpp
tasks_processor()
    : ios_()
    , work_(ios_)
    , signals_(ios_)
{}
```

5. And now we need a function for registering the signals handler:

```cpp
// This function is not threads safe!
// Must be called before all the 'start()' calls
// Function can be called only once
template <class Func>
void register_signals_handler(
        const Func& f,
        const std::vector<int>& signals_to_wait)
{
```

```
        // Making sure that this is the first call
        assert(!users_signal_handler_);

        users_signal_handler_ = f;
        std::for_each(
            signals_to_wait.begin(),
            signals_to_wait.end(),
            boost::bind(
                &boost::asio::signal_set::add, &signals_, _1
            )
        );

        signals_.async_wait(boost::bind(
            &tasks_processor::handle_signals, this, _1, _2
        ));
    }
```

That's all. Now we are ready to process signals. Following is a test program:

```
void accept_3_signals_and_stop(int signal) {
    static int signals_count = 0;
    assert(signal == SIGINT);
    ++ signals_count;
    std::cout << "Captured " << signals_count << " SIGINT\n";
    if (signals_count == 3) {
        tasks_processor::get().stop();
    }
}

int main () {
    tasks_processor::get().register_signals_handler(
        &accept_3_signals_and_stop,
        std::vector<int>(1, SIGINT) // vector containing 1 element
    );

    tasks_processor::get().start();
}
```

This will give the following output:

```
Captured 1 SIGINT
Captured 2 SIGINT
Captured 3 SIGINT
Press any key to continue . . .
```

How it works...

Nothing is difficult here (compared to some previous recipes from this chapter). The `register_signals_handler` function adds the signal numbers that will be processed. It is done via a call to the `boost::asio::signal_set::add` function for each element of the `signals_to_wait` vector (we do it using `std::for_each` and some magic of `boost::bind`).

Next, the instruction makes `signals_` member wait for the signal and calls the `tasks_processor::handle_signals` member function for `this` on the signal capture. The `tasks_processor::handle_signals` function checks for errors and if there is no error, it creates a functional object by referring to `users_signal_handler_` and the signal number. This functional object will be wrapped in the `task_wrapped` structure (that handles all the exceptions) and executed.

After that, we make `signals_` member wait for a signal again.

There's more...

When a thread-safe dynamic adding and removing of signals is required, we may modify this example to look like `detail::timer_task` from the *Making timers and processing timer events as tasks* recipe of this chapter. When multiple `boost::asio::signal_set` objects are registered as waiting on the same signals, a handler from each of `signal_set` will be called on a single signal.

C++ has been capable of processing signals for a long time using the `signal` function from the `<csignal>` header. However, it is incapable of using functional objects (which is a huge disadvantage).

See also

> ▸ The *Binding a value as a function parameter* and *Reordering the parameters of function* recipes from *Chapter 1, Starting to Write Your Application*, provide a lot of information about `boost::bind`. The official documentation may also help: http://www.boost.org/doc/libs/1_53_0/libs/bind/bind.html

> ▸ The *Storing any functional object in a variable* recipe (on `Boost.Function`) from *Chapter 3, Managing Resources*, provides information about `boost::function`.

> ▸ See the official `Boost.Asio` documentation has more information and examples on `boost::asio::signal_set` and other features of this great library at http://www.boost.org/doc/libs/1_53_0/doc/html/boost_asio.html.

7
Manipulating Strings

In this chapter we will cover:

- ▸ Changing cases and case-insensitive comparison
- ▸ Matching strings using regular expressions
- ▸ Searching and replacing strings using regular expressions
- ▸ Formatting strings using safe printf-like functions
- ▸ Replacing and erasing strings
- ▸ Representing a string with two iterators
- ▸ Using a reference to string type

Introduction

This whole chapter is devoted to different aspects of changing, searching, and representing strings. We'll see how some common string-related tasks can be easily done using the Boost libraries. This chapter is easy enough; it addresses very common string manipulation tasks. So, let's begin!

Changing cases and case-insensitive comparison

This is a pretty common task. We have two non-Unicode or ANSI character strings:

```
#include <string>
std::string str1 = "Thanks for reading me!";
std::string str2 = "Thanks for reading ME!";
```

We need to compare them in a case-insensitive manner. There are a lot of methods to do that; let's take a look at Boost's.

Getting ready

Basic knowledge of `std::string` is all we need here.

How to do it...

Here are some different ways to do case-insensitive comparisons:

1. The most trivial one is:

   ```
   #include <boost/algorithm/string/predicate.hpp>

   boost::iequals(str1, str2)
   ```

2. Using the Boost predicate and STL method:

   ```
   #include <boost/algorithm/string/compare.hpp>
   #include <algorithm>

   str1.size() == str2.size() && std::equal(
     str1.begin(),
     str1.end(),
     str2.begin(),
     boost::is_iequal()
   )
   ```

3. Making a lowercase copy of both the strings:

   ```
   #include <boost/algorithm/string/case_conv.hpp>

   std::string str1_low = boost::to_lower_copy(str1);
   std::string str2_low = boost::to_lower_copy(str2);
   assert(str1_low == str2_low);
   ```

4. Making an uppercase copy of the original strings:

   ```
   #include <boost/algorithm/string/case_conv.hpp>

   std::string str1_up = boost::to_upper_copy(str1);
   std::string str2_up = boost::to_upper_copy(str2);
   assert(str1_up == str2_up);
   ```

5. Converting the original strings to lowercase:

```
#include <boost/algorithm/string/case_conv.hpp>

boost::to_lower(str1);
boost::to_lower(str2);
assert(str1 == str2);
```

How it works...

The second method is not an obvious one. In the second method, we compare the length of the strings; if they have the same length, we compare the strings character by character using an instance of the `boost::is_iequal` predicate. The `boost::is_iequal` predicate compares two characters in a case-insensitive way.

> The `Boost.StringAlgorithm` library uses `i` in the name of the method or class, if this method is case-insensitive. For example, `boost::is_iequal`, `boost::iequals`, `boost::is_iless`, and others.

There's more...

Each function and the functional object of the `Boost.StringAlgorithm` library that work with cases accept `std::locale`. By default (and in our examples), methods and classes use a default constructed `std::locale`. If we work a lot with strings, it may be a good optimization to construct a `std::locale` variable once and pass it to all the methods. Another good optimization would be to use the 'C' locale (if your application logic permits that) via `std::locale::classic()`:

```
// On some platforms std::locale::classic() works
// faster than std::locale()
boost::iequals(str1, str2, std::locale::classic());
```

> Nothing forbids you to use both optimizations.

Unfortunately, C++11 has no string functions from `Boost.StringAlgorithm`. All the algorithms are fast and reliable, so do not be afraid to use them in your code.

See also

- Official documentation on the Boost String Algorithms library can be found at `http://www.boost.org/doc/libs/1_53_0/doc/html/string_algo.html`
- See the *C++ Coding Standards* book by Andrei Alexandrescu and Herb Sutter for an example on how to make a case-insensitive string with a few lines of code

Matching strings using regular expressions

Let's do something useful! It's common that the user's input must be checked using some regular expression-specific pattern that provides a flexible means of match. The problem is that there are a lot of regex syntaxes; expressions written using one syntax are not handled well by the other syntax. Another problem is that long regexes are not easy to write.

So in this recipe, we'll write a program that may use different types of regular expression syntaxes and checks that the input strings match the specified regexes.

Getting ready

This recipe requires basic knowledge of STL. Knowledge of regular expression syntax can be helpful, but it is not really required.

Linking examples against the `libboost_regex` library is required.

How to do it...

This regex matcher consists of a few lines of code in the `main()` function; however, I use it a lot. It'll help you some day.

1. To implement it, we'll need the following headers:

```
#include <boost/regex.hpp>
#include <iostream>
```

2. At the start of the program, we need to output the available regex syntaxes:

```
int main() {
  std::cout
    << "Available regex syntaxes:\n"
    << "\t[0] Perl\n"
    << "\t[1] Perl case insensitive\n"
    << "\t[2] POSIX extended\n"
    << "\t[3] POSIX extended case insensitive\n"
    << "\t[4] POSIX basic\n"
    << "\t[5] POSIX basic case insensitive\n"
    << "Choose regex syntax: ";
```

3. Now correctly set up flags, according to the chosen syntax:

```
boost::regex::flag_type flag;
switch (std::cin.get()) {
  case '0': flag = boost::regex::perl;
    break;
  case '1': flag = boost::regex::perl|boost::regex::icase;
```

```
        break;

    case '2': flag = boost::regex::extended;
      break;
    case '3': flag = boost::regex::extended|boost::regex::icase;
      break;
    case '4': flag = boost::regex::basic;
      break;

    case '5': flag = boost::regex::basic|boost::regex::icase;
      break;
    default:
      std::cout << "Inccorect number of regex syntax."
                << "Exiting... \n";
      return -1;
  }
  // Disabling exceptions
  flag |= boost::regex::no_except;
```

4. Now we'll be requesting regex patterns in a loop:

```
    // Restoring std::cin
    std::cin.ignore();
    std::cin.clear();

    std::string regex, str;
    do {
      std::cout << "Input regex: ";
      if (!std::getline(std::cin, regex) || regex.empty()) {
        return 0;
      }

      // Without `boost::regex::no_except`flag this
      // constructor may throw
      const boost::regex e(regex, flag);
      if (e.status()) {
        std::cout << "Incorrect regex pattern!\n";
        continue;
      }
    }
```

5. Getting a string to match in a loop:

```
    std::cout << "String to match: ";
    while (std::getline(std::cin, str) && !str.empty()) {
```

6. Applying regex to it and outputting the result:

```
bool matched = boost::regex_match(str, e);
std::cout << (matched ? "MATCH\n" : "DOES NOT MATCH\n");
std::cout << "String to match: ";
} // end of `while (std::getline(std::cin, str))`
```

7. Finishing our example by restoring `std::cin` and requesting new regex patterns:

```
// Restoring std::cin
std::cin.ignore();
std::cin.clear();
} while (1);
} // int main()
```

Now if we run the preceding example, we'll get the following output:

```
Available regex syntaxes:
        [0] Perl
        [1] Perl case insensitive
        [2] POSIX extended
        [3] POSIX extended case insensitive
        [4] POSIX basic
        [5] POSIX basic case insensitive
Choose regex syntax: 0
Input regex: (\d{3}[#-]){2}
String to match: 123-123#
MATCH
String to match: 312-321-
MATCH
String to match: 21-123-
DOES NOT MATCH
String to match: ^Z
Input regex: \l{3,5}
String to match: qwe
MATCH
String to match: qwert
MATCH
String to match: qwerty
DOES NOT MATCH
String to match: QWE
```

```
DOES NOT MATCH
String to match: ^Z


Input regex: ^Z
Press any key to continue . . .
```

How it works...

All this is done by the `boost::regex` class. It constructs an object that is capable of regex parsing and compilation. The `flags` variable adds additional configuration options.

If the regular expression is incorrect, it throws an exception; if the `boost::regex::no_except` flag was passed, it reports an error returning as non-zero in the `status()` call (just like in our example):

```
if (e.status()) {
    std::cout << "Incorrect regex pattern!\n";
    continue;
}
```

This will result in:

```
Input regex: (incorrect regex(
Incorrect regex pattern!
Input regex:
```

Regular expression matching is done by a call to the `boost::regex_match` function. It returns `true` in case of a successful match. Additional flags may be passed to `regex_match`, but we avoided their usage for brevity of the example.

There's more...

C++11 contains almost all the `Boost.Regex` classes and flags. They can be found in the `<regex>` header of the `std::` namespace (instead of `boost::`). Official documentation provides information about the differences between C++11 and `Boost.Regex`. It also contains some performance measures that tell `Boost.Regex` is fast.

See also

- ▶ The *Searching and replacing strings using regular expressions* recipe will give you more information about `Boost.Regex` usage

- ▶ You may also consider official documentation to get more information about flags, performance measures, regular expression syntaxes, and C++11 conformance at `http://www.boost.org/doc/libs/1_53_0/libs/regex/doc/html/index.html`

Searching and replacing strings using regular expressions

My wife enjoyed the *Matching strings using regular expressions* recipe very much and told me that I'll get no food until I improve it to be able to replace parts of the input string according to a regex match. Each matched subexpression (part of the regex in parenthesis) must get a unique number starting from 1; this number will be used to create a new string.

This is how an updated program will work like:

```
Available regex syntaxes:
        [0] Perl
        [1] Perl case insensitive
        [2] POSIX extended
        [3] POSIX extended case insensitive
        [4] POSIX basic
        [5] POSIX basic case insensitive
Choose regex syntax: 0

Input regex: (\d)(\d)
String to match: 00
MATCH: 0, 0,
Replace pattern: \1#\2
RESULT: 0#0
String to match: 42
MATCH: 4, 2,
Replace pattern: ###\1-\1-\2-\1-\1###
RESULT: ###4-4-2-4-4###
...
```

Getting ready

We'll be using the code from the *Matching strings using regular expressions* recipe. You should read it before getting your hands on this one.

Linking the example against the `libboost_regex` library is required.

How to do it...

This recipe is based on the code from the previous one. Let's see what must be changed.

1. No additional headers will be included; however, we'll need an additional string to store the replace pattern:

```
std::string regex, str, replace_string;
```

2. We'll replace `boost::regex_match` with `boost::regex_find` and output matched results:

```
std::cout << "String to match: ";
while (std::getline(std::cin, str) && !str.empty()) {
  boost::smatch results;
  bool matched = regex_search(str, results, e);
  if (matched) {
    std::cout << "MATCH: ";
    std::copy(
      results.begin() + 1,
      results.end(),
      std::ostream_iterator<std::string>( std::cout, ", ")
    );
```

3. After that, we need to get the replace pattern and apply it:

```
std::cout << "\nReplace pattern: ";
if (std::getline(std::cin, replace_string)
    && !replace_string.empty())
{
  std::cout << "RESULT: "
      << boost::regex_replace(str, e, replace_string);
} else {
  // Restoring std::cin
  std::cin.ignore();
  std::cin.clear();
}
} else { // `if (matched) `
  std::cout << "DOES NOT MATCH";
}
```

That's it! Everyone's happy and I'm fed.

How it works...

The `boost::regex_search` function doesn't only return a true or a false (such as the `boost::regex_match` function does) value, but also stores matched parts. We output matched parts using the following construction:

```
std::copy(
    results.begin() + 1,
    results.end(),
    std::ostream_iterator<std::string>( std::cout, ", ")
);
```

Note that we outputted the results by skipping the first result (`results.begin() + 1`); that is because `results.begin()` contains the whole regex match.

The `boost::regex_replace` function does all the replacing and returns the modified string.

There's more...

There are different variants of the `regex_*` function; some of them receive bidirectional iterators instead of strings and some provide output to the iterator.

`boost::smatch` is a `typedef` for `boost::match_results<std::string::const_iterator>`; so if you are using some other bidirectional iterators instead of `std::string::const_iterator`, you will need to use the type of your bidirectional iterators as a template parameter for `match_results`.

`match_results` has a format function, so we can tune our example with it. Instead of:

```
std::cout << "RESULT: " << boost::regex_replace(str, e, replace_
string);
```

We may use the following:

```
std::cout << "RESULT: " << results.format(replace_string);
```

By the way, `replace_string` may have different formats:

```
Input regex: (\d)(\d)
String to match: 12
MATCH: 1, 2,
Replace pattern: $1-$2---$&---$$
RESULT: 1-2---12---$
```

All the classes and functions from this recipe exist in C++11, in the `std::` namespace of the `<regex>` header.

► The official documentation on `Boost.Regex` will give you more examples and information about performance, C++11 standard compatibility, and regular expression syntax at `http://www.boost.org/doc/libs/1_53_0/libs/regex/doc/html/index.html`. The *Matching strings using regular expressions* recipe will tell you the basics of `Boost.Regex`.

Formatting strings using safe printf-like functions

The `printf` family of functions is a threat to security. It is a very bad design to allow users to put their own strings as a type and format the specifiers. So what do we do when user-defined format is required? How shall we implement the `std::string to_string(const std::string& format_specifier) const;` member function of the following class?

```
class i_hold_some_internals {
  int i;
  std::string s;
  char c;
  // ...
};
```

Getting ready

Basic knowledge of STL is more than enough for this recipe.

How to do it...

We wish to allow users to specify their own output format for a string.

1. To do that in a safe manner, we'll need the following header:

   ```
   #include <boost/format.hpp>
   ```

2. Now we will add some comments for the user:

   ```
   // fmt parameter must contain the following:
   //   $1$ for outputting integer 'i'
   //   $2$ for outputting string 's'
   //   $3$ for outputting character 'c'
   std::string
     to_string(const std::string& format_specifier) const {
   ```

3. Now it is time to make all of them work:

```
    boost::format f(format_specifier);
    unsigned char flags = boost::io::all_error_bits;
    flags ^= boost::io::too_many_args_bit;
    f.exceptions(flags);
    return (f % i % s % c).str();
}
```

That's all. Take a look at this code:

```
i_hold_some_internals class_instance;

std::cout << class_instance.to_string(
    "Hello, dear %2%! "
    "Did you read the book for %1% %% %3%\n"
);

std::cout << class_instance.to_string(
    "%1% == %1% && %1%%% != %1%\n\n"
);
```

Imagine that `class_instance` has a member i equal to `100`, an s member equal to `"Reader"`, and a member c equal to `'!'`. Then, the program will output the following:

```
Hello, dear Reader! Did you read the book for 100 % !
100 == 100 && 100% != 100
```

How it works...

The `boost::format` class accepts the string that specifies the resulting string. Arguments are passed to `boost::format` using `operator%`. Values %1%, %2%, %3%, %4%, and so on, in the format specifying string, will be replaced by arguments passed to `boost::format`.

We disable the exceptions for cases when a format string contains fewer arguments than passed to `boost::format`:

```
    boost::format f(format_specifier);
    unsigned char flags = boost::io::all_error_bits;
    flags ^= boost::io::too_many_args_bit;
```

This is done to allow some formats like this:

```
// Outputs 'Reader'
std::cout << class_instance.to_string("%2%\n\n");
```

There's more...

And what will happen in case of an incorrect format?

```
try {
  class_instance.to_string("%1% %2% %3% %4% %5%\n");
  assert(false);
} catch (const std::exception& e) {
  // boost::io::too_few_args exception must be caught
  std::cout << e.what() << '\n';
}
```

Well, in that case, no assertion will be triggered and the following lines will be outputted to the console:

```
boost::too_few_args: format-string referred to more arguments than
were passed
```

C++11 has no `std::format`. The `Boost.Format` library is not a very fast library; try not to use it much in performance critical sections.

See also

- ▶ The official documentation contains more information about the performance of the `Boost.Format` library. More examples and documentation on extended printf-like format is available at `http://www.boost.org/doc/libs/1_53_0/libs/format/`

Replacing and erasing strings

Situations where we need to erase something in a string, replace a part of the string, or erase the first or last occurrence of some substring are very common. STL allows us to do most of this, but it usually involves writing too much code.

We saw the `Boost.StringAlgorithm` library in action in the *Changing cases and case-insensitive comparison* recipe. Let's see how it can be used to simplify our lives when we need to modify some strings:

```
#include <string>
const std::string str = "Hello, hello, dear Reader.";
```

Getting ready

Basic knowledge of C++ is required for this example.

How to do it...

This recipe shows how different string-erasing and replacing methods from the `Boost.StringAlgorithm` library work.

Erasing requires the `#include <boost/algorithm/string/erase.hpp>` header:

```
namespace ba = boost::algorithm;
std::cout << "\n erase_all_copy    :" << ba::erase_all_copy(str, ",");
std::cout << "\n erase_first_copy :" << ba::erase_first_copy(str,
",");
std::cout << "\n erase_last_copy   :" << ba::erase_last_copy(str, ",");
std::cout << "\n ierase_all_copy   :" << ba::ierase_all_copy(str,
"hello");
std::cout << "\n ierase_nth_copy   :" << ba::ierase_nth_copy(str, ",",
1);
```

This code will output the following:

```
erase_all_copy       :Hello hello dear Reader.
erase_first_copy     :Hello hello, dear Reader.
erase_last_copy      :Hello, hello dear Reader.
ierase_all_copy      :, , dear Reader.
ierase_nth_copy      :Hello, hello dear Reader.
```

Replacing requires the `<boost/algorithm/string/replace.hpp>` header:

```
namespace ba = boost::algorithm;

std::cout << "\n replace_all_copy   :" << ba::replace_all_copy(str,
",", "!");
std::cout << "\n replace_first_copy   :" << ba::replace_first_copy(str,
",", "!");
std::cout << "\n replace_head_copy   :" << ba::replace_head_copy(str,
6, "Whaaaaaaa!");
```

This code will output the following:

```
replace_all_copy     :Hello! hello! dear Reader.
replace_first_copy   :Hello! hello, dear Reader.
replace_head_copy    :Whaaaaaaa! hello, dear Reader.
```

How it works...

All the examples are self-documenting. The only one that is not obvious is the `replace_head_copy` function. It accepts a number of bytes to replace as a second parameter and a replace string as the third parameter. So, in the preceding example, `Hello` gets replaced with `Whaaaaaaa!`.

There's more...

There are also methods that modify strings in-place. They don't just end on _copy and return void. All the case insensitive methods (the ones that start with i) accept std::locale as the last parameter, and use a default constructed locale as a default parameter.

C++11 does not have Boost.StringAlgorithm methods and classes.

See also

▶ The official documentation contains a lot of examples and a full reference on all the methods at http://www.boost.org/doc/libs/1_53_0/doc/html/string_algo.html

▶ See the *Changing cases and case-insensitive comparison* recipe from this chapter for more information about the Boost.StringAlgorithm library.

Representing a string with two iterators

There are situations when we need to split some strings into substrings and do something with those substrings. For example, count whitespaces in the string and, of course, we want to use Boost and be as efficient as possible.

Getting ready

You'll need some basic knowledge of STL algorithms for this recipe.

How to do it...

We won't be counting whitespaces; instead we'll split the string into sentences. You'll see that it is very easy with Boost.

1. First of all, include the right headers:

```
#include <boost/algorithm/string/split.hpp>
#include <boost/algorithm/string/classification.hpp>
#include <algorithm>
```

2. Now let's define our test string:

```
int main() {
  const char str[]
    = "This is a long long character array."
      "Please split this character array to sentences!"
      "Do you know, that sentences are separated using period, "
      "exclamation mark and question mark? :-)"
  ;
```

3. Now we make a `typedef` for our splitting iterator:

```
typedef boost::split_iterator<const char*> split_iter_t;
```

4. Construct that iterator:

```
split_iter_t sentences = boost::make_split_iterator(str,
  boost::algorithm::token_finder(boost::is_any_of("?!."))
);
```

5. Now we can iterate between matches:

```
for (unsigned int i = 1; !sentences.eof(); ++sentences, ++i) {
  boost::iterator_range<const char*> range = *sentences;
  std::cout << "Sentence #" << i << " : \t" << range << '\n';
```

6. Count the number of characters:

```
std::cout << "Sentence has " << range.size() << "
characters.\n";
```

7. And count the whitespaces:

```
std::cout
  << "Sentence has "
  << std::count(range.begin(), range.end(), ' ')
  << " whitespaces.\n\n";
} // end of for(...) loop
} // end of main()
```

That's it. Now if we run this example, it will output:

```
Sentence #1 :    This is a long long character array
Sentence has 35 characters.
Sentence has 6 whitespaces.


Sentence #2 :    Please split this character array to sentences
Sentence has 46 characters.
Sentence has 6 whitespaces.


Sentence #3 :    Do you know, that sentences are separated using
dot,
exclamation mark and question mark
Sentence has 87 characters.
Sentence has 13 whitespaces.
```

```
Sentence #4 :     :-)
Sentence has 4 characters.
Sentence has 1 whitespaces.
```

How it works...

The main idea of this recipe is that we do not need to construct `std::string` from substrings. We even do not need to tokenize the whole string at once. All we need to do is find the first substring and return it as a pair of iterators to the beginning and to the end of substring. If we need more substrings, find the next substring and return a pair of iterators for that substring.

Now let's take a closer look at `boost::split_iterator`. We constructed one using the `boost::make_split_iterator` function that takes `range` as the first argument and a binary finder predicate (or binary predicate) as the second. When `split_iterator` is dereferenced, it returns the first substring as `boost::iterator_range<const char*>`, which just holds a pair of iterators and has a few methods to work with them. When we increment `split_iterator`, it will try to find the next substring, and if there is no substring found, `split_iterator::eof()` will return `true`.

There's more...

The `boost::iterator_range` class is widely used across all the Boost libraries. You may find it useful for your own code and libraries in situations where a pair of iterators must be returned or where a function should accept/work with a pair of iterators.

The `boost::split_iterator<>` and `boost::iterator_range<>` classes accept a forward iterator type as a template parameter. Because we were working with a character array in the preceding example, we provided `const char*` as iterators. If we were working with `std::wstring`, we would need to use the `boost::split_iterator<std::wstring::const_iterator>` and `boost::iterator_range<std::wstring::const_iterator>` types.

C++11 has neither `iterator_range` nor `split_iterator`.

As the `boost::iterator_range` class has no virtual functions and no dynamic memory allocations, it is fast and efficient. However, its output stream operator `<<` has no specific optimizations for character arrays, so streaming it is slow.

The `boost::split_iterator` class has a `boost::function` class in it, so constructing it may be slow; however, iterating adds only a tiny overhead that you won't notice even in performance critical sections.

See also

▸ The next recipe will tell you about a nice replacement for `boost::iterator_range<const char*>`.

▸ The official documentation for `Boost.StringAlgorithm` will provide you with more detailed information about classes and a whole bunch of examples at `http://www.boost.org/doc/libs/1_53_0/doc/html/string_algo.html`.

▸ More information about `boost::iterator_range` can be found here: `http://www.boost.org/doc/libs/1_53_0/libs/range/doc/html/range/reference/utilities.html`. It is a part of the `Boost.Range` library that is not described in this book, but you may wish to study it by yourself.

Using a reference to string type

This recipe is the most important recipe in this chapter! Let's take a look at a very common case, where we write a function that accepts a string and returns the part of the string between character values passed in the `starts` and `ends` arguments:

```cpp
#include <string>
#include <algorithm>

std::string between_str(const std::string& input, char starts,
    char ends)
{
  std::string::const_iterator pos_beg
    = std::find(input.begin(), input.end(), starts);

  if (pos_beg == input.end()) {
    return std::string(); // Empty
  }

  ++ pos_beg;
  std::string::const_iterator pos_end
    = std::find(input.begin(), input.end(), ends);
```

```
    return std::string(pos_beg, pos_end);
}
```

Do you like this implementation? In my opinion, it looks awful; consider the following call to it:

```
between_str("Getting expression (between brackets)", '(', ')');
```

In this example, a temporary `std::string` variable will be constructed from `"Getting expression (between brackets)"`. The character array is long enough, so there is a big chance that dynamic memory allocation will be called inside the `std::string` constructor and the character array will be copied into it. Then, somewhere inside the `between_str` function, new `std::string` will be constructed, which may also lead to another dynamic memory allocation and result in copying.

So, this simple function may, and in most cases will:

▸ Call dynamic memory allocation (twice)

▸ Copy string (twice)

▸ Deallocate memory (twice)

Can we do better?

Getting ready

This recipe requires basic knowledge of STL and C++.

How to do it...

We do not really need a `std::string` class here, we only need some pointer to the character array and the array's size. Boost has the `std::string_ref` class.

1. To use the `boost::string_ref` class, include the following header:

   ```
   #include <boost/utility/string_ref.hpp>
   ```

2. Change the method's signature:

   ```
   boost::string_ref between(
     const boost::string_ref& input,
     char starts,
     char ends)
   ```

3. Change `std::string` to `boost::string_ref` everywhere inside the function body:

   ```
   {
     boost::string_ref::const_iterator pos_beg
   ```

```
   = std::find(input.cbegin(), input.cend(), starts);
if (pos_beg == input.cend()) {
  return boost::string_ref(); // Empty
}
++ pos_beg;
boost::string_ref::const_iterator pos_end
   = std::find(input.cbegin(), input.cend(), ends);
// ...
```

4. The `boost::string_ref` constructor accepts size as a second parameter, so we need to slightly change the code:

```
if (pos_end == input.cend()) {
  return boost::string_ref(pos_beg, input.end() - pos_beg);
}
return boost::string_ref(pos_beg, pos_end - pos_beg);
}
```

That's it! Now we may call `between("Getting expression (between brackets)", '(', ')')` and it will work without any dynamic memory allocation and characters copying. And we can still use it for `std::string`:

```
between(std::string("(expression)"), '(', ')')
```

How it works...

As already mentioned, `boost::string_ref` contains only a pointer to the character array and size of data. It has a lot of constructors and may be initialized in different ways:

```
boost::string_ref r0("^_^");

std::string O_O("O__O");
boost::string_ref r1 = O_O;

std::vector<char> chars_vec(10, '#');
boost::string_ref r2(&chars_vec.front(), chars_vec.size());
```

The `boost::string_ref` class has all the methods required by the container class, so it is usable with STL algorithms and Boost algorithms:

```
#include <boost/algorithm/string/case_conv.hpp>
#include <boost/algorithm/string/replace.hpp>
#include <boost/lexical_cast.hpp>
#include <iterator>

void string_ref_algorithms_examples() {
  boost::string_ref r("O_O");
```

```
// Finding symbol
std::find(r.cbegin(), r.cend(), '_');

// Will print 'o_o'
boost::to_lower_copy(std::ostream_iterator<char>(std::cout), r);
std::cout << '\n';

// Will print 'O_O'
std::cout << r << '\n';

// Will print '^_^'
boost::replace_all_copy(
    std::ostream_iterator<char>(std::cout), r, "O", "^"
);
}
```

 The boost::string_ref class does not really own string, so all its methods return constant iterators. Because of that, we cannot use it in methods that modify data, such as boost::to_lower(r).

While working with boost::string_ref, we should take additional care about data that it refers to; it must exist and be valid for the whole lifetime of boost::string_ref.

There's more...

The boost::string_ref class is not a part of C++11, but it is proposed for inclusion in the next standard.

The string_ref classes are fast and efficient; use them wherever it is possible.

The boost::string_ref class is actually a typedef in the boost:: namespace:

```
typedef basic_string_ref<char, std::char_traits<char> >
    string_ref;
```

You may also find useful the following typedefs for wide characters in the boost:: namespace:

```
typedef basic_string_ref<wchar_t,  std::char_traits<wchar_t> >
    wstring_ref;

typedef basic_string_ref<char16_t, std::char_traits<char16_t> >
    u16string_ref;

typedef basic_string_ref<char32_t, std::char_traits<char32_t> >
    u32string_ref;
```

See also

▸ The official `string_ref` proposal for inclusion in C++ standard can be found at `http://www.open-std.org/jtc1/sc22/wg21/docs/papers/2012/n3442.html`

▸ Boost documentation for `string_ref` could be found at `http://www.boost.org/doc/libs/1_53_0/libs/utility/doc/html/string_ref.html`

8
Metaprogramming

In this chapter we will cover:

- ► Using type "vector of types"
- ► Manipulating a vector of types
- ► Getting a function's result type at compile time
- ► Making a higher-order metafunction
- ► Evaluating metafunctions lazily
- ► Converting all the tuple elements to strings
- ► Splitting tuples

Introduction

This chapter is devoted to some cool and hard to understand metaprogramming methods. These methods are not for everyday use, but they will be a real help in the development of generic libraries.

Chapter 4, Compile-time Tricks, already covered the basics of metaprogramming. Reading it is recommended for better understanding. In this chapter we'll go deeper and see how multiple types can be packed into a single tuple like type. We'll make functions for manipulating collections of types, we'll see how types of compile-time collections can be changed, and how compile-time tricks can be mixed with runtime. All this is metaprogramming.

Fasten your seat belts and get ready, here we go!

Using type "vector of types"

There are situations when it would be great to work with all the template parameters as if they were in a container. Imagine that we are writing something such as `Boost.Variant`:

```
#include <boost/mpl/aux_/na.hpp>

// boost::mpl::na == n.a. == not available
template <
    class T0 = boost::mpl::na,
    class T1 = boost::mpl::na,
    class T2 = boost::mpl::na,
    class T3 = boost::mpl::na,
    class T4 = boost::mpl::na,
    class T5 = boost::mpl::na,
    class T6 = boost::mpl::na,
    class T7 = boost::mpl::na,
    class T8 = boost::mpl::na,
    class T9 = boost::mpl::na
>
struct variant;
```

And the preceding code is where all the following interesting tasks start to happen:

▸ How can we remove constant and volatile qualifiers from all the types?

▸ How can we remove duplicate types?

▸ How can we get the sizes of all the types?

▸ How can we get the maximum size of the input parameters?

All these tasks can be easily solved using `Boost.MPL`.

Getting ready

A basic knowledge of *Chapter 4, Compile-time Tricks*, is required for this recipe. Gather your courage before reading—there will be a lot of metaprogramming in this recipe.

How to do it...

We have already seen how a type can be manipulated at compile time. Why can't we go further and combine multiple types in an array and perform operations for each element of that array?

1. First of all, let's pack all the types in one of the Boost.MPL types containers:

```
#include <boost/mpl/vector.hpp>
template <
    class T0, class T1, class T2, class T3, class T4,
    class T5, class T6, class T7, class T8, class T9
>
struct variant {
    typedef boost::mpl::vector<T0, T1, T2, T3, T4, T5, T6, T7,
        T8, T9> types;
};
```

2. Let's make our example less abstract and see how it will work if we specify types:

```
#include <string>

struct declared{ unsigned char data[4096]; };

struct non_defined;

typedef variant<
    volatile int,
    const int,
    const long,
    declared,
    non_defined,
    std::string
>::types types;
```

3. We can check everything at compile time. Let's assert that types is not empty:

```
#include <boost/static_assert.hpp>
#include <boost/mpl/empty.hpp>
BOOST_STATIC_ASSERT((!boost::mpl::empty<types>::value));
```

4. We can also check that, for example, the non_defined types is still at the index 4 position:

```
#include <boost/mpl/at.hpp>
#include <boost/type_traits/is_same.hpp>
BOOST_STATIC_ASSERT((boost::is_same<
    non_defined,
    boost::mpl::at_c<types, 4>::type
>::value));
```

5. And that the last type is still `std::string`:

```
#include <boost/mpl/back.hpp>
BOOST_STATIC_ASSERT((boost::is_same<
    boost::mpl::back<types>::type,
    std::string
>::value));
```

6. Now, when we are sure that types really contain all the types passed to our variant structure, we can do some transformations. We'll start with removing constant and volatile qualifiers:

```
#include <boost/mpl/transform.hpp>
#include <boost/type_traits/remove_cv.hpp>
typedef boost::mpl::transform<
    types,
    boost::remove_cv<boost::mpl::_1>
>::type noncv_types;
```

7. Now we remove the duplicate types:

```
#include <boost/mpl/unique.hpp>


typedef boost::mpl::unique<
    noncv_types,
    boost::is_same<boost::mpl::_1, boost::mpl::_2>
>::type unique_types;
```

8. We can now check that the vector contains only 5 types:

```
#include <boost/mpl/size.hpp>
BOOST_STATIC_ASSERT((boost::mpl::size<unique_types>::value == 5));
```

9. The next step is to compute sizes:

```
// Without this we'll get an error:
// use of undefined type 'non_defined'
struct non_defined{};


#include <boost/mpl/sizeof.hpp>
typedef boost::mpl::transform<
    unique_types,
    boost::mpl::sizeof_<boost::mpl::_1>
>::type sizes_types;
```

10. The final step is getting the maximum size:

```
#include <boost/mpl/max_element.hpp>
typedef boost::mpl::max_element<sizes_types>::type max_size_type;
```

We can assert that the maximum size of the type is equal to the declared size of the structure, which must be the largest one in our example:

```
BOOST_STATIC_ASSERT(max_size_type::type::value ==
sizeof(declared));
```

How it works...

The `boost::mpl::vector` class is a compile-time container that holds types. To be more precise, it is a type that holds types. We don't make instances of it; instead we are just using it in typedefs.

Unlike the STL containers, the `Boost.MPL` containers have no member methods. Instead, methods are declared in a separate header. So to use some methods we need to:

▶ Include the correct header

▶ Call that method, usually by specifying the container as the first parameter

Here is another example:

```
#include <boost/mpl/size.hpp>
#include <cassert>

template <class Vector>
int foo_size() {
    return boost::mpl::size<Vector>::value;
}

int main() {
    typedef boost::mpl::vector<int,int,int> vector1_type;
    assert(foo_size<vector1_type>() == 3);
}
```

These methods should be familiar to you. We have already seen metafunctions in *Chapter 4, Compile-time Tricks*. By the way, we are also using some metafunctions (such as `boost::is_same`) from the familiar `Boost.TypeTraits` library.

So, in step 3, step 4, and step 5 we are just calling metafunctions for our container type.

The hardest part is coming up!

Remember, placeholders are widely used with the `boost::bind` and `Boost.Asio` libraries. `Boost.MPL` has them too and they are required for combining the metafunctions:

```
typedef boost::mpl::transform<
    types,
    boost::remove_cv<boost::mpl::_1>
>::type noncv_types;
```

Here, `boost::mpl::_1` is a placeholder and the whole expression means "for each type in types, do `boost::remove_cv<>::type` and push back that type to the resulting vector. Return the resulting vector via `::type`".

Let's move to step 7. Here, we specify a comparison metafunction for `boost::mpl::unique` using the `boost::is_same<boost::mpl::_1, boost::mpl::_2>` template parameter, where `boost::mpl::_1` and `boost::mpl::_2` are placeholders. You may find it similar to `boost::bind(std::equal_to(), _1, _2)`, and the whole expression in step 7 is similar to the following pseudo code:

```
std::vector<type> types;
// ...
std::unique(types.begin(), types.end(),
    boost::bind(std::equal_to<type>(), _1, _2));
```

There is something interesting, which is required for better understanding, in step 9. In the preceding code `sizes_types` is not a vector of values, but rather a vector of integral constants—types representing numbers. The `sizes_types` typedef is actually the following type:

```
struct boost::mpl::vector<
    struct boost::mpl::size_t<4>,
    struct boost::mpl::size_t<4>,
    struct boost::mpl::size_t<4096>,
    struct boost::mpl::size_t<1>,
    struct boost::mpl::size_t<32>
    >
```

The final step should be clear now. It just gets the maximum element from the `sizes_types` typedef.

 We can use the `Boost.MPL` metafunctions in any place where typedefs are allowed.

There's more...

The `Boost.MPL` library usage results in longer compilation time, but gives you the ability to do everything you want with types. It does not add runtime overhead and won't add even a single instruction to the binary. C++11 has no `Boost.MPL` classes, and `Boost.MPL` does not use features of C++11, such as the variadic templates. This makes the `Boost.MPL` compilation time longer on C++11 compilers, but makes it usable on C++03 compilers.

▶ See *Chapter 4, Compile-time Tricks*, for the basics of metaprogramming

▶ The *Manipulating a vector of types* recipe will give you even more information on metaprogramming and the `Boost.MPL` library

▶ See the official `Boost.MPL` documentation for more examples and full references at `http://www.boost.org/doc/libs/1_53_0/libs/mpl/doc/index.html`

Manipulating a vector of types

The task of this recipe will be to modify the content of one `boost::mpl::vector` function depending on the content of a second `boost::mpl::vector` function. We'll be calling the second vector as the vector of modifiers and each of those modifiers can have the following type:

```
// Make unsigned
struct unsigne; // No typo: 'unsigned' is a keyword, we cannot use it.

// Make constant
struct constant;

// Otherwise we do not change type
struct no_change;
```

So where shall we start?

Getting ready

A basic knowledge of `Boost.MPL` is required. Reading the *Using type "vector of types"* recipe and *Chapter 4, Compile-time Tricks*, may help.

How to do it...

This recipe is similar to the previous one, but it also uses conditional compile-time statements. Get ready, it won't be easy!

1. We shall start with headers:

```
// we'll need this at step 3
#include <boost/mpl/size.hpp>
#include <boost/type_traits/is_same.hpp>
#include <boost/static_assert.hpp>
```

```
// we'll need this at step 4
#include <boost/mpl/if.hpp>
#include <boost/type_traits/make_unsigned.hpp>
#include <boost/type_traits/add_const.hpp>

// we'll need this at step 5
#include <boost/mpl/transform.hpp>
```

2. Now, let's put all the metaprogramming magic inside the structure, for simpler re-use:

```
template <class Types, class Modifiers>
struct do_modifications {
```

3. It is a good idea to check that the passed vectors have the same size:

```
BOOST_STATIC_ASSERT((boost::is_same<
   typename boost::mpl::size<Types>::type,
   typename boost::mpl::size<Modifiers>::type
 >::value));
```

4. Now let's take care of modifying the metafunction:

```
typedef boost::mpl::if_<
   boost::is_same<boost::mpl::_2, unsigne>,
   boost::make_unsigned<boost::mpl::_1>,
   boost::mpl::if_<
     boost::is_same<boost::mpl::_2, constant>,
     boost::add_const<boost::mpl::_1>,
     boost::mpl::_1
   >
 > binary_operator_t;
```

5. And the final step:

```
typedef typename boost::mpl::transform<
   Types,
   Modifiers,
   binary_operator_t
 >::type type;
};
```

We can now run some tests and make sure that our metafunction works correctly:

```
#include <boost/mpl/vector.hpp>
typedef boost::mpl::vector<unsigne, no_change, constant, unsigne>
modifiers;
typedef boost::mpl::vector<int, char, short, long> types;
typedef do_modifications<types, modifiers>::type result_type;
```

```
#include <boost/mpl/at.hpp>
BOOST_STATIC_ASSERT((boost::is_same<
    boost::mpl::at_c<result_type, 0>::type,
    unsigned int
>::value));

BOOST_STATIC_ASSERT((boost::is_same<
    boost::mpl::at_c<result_type, 1>::type,
    char
>::value));

BOOST_STATIC_ASSERT((boost::is_same<
    boost::mpl::at_c<result_type, 2>::type,
    const short
>::value));

BOOST_STATIC_ASSERT((boost::is_same<
    boost::mpl::at_c<result_type, 3>::type,
    unsigned long
>::value));
```

How it works...

In step 3 we assert that the sizes are equal, but we do it in an unusual way. The `boost::mpl::size<Types>::type` metafunction actually returns the integral constant struct `boost::mpl::long_<4>`, so in a static assertion we actually compare two types, not two numbers. This can be rewritten in a more familiar way:

```
BOOST_STATIC_ASSERT((
    boost::mpl::size<Types>::type::value
    ==
    boost::mpl::size<Modifiers>::type::value
));
```

Notice the `typename` keyword we use. Without it the compiler won't be able to decide if `::type` is actually a type or some variable. Previous recipes did not require it, because parameters for the metafunction were fully known at the point where we were using them. But in this recipe, the parameter for the metafunction is a template.

We'll take a look at step 5, before taking care of step 4. In step 5, we provide the `Types`, `Modifiers`, and `binary_operator_t` parameters from step 4 to the `boost::mpl::transform` metafunction. This metafunction is rather simple—for each passed vector it takes an element and passes it to a third parameter—a binary metafunction. If we rewrite it in pseudo code, it will look like the following:

```
vector result;

for (std::size_t i = 0; i < Types.size(); ++i) {
  result.push_back(
    binary_operator_t(Types[i], Modifiers[i])
  );
}

return result;
```

Step 4 may make someone's head hurt. At this step we are writing a metafunction that will be called for each pair of types from the `Types` and `Modifiers` vectors (see the preceding pseudo code). As we already know, `boost::mpl::_2` and `boost::mpl::_1` are placeholders. In this recipe, `_1` is a placeholder for a type from the `Types` vector and `_2` is a placeholder for a type from the `Modifiers` vector.

So the whole metafunction works like this:

- Compares the second parameter passed to it (via `_2`) with an `unsigned` type
- If the types are equal, makes the first parameter passed to it (via `_1`) `unsigned` and returns that type
- Otherwise, compares the second parameter passed to it (via `_2`) with a constant type
- If the types are equal, makes the first parameter passed to it (via `_1`) constant and returns that type
- Otherwise, returns the first parameter passed to it (via `_1`)

We need to be very careful while constructing this metafunction. Additional care should be taken so as to not call `::type` at the end of it:

```
>::type binary_operator_t; // INCORRECT!
```

If we call `::type`, the compiler will attempt to evaluate the binary operator at this point and this will lead to a compilation error. In pseudo code, such an attempt would look like this:

```
binary_operator_t foo;
// Attempt to call binary_operator_t::operator() without parameters,
// when it has version only with two parameters
foo();
```

There's more...

Working with metafunctions requires some practice. Even your humble servant cannot write some functions correctly at the first attempt (second and third attempts are also not good though). Do not be afraid to experiment!

The `Boost.MPL` library is not a part of C++11 and does not use C++11 features, but it can be used with C++11 variadic templates:

```
template <class... T>
struct vt_example {
    typedef typename boost::mpl::vector<T...> type;
};

BOOST_STATIC_ASSERT((boost::is_same<
    boost::mpl::at_c<vt_example<int, char, short>::type, 0>::type,
    int
>::value));
```

As always, metafunctions won't add a single instruction to the resulting binary file and do not make performance worse. However, by using them you can make your code more tuned to a specific situation.

See also

▶ Read this chapter from the beginning to get more simple examples of `Boost.MPL` usage

▶ See *Chapter 4, Compile-time Tricks*, especially the *Selecting an optimal operator for a template parameter* recipe, which contains code similar to the `binary_operator_t` metafunction

▶ The official documentation for `Boost.MPL` has more examples and a full table of contents at `http://www.boost.org/doc/libs/1_53_0/libs/mpl/doc/index.html`

Getting a function's result type at compile time

Many features were added to C++11 to simplify the metaprogramming. One such feature is the alternative function syntax. It allows deducing the result type of a template function. Here is an example:

```
template <class T1, class T2>
auto my_function_cpp11(const T1& v1, const T2& v2)
  -> decltype(v1 + v2)
{
  return v1 + v2;
}
```

It allows us to write generic functions more easily and work in difficult situations:

```
#include <cassert>
struct s1 {};
struct s2 {};
struct s3 {};

inline s3 operator + (const s1& /*v1*/, const s2& /*v2*/) {
  return s3();
}

inline s3 operator + (const s2& /*v1*/, const s1& /*v2*/) {
  return s3();
}

int main() {
  s1 v1;
  s2 v2;
  my_function_cpp11(v1, v2);
  my_function_cpp11(v1, v2);
  assert(my_function_cpp11('\0', 1) == 1);
}
```

But Boost has a lot of functions like these and it does not require C++11 to work.

How is that possible and how can we make a C++03 version of the `my_function_cpp11` function?

Getting ready

A basic knowledge of C++ and templates is required for this recipe.

How to do it...

C++11 greatly simplifies metaprogramming. A lot of code must be written in C++03 to make something close to the alternative functions syntax.

1. We'll need to include the following header:

```
#include <boost/type_traits/common_type.hpp>
```

2. Now we need to make a metafunction in the `result_of` namespace for any types:

```
namespace result_of {

    template <class T1, class T2>
    struct my_function_cpp03 {
        typedef typename boost::common_type<T1, T2>::type type;
    };
```

3. And specialize it for types `s1`, and `s2`:

```
    template <>
    struct my_function_cpp03<s1, s2> {
        typedef s3 type;
    };

    template <>
    struct my_function_cpp03<s2, s1> {
        typedef s3 type;
    };
} // namespace result_of
```

4. Now we are ready to write the `my_function_cpp03` function:

```
template <class T1, class T2>
inline typename result_of::my_function_cpp03<T1, T2>::type
    my_function_cpp03(const T1& v1, const T2& v2)
{
    return v1 + v2;
}
```

That's it! Now we can use this function almost like a C++11 one:

```
s1 v1;
s2 v2;

my_function_cpp03(v1, v2);
my_function_cpp03(v2, v1);
assert(my_function_cpp03('\0', 1) == 1);
```

How it works...

The main idea of this recipe is that we can make a special metafunction that will deduce the resulting type. Such a technique can be seen all through the Boost libraries, for example, in the `Boost.Variants` implementation of `boost::get<>` or in almost any function from `Boost.Fusion`.

Now, let's move through this step by step. The `result_of` namespace is just a kind of tradition, but you can use your own and it won't matter. The `boost::common_type<>` metafunction deduces a type common to several types, so we use it as a general case. We also added two template specializations of the `my_function_cpp03` structures for the `s1` and `s2` types.

 The disadvantage of writing metafunctions in C++03 is that sometimes we are required to write a lot of code. Compare the amount of code for `my_function_cpp11` and `my_function_cpp03` including the `result_of` namespace to see the difference.

When the metafunction is ready, we can deduce the resulting type without C++11, so writing `my_function_cpp03` will be as easy as a pie:

```
template <class T1, class T2>
inline typename result_of::my_function_cpp03<T1, T2>::type
  my_function_cpp03(const T1& v1, const T2& v2)
{
  return v1 + v2;
}
```

There's more...

This technique does not add runtime overhead but it may slow down compilation a little bit. You can use it with C++11 compilers as well.

See also

▸ The recipes *Enabling the usage of templated functions for integral types, Disabling templated functions' usage for real types*, and *Selecting an optimal operator for a template parameter* from *Chapter 4, Compile-time Tricks*, will give you much more information about `Boost.TypeTraits` and metaprogramming.

▸ Consider the official documentation of `Boost.Typetraits` for more information about ready metafunctions at `http://www.boost.org/doc/libs/1_53_0/libs/type_traits/doc/html/index.html`

Making a higher-order metafunction

Functions that accept other functions as an input parameter or functions that return other functions are called higher-order functions. For example, the following functions are higher-order:

```
function_t higher_order_function1();
void higher_order_function2(function_t f);
function_t higher_order_function3(function_t f);
```

We have already seen higher-order metafunctions in the recipes *Using type "vector of types"* and *Manipulating a vector of types* from this chapter, where we used `boost::transform`.

In this recipe, we'll try to make our own higher-order metafunction named `coalesce`, which accepts two types and two metafunctions. The `coalesce` metafunction applies the first type-parameter to the first metafunction and compares the resulting type with the `boost::mpl::false_` type metafunction. If the resulting type is the `boost::mpl::false_` type metafunction, it returns the result of applying the second type-parameter to the second metafunction, otherwise, it returns the first result type:

```
template <class Param1, class Param2, class Func1, class Func2>
struct coalesce;
```

Getting ready

This recipe (and chapter) is a tricky one. Reading this chapter from the beginning is highly recommended.

How to do it...

The `Boost.MPL` metafunctions are actually structures, which can be easily passed as a template parameter. The hard part is to do it correctly.

1. We'll need the following headers to write a higher-order metafunction:

```
#include <boost/mpl/apply.hpp>
#include <boost/mpl/if.hpp>
#include <boost/type_traits/is_same.hpp>
```

2. The next step is to evaluate our functions:

```
template <class Param1, class Param2, class Func1, class Func2>
struct coalesce {
    typedef typename boost::mpl::apply<Func1, Param1>::type type1;
    typedef typename boost::mpl::apply<Func2, Param2>::type type2;
```

3. Now we need to choose the correct result type:

```
typedef typename boost::mpl::if_<
  boost::is_same< boost::mpl::false_, type1>,
  type2,
  type1
>::type type;
};
```

That's it! we have completed a higher-order metafunction! Now we can use it, just like that:

```
#include <boost/static_assert.hpp>
#include <boost/mpl/not.hpp>
using boost::mpl::_1;
using boost::mpl::_2;

typedef coalesce<
  boost::mpl::true_,
  boost::mpl::true_,
  boost::mpl::not_<_1>,
  boost::mpl::not_<_1>
>::type res1_t;
BOOST_STATIC_ASSERT((!res1_t::value));

typedef coalesce<
  boost::mpl::true_,
  boost::mpl::false_,
  boost::mpl::not_<_1>,
  boost::mpl::not_<_1>
>::type res2_t;
BOOST_STATIC_ASSERT((res2_t::value));
```

How it works...

The main problem with writing the higher-order metafunctions is taking care of the placeholders. That's why we should not call `Func1<Param1>::type` directly. Instead, we shall use the `boost::apply` metafunction, which accepts one function and up to five parameters that will be passed to this function.

 You can configure `boost::mpl::apply` to accept even more parameters, defining the `BOOST_MPL_LIMIT_ METAFUNCTION_ARITY` macro to the required amount of parameters, for example, to 6.

There's more...

C++11 has nothing close to the `Boost.MPL` library to apply a metafunction.

See also

► See the official documentation, especially the *Tutorial* section, for more information about `Boost.MPL` at `http://www.boost.org/doc/libs/1_53_0/libs/mpl/doc/index.html`

Evaluating metafunctions lazily

Lazy evaluation means that the function won't be called until we really need its result. Knowledge of this recipe is highly recommended for writing good metafunctions. The importance of lazy evaluation will be shown in the following example.

Imagine that we are writing a metafunction that accepts a function, a parameter, and a condition. The resulting type of that function must be a `fallback` type if the condition is `false` otherwise the result will be as follows:

```
struct fallback;

template <
    class Func,
    class Param,
    class Cond,
    class Fallback = fallback>
struct apply_if;
```

And the preceding code is the place where we cannot live without lazy evaluation.

Getting ready

Reading *Chapter 4, Compile-time Tricks*, is highly recommended. However, a good knowledge of metaprogramming should be enough.

How to do it...

We will see how this recipe is essential for writing good metafunctions:

1. We'll need the following headers:

```
#include <boost/mpl/apply.hpp>
#include <boost/mpl/eval_if.hpp>
#include <boost/mpl/identity.hpp>
```

2. The beginning of the function is simple:

```
template <class Func, class Param, class Cond, class Fallback>
struct apply_if {
  typedef typename boost::mpl::apply<
    Cond, Param
  >::type condition_t;
```

3. But we should be careful here:

```
  typedef boost::mpl::apply<Func, Param> applied_type;
```

4. Additional care must be taken when evaluating an expression:

```
  typedef typename boost::mpl::eval_if_c<
    condition_t::value,
    applied_type,
    boost::mpl::identity<Fallback>
  >::type type;
};
```

That's it! Now we are free to use it like this:

```
#include <boost/static_assert.hpp>
#include <boost/type_traits/is_integral.hpp>
#include <boost/type_traits/make_unsigned.hpp>
#include <boost/type_traits/is_same.hpp>

using boost::mpl::_1;
using boost::mpl::_2;

typedef apply_if<
  boost::make_unsigned<_1>,
  int,
  boost::is_integral<_1>
>::type res1_t;
BOOST_STATIC_ASSERT((
  boost::is_same<res1_t, unsigned int>::value
));

typedef apply_if<
  boost::make_unsigned<_1>,
  float,
  boost::is_integral<_1>
>::type res2_t;
BOOST_STATIC_ASSERT((
  boost::is_same<res2_t, fallback>::value
));
```

How it works...

The main idea of this recipe is that we should not execute the metafunction if the condition is `false`. Because when the condition is `false`, there is a chance that the metafunction for that type won't work:

```
// will fail with static assert somewhere deep in implementation
// of boost::make_unsigned<_1> if we won't be evaluating function
// lazy.
typedef apply_if<
    boost::make_unsigned<_1>,
    float,
    boost::is_integral<_1>
>::type res2_t;
BOOST_STATIC_ASSERT((
    boost::is_same<res2_t, fallback>::value
));
```

So, how do we evaluate a metafunction lazily?

The compiler won't look inside the metafunction if there is no access to the metafunction's internal types or values. In other words, the compiler will try to compile the metafunction when we try to get one of its members via `::`. This can be a call to `::type` or `::value`. That is what an incorrect version of `apply_if` looks like:

```
template <class Func, class Param, class Cond, class Fallback>
struct apply_if {
  typedef boost::mpl::apply<Cond, Param> condition_t;

  // Incorrect, metafunction is evaluated when `::type` called
  typedef typename boost::mpl::apply<Func, Param>::type applied_type;

  typedef typename boost::mpl::if_c<
    condition_t::value,
    applied_type,
    boost::mpl::identity<Fallback>
  >::type type;
};
```

This differs from our example, where we did not call `::type` at step 3 and implemented step 4 using `eval_if_c`, which calls `::type` only for one of its parameters. The `boost::mpl::eval_if_c` metafunction is implemented like this:

```
template<bool C, typename F1, typename F2>
struct eval_if_c {
  typedef typename if_c<C,F1,F2>::type f_;
  typedef typename f_::type type;
};
```

Because `boost::mpl::eval_if_c` calls `::type` for a success condition and `fallback` may have no `::type`, we were required to wrap `fallback` into the `boost::mpl::identity`. `boost::mpl::identity` class. This class is a very simple but useful structure that returns its template parameter via a `::type` call:

```
template <class T>
struct identity {
    typedef T type;
};
```

There's more...

As we previously mentioned, C++11 has no classes of `Boost.MPL`, but we can use `std::common_type<T>` with a single argument just like `boost::mpl::identity<T>`.

Just as always, metafunctions do not add a single line to the output binary file. So you can use metafunctions as many times as you want. The more you do at compile-time, the less will remain for runtime.

See also

▶   The `boost::mpl::identity` type can be used to disable **Argument Dependent Lookup (ADL)** for template functions. See the sources of `boost::implicit_cast` in the `<boost/implicit_cast.hpp>` header.

▶   Reading this chapter from the beginning and the official documentation for `Boost.MPL` may help: `http://www.boost.org/doc/libs/1_53_0/libs/mpl/doc/index.html`

Converting all the tuple elements to strings

This recipe and the next one are devoted to a mix of compile time and runtime features. We'll be using the `Boost.Fusion` library to see what it can do.

Remember that we were talking about tuples and arrays in the first chapter. Now we want to write a single function that can stream elements of tuples and arrays to strings.

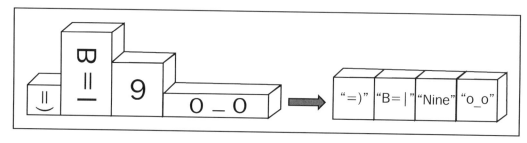

Getting ready

You should be aware of the `boost::tuple` and `boost::array` classes and of the `boost::lexical_cast` function.

How to do it...

We already know almost all the functions and classes that will be used in this recipe. We just need to gather all of them together.

1. We need to write a functor that converts any type to a string:

```
#include <boost/lexical_cast.hpp>
#include <boost/noncopyable.hpp>

struct stringize_functor: boost::noncopyable {
private:
  std::string& result;

public:
  explicit stringize_functor(std::string& res)
    : result(res)
  {}

  template <class T>
  void operator()(const T& v) const {
    result += boost::lexical_cast<std::string>(v);
  }
};
```

2. And this is the tricky part of the code:

```
#include <boost/fusion/include/for_each.hpp>

template <class Sequence>
std::string stringize(const Sequence& seq) {
  std::string result;
  boost::fusion::for_each(seq, stringize_functor(result));
  return result;
}
```

3. That's all! Now we can convert anything we want to a string:

```
struct cat{};

std::ostream& operator << (std::ostream& os, const cat& ) {
```

```
      return os << "Meow! ";
  }

  #include <iostream>
  #include <boost/fusion/adapted/boost_tuple.hpp>
  #include <boost/fusion/adapted/std_pair.hpp>
  #include <boost/fusion/adapted/boost_array.hpp>

  int main() {
    boost::fusion::vector<cat, int, std::string> tup1(cat(), 0, "_0");
    boost::tuple<cat, int, std::string> tup2(cat(), 0, "_0");
    std::pair<cat, cat> cats;
    boost::array<cat, 10> many_cats;

    std::cout << stringize(tup1) << '\n'
      << stringize(tup2) << '\n'
      << stringize(cats) << '\n'
      << stringize(many_cats) << '\n';
  }
```

The preceding example will output the following:

```
Meow! 0_0

Meow! 0_0

Meow! Meow!

Meow! Meow! Meow! Meow! Meow! Meow! Meow! Meow! Meow! Meow!
```

How it works...

The main problem with the `stringize` function is that neither `boost::tuple` nor `std::pair` have `begin()` or `end()` methods, so we cannot call `std::for_each`. And this is where `Boost.Fusion` steps in.

The `Boost.Fusion` library contains lots of terrific algorithms that can manipulate structures at compile time.

The `boost::fusion::for_each` function iterates through elements in sequence and applies a functor to each of the elements.

Note that we have included:

```
  #include <boost/fusion/adapted/boost_tuple.hpp>
  #include <boost/fusion/adapted/std_pair.hpp>
  #include <boost/fusion/adapted/boost_array.hpp>
```

This is required because, by default, `Boost.Fusion` works only with its own classes. `Boost.Fusion` has its own tuple class, `boost::fusion::vector`, which is quite close to `boost::tuple`:

```
#include <boost/tuple/tuple.hpp>
#include <string>
#include <cassert>

void tuple_example() {
  boost::tuple<int, int, std::string> tup(1, 2, "Meow");
  assert(boost::get<0>(tup) == 1);
  assert(boost::get<2>(tup) == "Meow");
}

#include <boost/fusion/include/vector.hpp>
#include <boost/fusion/include/at_c.hpp>

void fusion_tuple_example() {
  boost::fusion::vector<int, int, std::string> tup(1, 2, "Meow");
  assert(boost::fusion::at_c<0>(tup) == 1);
  assert(boost::fusion::at_c<2>(tup) == "Meow");
}
```

But `boost::fusion::vector` is not as simple as `boost::tuple`. We'll see the difference in the *Splitting tuples* recipe.

There's more...

There is one fundamental difference between `boost::fusion::for_each` and `std::for_each`. The `std::for_each` function contains a loop inside it and determinates at runtime, how many iterations will be done. However, `boost::fusion::for_each` knows the iteration count at compile time and fully unrolls the loop, generating the following code for `stringize(tup2)`:

```
std::string result;

// Instead of
// boost::fusion::for_each(seq, stringize_functor(result));
// there'll be the following:
{
  stringize_functor functor(result);
  functor(boost::fusion::at_c<0>(tup2));
  functor(boost::fusion::at_c<1>(tup2));
  functor(boost::fusion::at_c<2>(tup2));
}
return result;
```

C++11 contains no `Boost.Fusion` classes. All the methods of `Boost.Fusion` are very effective. They do as much as possible at compile time and have some very advanced optimizations.

See also

▸ The *Splitting tuples* recipe will give more information about the true power of `Boost.Fusion`

▸ The official documentation for `Boost.Fusion` contains some interesting examples and full references which can be found at `http://www.boost.org/doc/libs/1_53_0/libs/fusion/doc/html/index.html`

Splitting tuples

This recipe will show a tiny piece of the `Boost.Fusion` library's abilities. We'll be splitting a single tuple into two tuples, one with arithmetic types and the other with all the other types.

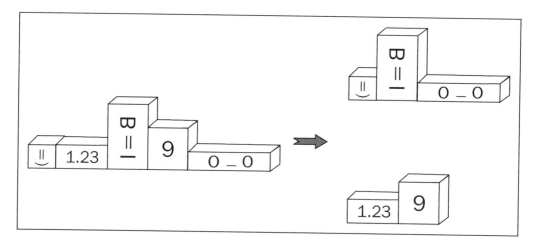

Getting ready

This recipe requires knowledge of `Boost.MPL`, placeholders, and `Boost.Tuple`. Read the following recipes from *Chapter 1, Starting to Write Your Application, Combining multiple values into one* for more information about tuples and *Reordering parameters of a function* for information about placeholders. Reading this chapter from the beginning is recommended.

How to do it...

This is possibly one of the hardest recipes in this chapter. Result types will be determined at compile time and values for those types will be filled at runtime.

1. To implement that mix, we'll need the following headers:

```
#include <boost/fusion/include/remove_if.hpp>
#include <boost/type_traits/is_arithmetic.hpp>
```

2. Now we are ready to make a function that returns non-arithmetic types:

```
template <class Sequence>
typename boost::fusion::result_of::remove_if<
    const Sequence,
    boost::is_arithmetic<boost::mpl::_1>
>::type get_nonarithmetics(const Sequence& seq)
{
    return boost::fusion::remove_if<
        boost::is_arithmetic<boost::mpl::_1>
    >(seq);
}
```

3. And a function that returns arithmetic types:

```
template <class Sequence>
typename boost::fusion::result_of::remove_if<
    const Sequence,
    boost::mpl::not_< boost::is_arithmetic<boost::mpl::_1> >
>::type get_arithmetics(const Sequence& seq)
{
    return boost::fusion::remove_if<
        boost::mpl::not_< boost::is_arithmetic<boost::mpl::_1> >
    >(seq);
}
```

That's it! Now we are capable of doing the following tasks:

```
#include <boost/fusion/include/vector.hpp>
#include <cassert>
#include <boost/fusion/include/at_c.hpp>

int main() {
    typedef boost::fusion::vector<
        int, boost::blank, boost::blank, float
    > tup1_t;
```

```
    tup1_t tup1(8, boost::blank(), boost::blank(), 0.0);
    boost::fusion::vector<boost::blank, boost::blank> res_na
      = get_nonarithmetics(tup1);

    boost::fusion::vector<int, float> res_a = get_arithmetics(tup1);
    assert(boost::fusion::at_c<0>(res_a) == 8);
}
```

How it works...

The idea behind `Boost.Fusion` is that the compiler knows the structure layout at compile time and whatever the compiler knows at compile time, we can change at the same time. `Boost.Fusion` allows us to modify different sequences, add and remove fields, and change field types. This is what we did in step 2 and step 3; we removed the non-required fields from the tuple.

Now let's take a very close look at `get_arithmetics`. First of all its result type is deduced using the following construction:

```
typename boost::fusion::result_of::remove_if<
  const Sequence,
  boost::is_arithmetic<boost::mpl::_1>
>::type
```

This should be familiar to us. We saw something like this in the *Getting a function's result type at compile time* recipe in this chapter. The `Boost.MPL` placeholder `boost::mpl::_1` should also be familiar.

Now let's move inside the function and we'll see the following code:

```
return boost::fusion::remove_if<
  boost::is_arithmetic<boost::mpl::_1>
>(seq);
```

Remember that the compiler knows all the types of `seq` at compile time. This means that `Boost.Fusion` can apply metafunctions to different elements of `seq` and get the metafunction results for them. This also means that `Boost.Fusion` will be capable of copying required fields from the old structure to the new one.

 However, `Boost.Fusion` tries not to copy fields if at all possible.

The code in step 3 is very similar to the code in step 2, but it has a negated predicate for removing non-required types.

Our functions can be used with any type supported by `Boost.Fusion` and not just with `boost::fusion::vector`.

There's more...

You can use `Boost.MPL` functions for the `Boost.Fusion` containers. You just need to include `#include <boost/fusion/include/mpl.hpp>`:

```cpp
#include <boost/fusion/include/mpl.hpp>
#include <boost/mpl/transform.hpp>
#include <boost/type_traits/remove_const.hpp>

template <class Sequence>
struct make_nonconst: boost::mpl::transform<
    Sequence,
    boost::remove_const<boost::mpl::_1>
> {};

typedef boost::fusion::vector<
    const int, const boost::blank, boost::blank
> type1;

typedef make_nonconst<type1>::type nc_type;

BOOST_STATIC_ASSERT((boost::is_same<
    boost::fusion::result_of::value_at_c<nc_type, 0>::type,
    int
>::value));
```

 We have used `boost::fusion::result_of::value_at_c` instead of `boost::fusion::result_of::at_c` because `boost::fusion::result_of::at_c` returns the exact type that will be used as a return type in the `boost::fusion::at_c` call, which is a reference. `boost::fusion::result_of::value_at_c` returns type without a reference.

The `Boost.Fusion` and `Boost.MPL` libraries are not a part of C++11. `Boost.Fusion` is extremely fast. It has many optimizations. All the metafunctions that you use with it will be evaluated at compile time.

It is worth mentioning that we saw only a tiny part of the `Boost.Fusion` abilities. A separate book could be written about it.

See also

▸ Good tutorials and full documentation for `Boost.Fusion` is available at the Boost site `http://www.boost.org/doc/libs/1_53_0/libs/fusion/doc/html/index.html`

▸ You may also wish to see the official documentation for `Boost.MPL` at `http://www.boost.org/doc/libs/1_53_0/libs/mpl/doc/index.html`

9
Containers

In this chapter we will cover:

- ▶ Comparing strings in an ultra-fast manner
- ▶ Using an unordered set and map
- ▶ Making a map, where value is also a key
- ▶ Using multi-index containers
- ▶ Getting the benefits of single-linked list and memory pool
- ▶ Using flat associative containers

Introduction

This chapter is devoted to the Boost containers and the things directly connected with them. This chapter provides information about the Boost classes that can be used in every day programming, and that will make your code much faster, and the development of new applications easier.

Containers differ not only by functionality, but also by the efficiency (complexity) of some of their members. The knowledge about complexities is essential for writing fast applications. This chapter doesn't just introduce some new containers to you; it gives you tips on when and when not to use a specific type of container or its methods.

So, let's begin!

Comparing strings in an ultra-fast manner

It is a common task to manipulate strings. Here we'll see how the operation of string comparison can be done quickly using some simple tricks. This recipe is a trampoline for the next one, where the techniques described here will be used to achieve constant time-complexity searches.

So, we need to make a class that is capable of quickly comparing strings for equality. We'll make a template function to measure the speed of comparison:

```cpp
#include <string>

template <class T>
std::size_t test_default() {
    // Constants
    const std::size_t ii_max = 20000000;
    const std::string s(
        "Long long long string that "
        "will be used in tests to compare "
        "speed of equality comparisons."
    );

    // Making some data, that will be
    // used in comparisons
    const T data[] = {
        T(s),
        T(s + s),
        T(s + ". Whooohooo"),
        T(std::string(""))
    };

    const std::size_t data_dimensions
            = sizeof(data) / sizeof(data[0]);
    std::size_t matches = 0u;
    for (std::size_t ii = 0; ii < ii_max; ++ii) {
        for (std::size_t i = 0; i < data_dimensions; ++i) {
            for (std::size_t j = 0; j < data_dimensions; ++j) {
                if (data[i] == data[j]) {
                    ++ matches;
                }
            }
        }
    }

    return matches;
}
```

Getting ready

This recipe requires only the basic knowledge of STL and C++.

How to do it...

We'll make `std::string` a public field in our own class, and add all the comparison code to our class, without writing helper methods to work with stored `std::string`, as shown in the following steps:

1. To do so, we'll need the following header:

```cpp
#include <boost/functional/hash.hpp>
```

2. Now we can create our fast comparison class:

```cpp
struct string_hash_fast {
    typedef std::size_t comp_type;

    const comp_type     comparison_;
    const std::string   str_;

    explicit string_hash_fast(const std::string& s)
        : comparison_(
            boost::hash<std::string>()(s)
        )
        , str_(s)
    {}
};
```

3. Do not forget to define the equality comparison operators:

```cpp
inline bool operator == (const string_hash_fast& s1,
    const string_hash_fast& s2)
{
    return s1.comparison_ == s2.comparison_
        && s1.str_ == s2.str_;
}

inline bool operator != (const string_hash_fast& s1,
    const string_hash_fast& s2)
{
    return !(s1 == s2);
}
```

4. And, that's it! Now we can run our tests and see the result using the following code:

```
#include <iostream>
int main(int argc, char* argv[]) {
    if (argc < 2) {
        assert(
            test_default<string_hash_fast>()
            ==
            test_default<std::string>()
        );
        return 0;
    }

    switch (argv[1][0]) {
    case 'h':
        std::cout << "HASH matched: "
                  << test_default<string_hash_fast>();
        break;

    case 's':
        std::cout << "STD matched: "
                  << test_default<std::string>();
        break;

    default:
        assert(false);
        return -2;
    }
}
```

How it works...

The comparison of strings is slow because we are required to compare all the characters of the string one-by-one, if the strings are of equal length. Instead of doing that, we replace the comparison of strings with the comparison of integers. This is done via the hash function—the function that makes some short-fixed length representation of the string. Let us talk about the hash values on apples. Imagine that you have two apples with labels, as shown in the following diagram, and you wish to check that the apples are of the same cultivar. The simplest way to compare those apples is to compare them by labels. Otherwise you'll lose a lot of time comparing the apples based on the color, size, form, and other parameters. A hash is something like a label that reflects the value of the object.

So, let's move step-by-step.

In step 1, we include the header file that contains the definitions of the hash functions. In step 2, we declare our new string class that contains `str_`, which is the original value of the string and `comparison_`, which is the computed hash value. Note the construction:

```
boost::hash<std::string>()(s)
```

Here, `boost::hash<std::string>` is a structure, a functional object just like `std::negate<>`. That is why we need the first parenthesis—we construct that functional object. The second parenthesis with `s` inside is a call to `std::size_t operator()(const std::string& s)`, which will compute the hash value.

Now take a look at step 3 where we define `operator==`. Look at the following code:

```
return s1.comparison_ == s2.comparison_ && s1.str_ == s2.str_;
```

And, take additional care about the second part of the expression. The hashing operation loses information, which means that there is a possibility that more than one string produces exactly the same hash value. It means that if the hashes mismatch, there is a 100 percent guarantee that the strings will not match, otherwise we are required to compare the strings using the traditional methods.

Well, it's time to compare numbers. If we measure the execution time using the default comparison method, it will give us 819 milliseconds; however, our hashing comparison works almost two times faster and finishes in 475 milliseconds.

There's more...

C++11 has the hash functional object, you may find it in the `<functional>` header in the `std::` namespace. You will know that the default Boost implementation of hash does not allocate additional memory and also does not have virtual functions. Hashing in Boost and STL is fast and reliable.

You can also specialize hashing for your own types. In Boost, it is done via specializing the `hash_value` function in the namespace of a custom type:

```
// Must be in namespace of string_hash_fast class
inline std::size_t hash_value(const string_hash_fast& v) {
    return v.comparison_;
}
```

This is different from STL specialization of `std::hash`, where you are required to make a template specialization of the `hash<>` structure in the `std::` namespace.

Hashing in Boost is defined for all the basic type arrays (such as `int`, `float`, `double`, and `char`), and for all the STL containers including `std::array`, `std::tuple`, and `std::type_index`. Some libraries also provide hash specializations, for example, `Boost.Variant` can hash any `boost::variant` class.

See also

▸ Read the *Using an unordered set and map* recipe for more information about the hash functions' usage.

▸ The official documentation of `Boost.Functional/Hash` will tell you how to combine multiple hashes and provides more examples. Read about it at `http://www.boost.org/doc/libs/1_53_0/doc/html/hash.html`.

Using an unordered set and map

In the previous recipe, we saw how string comparison can be optimized using hashing. After reading it, the following question may arise, "Can we make a container that will cache hashed values to use faster comparison?".

The answer is yes, and we can do much more. We can achieve almost constant time complexities for search, insertion, and removal of elements.

Getting ready

Basic knowledge of C++ and STL containers is required. Reading the previous recipe will also help.

How to do it...

This will be the simplest of all recipes:

1. All you need to do is just include the `<boost/unordered_map.hpp>` header, if we wish to use maps or the `<boost/unordered_set.hpp>` header, if we wish to use sets.

2. Now you are free to use `boost::unordered_map`, instead of `std::map` and `boost::unordered_set` instead of `std::set`:

```
#include <boost/unordered_set.hpp>
void example() {
    boost::unordered_set<std::string> strings;

    strings.insert("This");
    strings.insert("is");
    strings.insert("an");
    strings.insert("example");

    assert(strings.find("is") != strings.cend());
}
```

How it works...

Unordered containers store values and remember the hash of each value. Now if you wish to find a value in them, they will compute the hash of that value and search for that hash in the container. After the hash is found, the containers check for equality between the found value and the searched value. Then, the iterator to the value, or to the end of the container is returned.

Because the container can search for a constant width integral hash value, it may use some optimizations and algorithms suitable only for integers. Those algorithms guarantee constant search complexity O(1), when traditional `std::set` and `std::map` provide worse complexity O(log(N)), where N is the number of elements in the container. This leads us to a situation where the more elements in traditional `std::set` or `std::map`, the slower it works. However, the performance of unordered containers does not depend on the element count.

Such good performance never comes free of cost. In unordered containers, values are unordered (you are not surprised, are you?). It means that if we'll be outputting elements of containers from `begin()` to `end()`, as follows:

```
template <class T>
void output_example() {
    T strings;
```

```
        strings.insert("CZ"); strings.insert("CD");
        strings.insert("A"); strings.insert("B");
        std::copy(
            strings.begin(),
            strings.end(),
            std::ostream_iterator<std::string>(std::cout, "  ")
        );
    }
```

We'll get the following output for `std::set` and `boost::unordered_set`:

```
boost::unordered_set<std::string> : B   A   CD   CZ
std::set<std::string> : A   B   CD   CZ
```

So, how much does the performance differ? Have a look at the following output:

```
$ TIME="%E" time ./unordered s

STD matched: 20000000

0:31.39

$ TIME="%E" time ./unordered h

HASH matched: 20000000

0:26.93
```

The performance was measured using the following code:

```
    template <class T>
    std::size_t test_default() {
        // Constants
        const std::size_t ii_max = 20000000;
        const std::string s("Test string");

        T map;

        for (std::size_t ii = 0; ii < ii_max; ++ii) {
            map[s + boost::lexical_cast<std::string>(ii)] = ii;
        }

        // Inserting once more
        for (std::size_t ii = 0; ii < ii_max; ++ii) {
            map[s + boost::lexical_cast<std::string>(ii)] = ii;
        }
```

```
            return map.size();
    }
```

Note that the code contains a lot of string constructions, so it is not 100 percent correct to measure the speedup using this test. It is here to show that unordered containers are usually faster than ordered ones.

Sometimes a task might arise where we need to use a user-defined type in unordered containers:

```
struct my_type {
    int          val1_;
    std::string val2_;
};
```

To do that, we need to write a comparison operator for that type:

```
inline bool operator == (const my_type& v1, const my_type& v2) {
    return v1.val1_ == v2.val1_ && v1.val2_ == v2.val2_;}
```

Now, specialize the hashing function for that type. If the type consists of multiple fields, we usually just need to combine the hashes of all the fields that participate in equal comparison:

```
std::size_t hash_value(const my_type& v) {
    std::size_t ret = 0u;

    boost::hash_combine(ret, v.val1_);
    boost::hash_combine(ret, v.val2_);
    return ret;
}
```

 It is highly recommended to combine hashes using the `boost::hash_combine` function.

There's more...

Multiversions of containers are also available: `boost::unordered_multiset` is defined in the `<boost/unordered_set.hpp>` header, and `boost::unordered_multimap` is defined in the `<boost/unordered_map.hpp>` header. Just like in the case of STL, multiversions of containers are capable of storing multiple equal key values.

All the unordered containers allow you to specify your own hashing functor, instead of the default `boost::hash`. They also allow you to specialize your own equal comparison functor, instead of the default `std::equal_to`.

C++11 has all the unordered containers from Boost. You may find them in the headers: `<unordered_set>` and `<unordered_map>`, in the `std::` namespace, instead of `boost::`. The Boost and the STL versions have the same performance, and must work in the same way. However, Boost's unordered containers are available even on C++03 compilers, and make use of the rvalue reference emulation of `Boost.Move`, so you can use those containers for the move-only classes in C++03.

C++11 has no `hash_combine` function, so you will need to write your own:

```
template <class T>
inline void hash_combine(std::size_t& seed, const T& v)
{
    std::hash<T> hasher;
    seed ^= hasher(v) + 0x9e3779b9 + (seed<<6) + (seed>>2);
}
```

Or just use `boost::hash_combine`.

See also

*   ▶ The recipe *Using the C++11 move emulation* in *Chapter 1, Starting to Write Your Application*, for more details on rvalue reference emulation of `Boost.Move`

*   ▶ More information about the unordered containers is available on the official site at `http://www.boost.org/doc/libs/1_53_0/doc/html/unordered.html`

*   ▶ More information about combining hashes and computing hashes for ranges is available at `http://www.boost.org/doc/libs/1_53_0/doc/html/hash.html`

Making a map, where value is also a key

Several times in a year, we need something that can store and index a pair of values. Moreover, we need to get the first part of the pair using the second, and get the second part using the first. Confused? Let me show you an example. We are creating a vocabulary class, wherein when the users put values into it, the class must return identifiers and when the users put identifiers into it, the class must return values.

To be more practical, users will be entering login names into our vocabulary, and wish to get the unique identifier of a person. They will also wish to get all the persons' names using identifiers.

Let's see how it can be implemented using Boost.

Getting ready

Basic knowledge of STL and templates are required for this recipe.

How to do it...

This recipe is about the abilities of the `Boost.Bimap` library. Let's see how it can be used to implement this task:

1. We'll need the following includes:

```
#include <boost/bimap.hpp>
#include <boost/bimap/multiset_of.hpp>
```

2. Now we are ready to make our vocabulary structure:

```
typedef boost::bimap<
    std::string,
    boost::bimaps::multiset_of<std::size_t>
> name_id_type;

name_id_type name_id;
```

3. It can be filled using the following syntax:

```
// Inserting keys <-> values
name_id.insert(name_id_type::value_type(
    "John Snow", 1
));

name_id.insert(name_id_type::value_type(
    "Vasya Pupkin", 2
));

name_id.insert(name_id_type::value_type(
    "Antony Polukhin", 3
));

// Same person as "Antony Polukhin"
name_id.insert(name_id_type::value_type(
    "Anton Polukhin", 3
));
```

4. We can work with the left part of bimap just like with a map:

```
std::cout << "Left:\n";
typedef name_id_type::left_const_iterator
  left_const_iterator;
for (left_const_iterator it = name_id.left.begin(),
    iend = name_id.left.end();
    it!= iend;
    ++it)
```

```
    {
        std::cout << it->first << " <=> " << it->second
            << '\n';
    }
```

5. The right part of bimap is almost the same as the left:

```
std::cout << "\nRight:\n";
typedef name_id_type::right_const_iterator
    right_const_iterator;
for (right_const_iterator it = name_id.right.begin(),
        iend = name_id.right.end();
        it!= iend;
        ++it)
    {
        std::cout << it->first << " <=> " << it->second
            << '\n';
    }
```

6. We also need to ensure that there is such a person in the vocabulary:

```
assert(
    name_id.find(name_id_type::value_type(
        "Anton Polukhin", 3
    )) != name_id.end()
);
```

7. That's it. Now, if we put all the code (except includes) inside int main(), we'll get the following output:

```
Left:
Anton Polukhin <=> 3
Antony Polukhin <=> 3
John Snow <=> 1
Vasya Pupkin <=> 2

Right:
1 <=> John Snow
2 <=> Vasya Pupkin
3 <=> Antony Polukhin
3 <=> Anton Polukhin
```

How it works...

In step 2, we define the `bimap` type:

```
typedef boost::bimap<
    std::string,
    boost::bimaps::multiset_of<std::size_t>
> name_id_type;
```

The first template parameter tells that the first key must have type `std::string`, and should work as `std::set`. The second template parameter tells that the second key must have type `std::size_t`. Multiple first keys can have a single second key value, just like in `std::multimap`.

We can specify the underlying behavior of `bimap` using classes from the `boost::bimaps::` namespace. We can use hash map as an underlying type for the first key:

```
#include <boost/bimap/unordered_set_of.hpp>
#include <boost/bimap/unordered_multiset_of.hpp>

typedef boost::bimap<
    boost::bimaps::unordered_set_of<std::string>,
    boost::bimaps::unordered_multiset_of<std::size_t>
> hash_name_id_type;
```

When we do not specify the behavior of the key, and just specify its type, `Boost.Bimap` uses `boost::bimaps::set_of` as a default behavior. Just like in our example, we can try to express the following code using STL:

```
#include <boost/bimap/set_of.hpp>

typedef boost::bimap<
    boost::bimaps::set_of<std::string>,
    boost::bimaps::multiset_of<std::size_t>
> name_id_type;
```

Using STL it would look like a combination of the following two variables:

```
// name_id.left
std::map<std::string, std::size_t> key1;

// name_id.right
std::multimap<std::size_t, std::string> key2;
```

As we can see from the preceding comments, a call to `name_id.left` (in step 4) will return a reference to something with an interface close to `std::map<std::string, std::size_t>`. A call to `name_id.right` from step 5 will return something with an interface close to `std::multimap<std::size_t, std::string>`.

In step 6, we work with a whole `bimap`, searching for a pair of keys, and making sure that they are in the container.

There's more...

Unfortunately, C++11 has nothing close to `Boost.Bimap`. Here we have some other bad news: `Boost.Bimap` does not support rvalue references, and on some compilers, insane numbers of warnings will be shown. Refer to your compiler's documentation to get the information about suppressing specific warnings.

The good news is that `Boost.Bimap` usually uses less memory than two STL containers, and makes searches as fast as STL containers. It has no virtual function calls inside, but does use dynamic allocations.

See also

- The next recipe, *Using multi-index containers*, will give you more information about multi-indexing, and about the Boost library that can be used instead of `Boost.Bimap`

- Read the official documentation for more examples and information about bimap at `http://www.boost.org/doc/libs/1_53_0/libs/bimap/doc/html/index.html`

Using multi-index containers

In the previous recipe, we made some kind of vocabulary, which is good when we need to work with pairs. But, what if we need much more advanced indexing? Let's make a program that indexes persons:

```
struct person {
    std::size_t    id_;
    std::string    name_;
    unsigned int   height_;
    unsigned int   weight_;
    person(std::size_t id, const std::string& name, unsigned int
      height, unsigned int weight)
        : id_(id)
        , name_(name)
```

```
        , height_(height)
        , weight_(weight)
    {}
};

inline bool operator < (const person& p1, const person& p2) {
    return p1.name_ < p2.name_;
}
```

We will need a lot of indexes; for example, by name, ID, height, and weight.

Getting ready

Basic knowledge of STL containers and unordered maps is required.

How to do it...

All the indexes can be constructed and managed by a single `Boost.Multiindex` container.

1. To do so, we will need a lot of includes:

```
#include <boost/multi_index_container.hpp>
#include <boost/multi_index/ordered_index.hpp>
#include <boost/multi_index/hashed_index.hpp>
#include <boost/multi_index/identity.hpp>
#include <boost/multi_index/member.hpp>
```

2. The hardest part is to construct the multi-index type:

```
typedef boost::multi_index::multi_index_container<
    person,
    boost::multi_index::indexed_by<
        // names are unique
        boost::multi_index::ordered_unique<
            boost::multi_index::identity<person>
        >,
        // IDs are not unique, but we do not need then
        //ordered
        boost::multi_index::hashed_non_unique<
            boost::multi_index::member<
                person, std::size_t, &person::id_
            >
        >,
        // Height may not be unique, but must be sorted
        boost::multi_index::ordered_non_unique<
```

```
            boost::multi_index::member<
                person, unsigned int, &person::height_
            >
        >,
        // Weight may not be unique, but must be sorted
        boost::multi_index::ordered_non_unique<
            boost::multi_index::member<
                person, unsigned int, &person::weight_
            >
        >
    > // closing for `boost::multi_index::indexed_by<
> indexes_t;
```

3. Now we may insert values into our multi-index:

```
indexes_t persons;

// Inserting values
persons.insert(person(1, "John Snow", 185, 80));
persons.insert(person(2, "Vasya Pupkin", 165, 60));
persons.insert(person(3, "Antony Polukhin", 183, 70));
// Same person as "Antony Polukhin"
persons.insert(person(3, "Anton Polukhin", 182, 70));
```

4. Let's construct a function for printing the index content:

```
template <std::size_t IndexNo, class Indexes>
void print(const Indexes& persons) {
    std::cout << IndexNo << ":\n";

    typedef typename Indexes::template nth_index<
            IndexNo
    >::type::const_iterator const_iterator_t;

    for (const_iterator_t it = persons.template
      get<IndexNo>().begin(),
        iend = persons.template get<IndexNo>().end();
        it != iend;
        ++it)
    {
        const person& v = *it;
        std::cout
            << v.name_   << ", "
            << v.id_     << ", "
            << v.height_ << ", "
            << v.weight_ << '\n'
```

```
        ;
    }

    std::cout << '\n';
}
```

5. Print all the indexes as follows:

```
print<0>(persons);
print<1>(persons);
print<2>(persons);
print<3>(persons);
```

6. Some code from the previous recipe can also be used:

```
assert(persons.get<1>().find(2)->name_ == "Vasya
  Pupkin");
assert(
    persons.find(person(
        77, "Anton Polukhin", 0, 0
    )) != persons.end()
);

// Won' compile
//assert(persons.get<0>().find("John Snow")->id_ == 1);
```

7. Now if we run our example, it will output the content of the indexes:

```
0:
Anton Polukhin, 3, 182, 70
Antony Polukhin, 3, 183, 70
John Snow, 1, 185, 80
Vasya Pupkin, 2, 165, 60

1:
John Snow, 1, 185, 80
Vasya Pupkin, 2, 165, 60
Anton Polukhin, 3, 182, 70
Antony Polukhin, 3, 183, 70

2:
Vasya Pupkin, 2, 165, 60
Anton Polukhin, 3, 182, 70
Antony Polukhin, 3, 183, 70
```

```
John Snow, 1, 185, 80

3:
Vasya Pupkin, 2, 165, 60
Antony Polukhin, 3, 183, 70
Anton Polukhin, 3, 182, 70
John Snow, 1, 185, 80
```

How it works...

The hardest part here is the construction of a multi-index type using `boost::multi_index::multi_index_container`. The first template parameter is a class that we are going to index. In our case, it is `person`. The second parameter is a type `boost::multi_index::indexed_by`, all the indexes must be described as a template parameter of that class.

Now, let's take a look at the first index description:

```
boost::multi_index::ordered_unique<
   boost::multi_index::identity<person>
>
```

The usage of the `boost::multi_index::ordered_unique` class means that the index must work like `std::set`, and have all of its members. The `boost::multi_index::identity<person>` class means that the index will use the `operator <` of a `person` class for orderings.

The next table shows the relation between the `Boost.MultiIndex` types and the STL containers:

The Boost.MultiIndex types	STL containers
`boost::multi_index::ordered_unique`	`std::set`
`boost::multi_index::ordered_non_unique`	`std::multiset`
`boost::multi_index::hashed_unique`	`std::unordered_set`
`boost::multi_index::hashed_non_unique`	`std::unordered_mutiset`
`boost::multi_index::sequenced`	`std::list`

Let's take a look at the second index:

```
boost::multi_index::hashed_non_unique<
  boost::multi_index::member<
     person, std::size_t, &person::id_
  >
>
```

The `boost::multi_index::hashed_non_unique` type means that the index will
work like `std::set`, and `boost::multi_index::member<person, std::size_t,
&person::id_>` means that the index will apply the hash function only to a single member
field of the person structure, to `person::id_`.

The remaining indexes won't be a trouble now, so let's take a look at the usage of indexes
in the print function instead. Getting the type of iterator for a specific index is done using the
following code:

```
typedef typename Indexes::template nth_index<
        IndexNo
>::type::const_iterator const_iterator_t;
```

This looks slightly overcomplicated because `Indexes` is a template parameter. The example
would be simpler, if we could write this code in the scope of `indexes_t`:

```
typedef indexes_t::nth_index<0>::type::const_iterator
  const_iterator_t;
```

The `nth_index` member metafunction takes a zero-based number of index to use. In our
example, index 1 is the index of IDs, index 2 is the index of heights and so on.

Now, let's take a look at how to use `const_iterator_t`:

```
for (const_iterator_t it = persons.template
  get<IndexNo>().begin(),
     iend = persons.template get<IndexNo>().end();
     it != iend;
     ++it)
{
     const person& v = *it;
     // ...
```

This can also be simplified for `indexes_t` being in scope:

```
for (const_iterator_t it = persons.get<0>().begin(),
        iend = persons.get<0>().end();
     it != iend;
     ++it)
{
```

```
const person& v = *it;
// ...
```

The function `get<indexNo>()` returns index. We can use that index almost like an STL container.

There's more...

C++11 has no multi-index library. The `Boost.MultiIndex` library is a fast library that uses no virtual functions. The official documentation of `Boost.MultiIndex` contains performance and memory usage measures, showing that this library in most cases uses less memory than STL-based handwritten code. Unfortunately, `boost::multi_index::multi_index_container` does not support C++11 features, and also has no rvalue references emulation using `Boost.Move`.

See also

▶ The official documentation of `Boost.MultiIndex` contains tutorials, performance measures, examples, and other `Boost.Multiindex` libraries' description of useful features. Read about it at `http://www.boost.org/doc/libs/1_53_0/libs/multi_index/doc/index.html`.

Getting the benefits of single-linked list and memory pool

Nowadays, we usually use `std::vector` when we need nonassociative and nonordered containers. This is recommended by *Andrei Alexandrescu* and *Herb Sutter* in the book *C++ Coding Standards*, and even those users who did not read the book usually use `std::vector`. Why? Well, `std::list` is slower, and uses much more resources than `std::vector`. The `std::deque` container is very close to `std::vector`, but stores values noncontinuously.

Everything is good until we do not need a container; however, if we need a container, erasing and inserting elements does not invalidate iterators. Then we are forced to choose the slower `std::list`.

But wait, there is a good solution in Boost for such cases!

Getting ready

Good knowledge of STL containers is required to understand the introductory part. After that, only basic knowledge of C++ and STL containers is required.

How to do it...

In this recipe, we'll be using two Boost libraries at the same time: `Boost.Pool` and single-linked list from `Boost.Container`.

1. We'll need the following headers:

```
#include <boost/pool/pool_alloc.hpp>
#include <boost/container/slist.hpp>
```

2. Now we need to describe the type of our list. This can be done as shown in the following code:

```
typedef boost::fast_pool_allocator<int> allocator_t;
typedef boost::container::slist<int, allocator_t> slist_t;
```

3. We can work with our single-linked list like with `std::list`. Take a look at the function that is used to measure the speed of both the list types:

```
template <class ListT>
void test_lists() {
    typedef ListT list_t;

    // Inserting 1000000 zeros
    list_t  list(1000000, 0);
    for (int i = 0; i < 1000; ++i) {
        list.insert(list.begin(), i);
    }

    // Searching for some value
    typedef typename list_t::iterator iterator;
    iterator it = std::find(list.begin(), list.end(), 777);
    assert(it != list.end());

    // Erasing some values
    for (int i = 0; i < 100; ++i) {
        list.pop_front();
    }

    // Iterator still valid and points to same value
    assert(it != list.end());
    assert(*it == 777);

    // Inserting more values
    for (int i = -100; i < 10; ++i) {
        list.insert(list.begin(), i);
    }
}
```

```
            // Iterator still valid and points to same value
            assert(it != list.end());
            assert(*it == 777);

            list_specific(list, it);
        }
```

4. Features specific for each type of list are moved to `list_specific` functions:

```
    void list_specific(slist_t& list, slist_t::iterator it) {
        typedef slist_t::iterator iterator;

        // Erasing element 776
        assert( *(++iterator(it)) == 776);
        assert(*it == 777);
        list.erase_after(it);
        assert(*it == 777);
        assert( *(++iterator(it)) == 775);

        // Freeing memory
        boost::singleton_pool<
            boost::pool_allocator_tag,
            sizeof(int)
        >::release_memory();
    }


    #include <list>
    typedef std::list<int> stdlist_t;

    void list_specific(stdlist_t& list, stdlist_t::iterator it)
        {
        typedef stdlist_t::iterator iterator;

        // Erasing element 776
        ++it;
        assert( *it == 776);
        it = list.erase(it);
        assert(*it == 775);
    }
```

How it works...

When we are using `std::list`, we may notice a slowdown because each node of the list needs a separate allocation. It means that usually when we insert 10 elements into `std::list`, the container calls new 10 times.

That is why we used boost::fast_pool_allocator<int> from Boost.Pool. This allocator tries to allocate bigger blocks of memory, so that at a later stage, multiple nodes can be constructed without any calls to allocate new ones.

The Boost.Pool library has a drawback—it uses memory for internal needs. Usually, an additional sizeof pointer is used per element. To workaround that issue, we are using a single linked list from Boost.Containers.

The boost::container::slist class is more compact, but its iterators can iterate only forward. Step 3 will be trivial for those readers who are aware of STL containers, so we move to step 4 to see some boost::container::slist specific features. Since the single-linked list iterator could iterate only forward, traditional algorithms of insertion and deletion will take linear time O(N). That's because when we are erasing or inserting, the previous element must be modified to point at new elements of the list. To workaround that issue, the single-linked list has the methods erase_after and insert_after that work for constant time O(1). These methods insert or erase elements right after the current position of the iterator.

 However, erasing and inserting values at the beginning of single-linked lists makes no big difference.

Take a careful look at the following code:

```
boost::singleton_pool<
    boost::pool_allocator_tag,
    sizeof(int)
>::release_memory();
```

It is required because boost::fast_pool_allocator does not free memory, so we must do it by hand. The *Doing something at scope exit* recipe from *Chapter 3, Managing Resources*, will be a help in freeing Boost.Pool.

Let's take a look at the execution results to see the difference:

```
$TIME="Runtime=%E RAM=%MKB" time ./slist_and_pool l

std::list: Runtime=0:00.05 RAM=32440KB

$ TIME="Runtime=%E RAM=%MKB" time ./slist_and_pool s

slist_t:   Runtime=0:00.02 RAM=17564KB
```

As we can see, slist_t uses half the memory, and is twice as fast compared to the std::list class.

There's more...

C++11 has `std::forward_list`, which is very close to `boost::containers::slist`. It also has the `*_after` methods, but has no `size()` method. They have the same performance and neither of them have virtual functions, so these containers are fast and reliable. However, the Boost version is also usable on C++03 compilers, and even has support for rvalue references emulation via `Boost.Move`.

Pools are not part of C++11. Use the version from Boost; it is fast and does not use virtual functions.

 Guessing why `boost::fast_pool_allocator` does not free the memory by itself? That's because C++03 has no stateful allocators, so the containers are not copying and storing allocators. That makes it impossible to implement a `boost::fast_pool_allocator` function that deallocates memory by itself.

See also

▶ The official documentation of `Boost.Pool` contains more examples and classes to work with memory pools. Read about it at `http://www.boost.org/doc/libs/1_53_0/libs/pool/doc/html/index.html`.

▶ The *Using flat associative containers* recipe will introduce you to some more classes from `Boost.Container`. You can also read the official documentation of `Boost.Container` to study that library by yourself, or get full reference documentation of its classes at `http://www.boost.org/doc/libs/1_53_0/doc/html/container.html`.

▶ Read about why stateful allocators may be required at `http://www.boost.org/doc/libs/1_53_0/doc/html/interprocess/allocators_containers.html#interprocess.allocators_containers.allocator_introduction`.

▶ *Vector vs List*, and other interesting topics from *Bjarne Stroustrup*, the inventor of the C++ programming language, can be found at `http://channel9.msdn.com/Events/GoingNative/GoingNative-2012/Keynote-Bjarne-Stroustrup-Cpp11-Style`.

Using flat associative containers

After reading the previous recipe, some of the readers may start using fast pool allocators everywhere; especially, for `std::set` and `std::map`. Well, I'm not going to stop you from doing that, but let's at least take a look at an alternative: flat associative containers. These containers are implemented on top of the traditional vector container and store the values ordered.

Getting ready

Basic knowledge of STL associative containers is required.

How to do it...

The flat containers are part of the `Boost.Container` library. We already saw how to use some of its containers in the previous recipes. In this recipe we'll be using a `flat_set` associative container:

1. We'll need to include only a single header file:

    ```
    #include <boost/container/flat_set.hpp>
    ```

2. After that, we are free to construct the flat container:

    ```
    boost::container::flat_set<int> set;
    ```

3. Reserving space for elements:

    ```
    set.reserve(4096);
    ```

4. Filling the container:

    ```
    for (int i = 0; i < 4000; ++i) {
        set.insert(i);
    }
    ```

5. Now we can work with it just like with `std::set`:

    ```
    // 5.1
    assert(set.lower_bound(500) - set.lower_bound(100) ==
      400);

    // 5.2
    set.erase(0);

    // 5.3
    set.erase(5000);
    ```

```
// 5.4
assert(std::lower_bound(set.cbegin(), set.cend(),
    900000) == set.cend());

// 5.5
assert(
    set.lower_bound(100) + 400
    ==
    set.find(500)
);
```

How it works...

Steps 1 and 2 are trivial, but step 3 requires attention. It is one of the most important steps while working with flat associative containers and `std::vector`.

The `boost::container::flat_set` class stores its values ordered in vector, which means that any insertion or deletion of elements takes linear time O(N), just like in case of `std::vector`. This is a necessary evil. But for that, we gain almost three times less memory usage per element, more processor cache friendly storage, and random access iterators. Take a look at step 5, `5.1`, where we were getting the distance between two iterators returned by calls to the `lower_bound` member functions. Getting distance with a flat set takes constant time O(1), while the same operation on iterators of `std::set` takes linear time O(N). In the case of `5.1`, getting the distance using `std::set` would be 400 times slower than getting the distance for flat set containers.

Back to step 3. Without reserving memory, insertion of elements can become at times slower and less memory efficient. The `std::vector` class allocates the required chunk of memory and the in-place construct elements on that chunk. When we insert some element without reserving the memory, there is a chance that there is no free space remaining on the preallocated chunk of memory, so `std::vector` will allocate twice the chunk of memory that was allocated previously. After that, `std::vector` will copy or move elements from the first chunk to the second, delete elements of the first chunk, and deallocate the first chunk. Only after that, insertion will occur. Such copying and deallocation may occur multiple times during insertions, dramatically reducing the speed.

 If you know the count of elements that `std::vector` or any flat container must store, reserve the space for those elements before insertion. There are no exceptions from that rule!

Step 4 is trivial, we are inserting elements here. Note that we are inserting ordered elements. This is not required, but recommended to speedup insertion. Inserting elements at the end of `std::vector` is much more cheaper than in the middle or at the beginning.

In step 5, `5.2` and `5.3` do not differ much, except of their execution speed. Rules for erasing elements are pretty much the same as for inserting them, so see the preceding paragraph for explanations.

 Maybe I'm telling you trivial things about containers, but I have seen some very popular products that use features of C++11, have an insane amount of optimizations and lame usage of STL containers, especially `std::vector`.

In step 5, `5.4` shows you that the `std::lower_bound` function will work faster with `boost::container::flat_set` than with `std::set`, because of random access iterators.

In step 5, `5.5` also shows you the benefit of random access iterators. Note that we did not use the `std::find` function here. This is because that function takes linear time O(N), while the member `find` functions take logarithmic time O(log(N)).

There's more...

When should we use flat containers, and when should we use usual ones? Well, it's up to you, but here is a list of differences from the official documentation of `Boost.Container` that will help you to decide:

- Faster lookup than standard associative containers
- Much faster iteration than standard associative containers
- Less memory consumption for small objects (and for large objects if `shrink_to_fit` is used)
- Improved cache performance (data is stored in contiguous memory)
- Nonstable iterators (iterators are invalidated when inserting and erasing elements)
- Non-copyable and non-movable value types can't be stored
- Weaker exception safety than standard associative containers (copy/move constructors can throw an exception when shifting values in erasures and insertions)
- Slower insertion and erasure than standard associative containers (specially for non-movable types)

C++11 unfortunately has no flat containers. Flat containers from Boost are fast, have a lot of optimizations, and do not use virtual functions. Classes from `Boost.Containers` have support of rvalue reference emulation via `Boost.Move` so you are free to use them even on C++03 compilers.

See also

▸ Refer to the *Getting the benefits of single-linked list and memory pool* recipe for more information about `Boost.Container`.

▸ The recipe *Using the C++11 move emulation* in *Chapter 1, Starting to Write Your Application*, will give you the basics of emulation rvalue references on C++03 compatible compilers.

▸ The official documentation of `Boost.Container` contains a lot of useful information about `Boost.Container` and full reference of each class. Read about it at `http://www.boost.org/doc/libs/1_53_0/doc/html/container.html`.

10
Gathering Platform and Compiler Information

In this chapter we will cover:

- ▶ Detecting int128 support
- ▶ Detecting RTTI support
- ▶ Speeding up compilation using C++11 extern templates
- ▶ Writing metafunctions using simpler methods
- ▶ Reducing code size and increasing performance of user-defined types (UDTs) in C++11
- ▶ The portable way to export and import functions and classes
- ▶ Detecting the Boost version and getting latest features

Introduction

Different projects and companies have different coding requirements. Some of them forbid exceptions or RTTI and some forbid C++11. If you are willing to write portable code that can be used by a wide range of projects, this chapter is for you.

Want to make your code as fast as possible and use the latest C++ features? You'll definitely need a tool for detecting compiler features.

Some compilers have unique features that may greatly simplify your life. If you are targeting a single compiler, you can save many hours and use those features. No need to implement their analogues from scratch!

This chapter is devoted to different helper macros used to detect compiler, platform, and Boost features. Those macro are widely used across Boost libraries and are essential for writing portable code that is able to work with any compiler flags.

Detecting int128 support

Some compilers have support for extended arithmetic types such as 128-bit floats or integers. Let's take a quick glance at how to use them using Boost. We'll be creating a method that accepts three parameters and returns the multiplied value of those methods.

Getting ready

Only basic knowledge of C++ is required.

How to do it...

What do we need to work with 128-bit integers? Macros that show that they are available and a few typedefs to have portable type names across platforms.

1. We'll need only a single header:

   ```
   #include <boost/config.hpp>
   ```

2. Now we need to detect int128 support:

   ```
   #ifdef BOOST_HAS_INT128
   ```

3. Add some typedefs and implement the method as follows:

   ```
   typedef boost::int128_type int_t;
   typedef boost::uint128_type uint_t;

   inline int_t mul(int_t v1, int_t v2, int_t v3) {
       return v1 * v2 * v3;
   }
   ```

4. For compilers that do not support the int128 type, we may require support of the int64 type:

   ```
   #else // BOOST_NO_LONG_LONG

   #ifdef BOOST_NO_LONG_LONG
   #error "This code requires at least int64_t support"
   #endif
   ```

5. Now we need to provide some implementation for compilers without int128 support using int64:

```
struct int_t { boost::long_long_type hi, lo; };
struct uint_t { boost::ulong_long_type hi, lo; };

inline int_t mul(int_t v1, int_t v2, int_t v3) {
    // Some hand written math
    // ...
}

#endif // BOOST_NO_LONG_LONG
```

How it works...

The header `<boost/config.hpp>` contains a lot of macros to describe compiler and platform features. In this example, we used `BOOST_HAS_INT128` to detect support of 128-bit integers and `BOOST_NO_LONG_LONG` to detect support of 64-bit integers.

As we may see from the example, Boost has typedefs for 64-bit signed and unsigned integers:

```
boost::long_long_type
boost::ulong_long_type
```

It also has typedefs for 128-bit signed and unsigned integers:

```
boost::int128_type
boost::uint128_type
```

There's more...

C++11 has support of 64-bit types via the `long long int` and `unsigned long long int` built-in types. Unfortunately, not all compilers support C++11, so `BOOST_NO_LONG_LONG` will be useful for you. 128-bit integers are not a part of C++11, so typedefs and macros from Boost are the only way to write portable code.

See also

► Read the recipe *Detecting RTTI support* for more information about `Boost.Config`.

► Read the official documentation of `Boost.Config` for more information about its abilities at `http://www.boost.org/doc/libs/1_53_0/libs/config/doc/html/index.html`.

► There is a library in Boost that allows constructing types of unlimited precision. Take a look at the `Boost.Multiprecision` library at `http://www.boost.org/doc/libs/1_53_0/libs/multiprecision/doc/html/index.html`.

Detecting RTTI support

Some companies and libraries have specific requirements for their C++ code, such as successful compilation without **Runtime type information** (**RTTI**). In this small recipe, we'll take a look at how we can detect disabled RTTI, how to store information about types, and compare types at runtime, even without `typeid`.

Getting ready

Basic knowledge of C++ RTTI usage is required for this recipe.

How to do it...

Detecting disabled RTTI, storing information about types, and comparing types at runtime are tricks that are widely used across Boost libraries. The examples are `Boost.Exception` and `Boost.Function`.

1. To do this, we first need to include the following header:

```
#include <boost/config.hpp>
```

2. Let's first look at the situation where RTTI is enabled and the C++11 `std::type_index` class is available:

```
#if !defined(BOOST_NO_RTTI) \
    && !defined(BOOST_NO_CXX11_HDR_TYPEINDEX)

#include <typeindex>
using std::type_index;

template <class T>
type_index type_id() {
    return typeid(T);
}
```

3. Otherwise, we need to construct our own `type_index` class:

```
#else

#include <cstring>

struct type_index {
    const char* name_;

    explicit type_index(const char* name)
        : name_(name)
    {}
};
```

```
inline bool operator == (const type_index& v1,
    const type_index& v2)
{
    return !std::strcmp(v1.name_, v2.name_);
}

inline bool operator != (const type_index& v1,
    const type_index& v2)
{
    // '!!' to supress warnings
    return !!std::strcmp(v1.name_, v2.name_);
}
```

4. The final step is to define the `type_id` function:

```
#include <boost/current_function.hpp>

template <class T>
inline type_index type_id() {
    return type_index(BOOST_CURRENT_FUNCTION);
}
#endif
```

5. Now we can compare types:

```
assert(type_id<unsigned int>() == type_id<unsigned>());
assert(type_id<double>() != type_id<long double>());
```

How it works...

The macro `BOOST_NO_RTTI` will be defined if RTTI is disabled, and the macro `BOOST_NO_CXX11_HDR_TYPEINDEX` will be defined when the compiler has no `<typeindex>` header and no `std::type_index` class.

The handwritten `type_index` structure from step 3 of the previous section only holds the pointer to some string; nothing really interesting here.

Take a look at the `BOOST_CURRENT_FUNCTION` macro. It returns the full name of the current function, including template parameters, arguments, and the return type. For example, `type_id<double>()` will be represented as follows:

`type_index type_id() [with T = double]`

So, for any other type, `BOOST_CURRENT_FUNCTION` will return a different string, and that's why the `type_index` variable from the example won't compare equal-to it.

There's more...

Different compilers have different macros for getting the full function name and RTTI. Using macros from Boost is the most portable solution. The `BOOST_CURRENT_FUNCTION` macro returns the name at compile time, so it implies minimal runtime penalty.

See also

- ▸ Read the upcoming recipes for more information on `Boost.Config`
- ▸ Browse to `https://github.com/apolukhin/type_index` and refer to the library there, which uses all the tricks from this recipe to implement `type_index`
- ▸ Read the official documentation of `Boost.Config` at `http://www.boost.org/doc/libs/1_53_0/libs/config/doc/html/index.html`

Speeding up compilation using C++11 extern templates

Remember some situations where you were using some complicated template class declared in the header file? Examples of such classes would be `boost::variant`, containers from `Boost.Container`, or `Boost.Spirit` parsers. When we use such classes or methods, they are usually compiled (instantiated) separately in each source file that is using them, and duplicates are thrown away during linking. On some compilers, that may lead to slow compilation speed.

If only there was some way to tell the compiler in which source file to instantiate it!

Getting ready

Basic knowledge of templates is required for this recipe.

How to do it...

This method is widely used in modern C++ standard libraries for compilers that do support it. For example, the STL library, which is shipped with GCC, uses this technique to instantiate `std::basic_string<char>` and `std::basic_fstream<char>`.

1. To do it by ourselves, we need to include the following header:

   ```
   #include <boost/config.hpp>
   ```

2. We also need to include a header file that contains a template class whose instantiation count we wish to reduce:

```
#include <boost/variant.hpp>
#include <boost/blank.hpp>
#include <string>
```

3. The following is the code for compilers with support for C++11 extern templates:

```
#ifndef BOOST_NO_CXX11_EXTERN_TEMPLATE

extern template class boost::variant<
    boost::blank,
    int,
    std::string,
    double
>;

#endif
```

4. Now we need to add the following code to the source file where we wish the template to be instantiated:

```
// Header with 'extern template'
#include "header.hpp"

#ifndef BOOST_NO_CXX11_EXTERN_TEMPLATE
template class boost::variant<
    boost::blank,
    int,
    std::string,
    double
>;
#endif
```

How it works...

The C++11 keyword `extern template` just tells the compiler not to instantiate the template without an explicit request to do that.

The code in step 4 is an explicit request to instantiate the template in this source file.

The `BOOST_NO_CXX11_EXTERN_TEMPLATE` macro is defined when the compiler has support of C++11 extern templates.

There's more...

Extern templates do not affect the runtime performance of your program, but can significantly reduce the compilation time of some template classes. Do not overuse them; they are nearly useless for small template classes.

See also

- ▸ Read the other recipes of this chapter to get more information about `Boost.Config`
- ▸ Read the official documentation of `Boost.Config` for information about macros that was not covered in this chapter, at `http://www.boost.org/doc/libs/1_53_0/libs/config/doc/html/index.html`

Writing metafunctions using simpler methods

Chapter 4, Compile-time Tricks, and *Chapter 8, Metaprogramming,* were devoted to metaprogramming. If you were trying to use techniques from those chapters, you may have noticed that writing a metafunction can take a lot of time. So it may be a good idea to experiment with metafunctions using more user-friendly methods, such as C++11 `constexpr`, before writing a portable implementation.

In this recipe, we'll take a look at how to detect `constexpr` support.

Getting ready

The `constexpr` functions are functions that can be evaluated at compile time. That is all we need to know for this recipe.

How to do it...

Currently, not many compilers support the `constexpr` feature, so a good new compiler may be required for experiments. Let's see how we can detect compiler support for the `constexpr` feature:

1. Just like in other recipes from this chapter, we start with the following header:

```
#include <boost/config.hpp>
```

2. Now we will work with `constexpr`:

```
#if !defined(BOOST_NO_CXX11_CONSTEXPR) \
    && !defined(BOOST_NO_CXX11_HDR_ARRAY)

template <class T>
constexpr int get_size(const T& val) {
    return val.size() * sizeof(typename T::value_type);
}
```

3. Let's print an error if C++11 features are missing:

```
#else
#error "This code requires C++11 constexpr and std::array"
#endif
```

4. That's it; now we are free to write code such as the following:

```
std::array<short, 5> arr;
assert(get_size(arr) == 5 * sizeof(short));

unsigned char data[get_size(arr)];
```

How it works...

The `BOOST_NO_CXX11_CONSTEXPR` macro is defined when C++11 `constexpr` is available.

The `constexpr` keyword tells the compiler that the function can be evaluated at compile time if all the inputs for that function are compile-time constants. C++11 imposes a lot of limitations on what a `constexpr` function can do. C++14 will remove some of the limitations.

The `BOOST_NO_CXX11_HDR_ARRAY` macro is defined when the C++11 `std::array` class and the `<array>` header are available.

There's more...

However, there are other usable and interesting macros for `constexpr` too, as follows:

▶   The `BOOST_CONSTEXPR` macro expands to `constexpr` or does not expand

▶   The `BOOST_CONSTEXPR_OR_CONST` macro expands to `constexpr` or `const`

▶   The `BOOST_STATIC_CONSTEXPR` macro is the same as `static BOOST_CONSTEXPR_OR_CONST`

Using those macros, it is possible to write code that takes advantage of C++11 constant expression features if they are available:

```
template <class T, T Value>
struct integral_constant {
    BOOST_STATIC_CONSTEXPR T value = Value;

    BOOST_CONSTEXPR operator T() const {
        return this->value;
    }
};
```

Now, we can use `integral_constant` as shown in the following code:

```
char array[integral_constant<int, 10>()];
```

In the example, `BOOST_CONSTEXPR operator T()` will be called to get the array size.

The C++11 constant expressions may improve compilation speed and diagnostic information in case of error. It's a good feature to use.

See also

 ▸ More information about `constexpr` usage can be read at `http://en.cppreference.com/w/cpp/language/constexpr`

 ▸ Read the official documentation of `Boost.Config` for more information about macros at `http://www.boost.org/doc/libs/1_53_0/libs/config/doc/html/index.html`

Reducing code size and increasing performance of user-defined types (UDTs) in C++11

C++11 has very specific logic when **user-defined types** (**UDTs**) are used in STL containers. Containers will use move assignment and move construction only if the move constructor does not throw exceptions or there is no copy constructor.

Let's see how we can ensure the `move_nothrow` assignment operator and `move_nothrow` constructor of our type do not throw exceptions.

Getting ready

Basic knowledge of C++11 rvalue references is required for this recipe. Knowledge of STL containers will also serve you well.

How to do it...

Let's take a look at how we can improve our C++ classes using Boost.

1. All we need to do is mark the `move_nothrow` assignment operator and `move_nothrow` constructor with the `BOOST_NOEXCEPT` macro:

```
#include <boost/config.hpp>
class move_nothrow {
    // Some class class members go here
    // ...
public:
    move_nothrow() BOOST_NOEXCEPT {}
    move_nothrow(move_nothrow&&) BOOST_NOEXCEPT
        // : members initialization
        // ...
    {}

    move_nothrow& operator=(move_nothrow&&) BOOST_NOEXCEPT
      {
        // Implementation
        // ...
        return *this;
      }

    move_nothrow(const move_nothrow&);
    move_nothrow& operator=(const move_nothrow&);
};
```

2. Now we may use the class with `std::vector` in C++11 without any modifications:

```
std::vector<move_nothrow> v(10);
v.push_back(move_nothrow());
```

3. If we remove `BOOST_NOEXCEPT` from the move constructor, we'll get the following error for GCC-4.7 and later compilers:

```
/usr/include/c++/4.7/bits/stl_construct.h:77: undefined
  reference to `move_nothrow::move_nothrow(move_nothrow
    const&)'
```

How it works...

The `BOOST_NOEXCEPT` macro expands to `noexcept` on compilers that support it. The STL containers use type traits to detect if the constructor throws an exception or not. Type traits make their decision mainly based on `noexcept` specifiers.

Why do we get an error without `BOOST_NOEXCEPT`? GCC's type traits return the move constructor that `move_nothrow` throws, so `std::vector` will try to use the copy constructor of `move_nothrow`, which is not defined.

There's more...

The `BOOST_NOEXCEPT` macro also reduces binary size irrespective of whether the definition of the `noexcept` function or method is in a separate source file or not.

```
// In header file
int foo() BOOST_NOEXCEPT;

// In source file
int foo() BOOST_NOEXCEPT {
    return 0;
}
```

That's because in the latter case, the compiler knows that the function will not throw exceptions and so there is no need to generate code that handles them.

 If a function marked as `noexcept` does throw an exception, your program will terminate without calling destructors for the constructed objects.

See also

- A document describing why move constructors are allowed to throw exceptions and how containers must move objects is available at `http://www.open-std.org/jtc1/sc22/wg21/docs/papers/2010/n3050.html`
- Read the official documentation of `Boost.Config` for more examples of `noexcept` macros existing in Boost, at `http://www.boost.org/doc/libs/1_53_0/libs/config/doc/html/index.html`

The portable way to export and import functions and classes

Almost all modern languages have the ability to make libraries, which is a collection of classes and methods that have a well-defined interface. C++ is no exception to this rule. We have two types of libraries: runtime (also called shared or dynamic load) and static. But writing libraries is not a trivial task in C++. Different platforms have different methods for describing which symbols must be exported from the shared library.

Let's have a look at how to manage symbol visibility in a portable way using Boost.

Getting ready

Experience in creating dynamic and static libraries will be useful in this recipe.

How to do it...

The code for this recipe consists of two parts. The first part is the library itself. The second part is the code that uses that library. Both parts use the same header, in which the library methods are declared. Managing symbol visibility in a portable way using Boost is simple and can be done using the following steps:

1. In the header file, we'll need definitions from the following `include` header:

    ```
    #include <boost/config.hpp>
    ```

2. The following code must also be added to the header file:

    ```
    #if defined(MY_LIBRARY_LINK_DYNAMIC)
    # if defined(MY_LIBRARY_COMPILATION)
    #    define MY_LIBRARY_API BOOST_SYMBOL_EXPORT
    # else
    #    define MY_LIBRARY_API BOOST_SYMBOL_IMPORT
    # endif
    #else
    # define MY_LIBRARY_API
    #endif
    ```

3. Now all the declarations must use the `MY_LIBRARY_API` macro:

    ```
    int MY_LIBRARY_API foo();
    class MY_LIBRARY_API bar {
    public:
        /* ... */
        int meow() const;
    };
    ```

4. Exceptions must be declared with `BOOST_SYMBOL_VISIBLE`, otherwise they can be caught only using `catch(...)` in the code that will use the library:

```
#include <stdexcept>
struct BOOST_SYMBOL_VISIBLE bar_exception
    : public std::exception
{};
```

5. Library source files must include the header file:

```
#define MY_LIBRARY_COMPILATION
#include "my_library.hpp"
```

6. Definitions of methods must also be in the source files of the library:

```
int MY_LIBRARY_API foo() {
    // Implementation
    // ...
    return 0;
}
int bar::meow() const {
    throw bar_exception();
}
```

7. Now we can use the library as shown in the following code:

```
#include "../my_library/my_library.hpp"
#include <cassert>

int main() {
    assert(foo() == 0);
    bar b;
    try {
        b.meow();
        assert(false);
    } catch (const bar_exception&) {}
}
```

How it works...

All the work is done in step 2. There we are defining the macro `MY_LIBRARY_API`, which will be applied to classes and methods that we wish to export from our library. In step 2, we check for `MY_LIBRARY_LINK_DYNAMIC`; if it is not defined, we are building a static library and there is no need to define `MY_LIBRARY_API`.

The developer must take care of MY_LIBRARY_LINK_DYNAMIC! It will not define itself. So we need to make our build system to define it, if we are making a dynamic library.

If MY_LIBRARY_LINK_DYNAMIC is defined, we are building a runtime library, and that's where the workarounds start. You, as the developer, must tell the compiler that we are now exporting these methods to the user. The user must tell the compiler that he/she is importing methods from the library. To have a single header file for both library import and export, we use the following code:

```
# if defined(MY_LIBRARY_COMPILATION)
#    define MY_LIBRARY_API BOOST_SYMBOL_EXPORT
# else
#    define MY_LIBRARY_API BOOST_SYMBOL_IMPORT
# endif
```

When exporting the library (or, in other words, compiling it), we must define MY_LIBRARY_COMPILATION. This leads to MY_LIBRARY_API being defined to BOOST_SYMBOL_EXPORT. For example, see step 5, where we defined MY_LIBRARY_COMPILATION before including my_library.hpp. If MY_LIBRARY_COMPILATION is not defined, the header is included by the user, who doesn't know anything about that macro. And, if the header is included by the user, the symbols must be imported from the library.

The BOOST_SYMBOL_VISIBLE macro must be used only for those classes that are not exported and are used by RTTI. Examples of such classes are exceptions and classes being cast using dynamic_cast.

There's more...

Some compilers export all the symbols by default but provide flags to disable such behavior. For example, GCC provides -fvisibility=hidden. It is highly recommended to use those flags because it leads to smaller binary size, faster loading of dynamic libraries, and better logical structuring of binary input. Some inter-procedural optimizations can perform better when fewer symbols are exported.

C++11 has generalized attributes that someday may be used to provide a portable way to work with visibilities, but until then we have to use macros from Boost.

See also

- ▶ Read this chapter from the beginning to get more examples of `Boost.Config` usage
- ▶ Consider reading the official documentation of `Boost.Config` for the full list of the `Boost.Config` macro and their description at `http://www.boost.org/doc/libs/1_53_0/libs/config/doc/html/index.html`

Detecting the Boost version and getting latest features

Boost is being actively developed, so each release contains new features and libraries. Some people wish to have libraries that compile for different versions of Boost and also want to use some of the features of the new versions.

Let's take a look at the `boost::lexical_cast` change log. According to it, Boost 1.53 has a `lexical_cast(const CharType* chars, std::size_t count)` function overload. Our task for this recipe will be to use that function overload for new versions of Boost, and work around that missing function overload for older versions.

Getting ready

Only basic knowledge of C++ and the `Boost.Lexical` library is required.

How to do it...

Well, all we need to do is get a version of Boost and use it to write optimal code. This can be done as shown in the following steps:

1. We need to include headers containing the Boost version and `boost::lexical_cast`:

```
#include <boost/version.hpp>
#include <boost/lexical_cast.hpp>
```

2. We will use the new feature of `Boost.LexicalCast` if it is available:

```
#if (BOOST_VERSION >= 105200)
int to_int(const char* str, std::size_t length) {
    return boost::lexical_cast<int>(str, length);
}
```

3. Otherwise, we are required to copy data to `std::string` first:

```
#else
int to_int(const char* str, std::size_t length) {
    return boost::lexical_cast<int>(
        std::string(str, length)
    );
}
#endif
```

4. Now we can use the code as shown here:

```
assert(to_int("10000000", 3) == 100);
```

How it works...

The `BOOST_VERSION` macro contains the Boost version written in the following format: a single number for the major version, followed by three numbers for the minor version, and then two numbers for the patch level. For example, Boost 1.46.1 will contain the `104601` number in the `BOOST_VERSION` macro.

So, we will check the Boost version in step 2 and choose the correct implementation of the `to_int` function according to the abilities of `Boost.LexicalCast`.

There's more...

Having a version macro is a common practice for big libraries. Some of the Boost libraries allow you to specify the version of the library to use; see `Boost.Thread` and its `BOOST_THREAD_VERSION` macro for an example.

See also

▸ Read the recipe *Creating an execution thread* in *Chapter 5, Multithreading*, for more information about `BOOST_THREAD_VERSION` and how it affects the `Boost.Thread` library, or read the documentation at `http://www.boost.org/doc/libs/1_53_0/doc/html/thread/changes.html`

▸ Read this chapter from the beginning or consider reading the official documentation of `Boost.Config` at `http://www.boost.org/doc/libs/1_53_0/libs/config/doc/html/index.html`

11
Working with the System

In this chapter we will cover:

- ▶ Listing files in a directory
- ▶ Erasing and creating files and directories
- ▶ Passing data quickly from one process to another
- ▶ Syncing interprocess communications
- ▶ Using pointers in shared memory
- ▶ The fastest way to read files
- ▶ Coroutines – saving the state and postponing the execution

Introduction

Each operating system has many system calls doing almost the same things in slightly different ways. Those calls differ in performance and differ from one operating system to another. Boost provides portable and safe wrappers around those calls. Knowledge of those wrappers is essential for writing good programs.

This chapter is devoted to working with the operating system. We have seen how to deal with network communications and signals in *Chapter 6, Manipulating Tasks*. In this chapter, we'll take a closer look at the filesystem and creating and deleting files. We'll see how data can be passed between different system processes, how to read files at maximum speed, and how to perform other tricks.

Listing files in a directory

There are STL functions and classes to read and write data to files. But there are no functions to list files in a directory, to get the type of a file, or to get access rights for a file.

Let's see how such iniquities can be fixed using Boost. We'll be creating a program that lists names, write accesses, and types of files in the current directory.

Getting ready

Some basics of C++ would be more than enough to use this recipe.

This recipe requires linking against the `boost_system` and `boost_filesystem` libraries.

How to do it...

This recipe and the next one are about portable wrappers for working with a filesystem:

1. We need to include the following two headers:

   ```
   #include <boost/filesystem/operations.hpp>
   #include <iostream>
   ```

2. Now we need to specify a directory:

   ```
   int main() {
       boost::filesystem::directory_iterator begin("./");
   ```

3. After specifying the directory, loop through its content:

   ```
   boost::filesystem::directory_iterator end;
   for (; begin != end; ++ begin) {
   ```

4. The next step is getting the file info:

   ```
   boost::filesystem::file_status fs =
       boost::filesystem::status(*begin);
   ```

5. Now output the file info:

   ```
   switch (fs.type()) {
   case boost::filesystem::regular_file:
       std::cout << "FILE        ";
       break;
   case boost::filesystem::symlink_file:
       std::cout << "SYMLINK     ";
       break;
   case boost::filesystem::directory_file:
   ```

```
        std::cout << "DIRECTORY    ";
        break;
    default:
        std::cout << "OTHER       ";
        break;
    }
    if (fs.permissions() & boost::filesystem::owner_write) {
        std::cout << "W ";
    } else {
        std::cout << "   ";
    }
```

6. The final step would be to output the filename:

```
        std::cout << *begin << '\n';
    } /*for*/
} /*main*/
```

That's it. Now, if we run the program, it will output something like this:

```
FILE W "./main.o"
FILE W "./listing_files"
DIRECTORY W "./some_directory"
FILE W "./Makefile"
```

How it works...

Functions and classes of `Boost.Filesystem` just wrap around system-specific functions to work with files.

Note the usage of / in step 2. POSIX systems use a slash to specify paths; Windows, by default, uses backslashes. However, Windows understands forward slashes too, so ./ will work on all of the popular operating systems, and it means "the current directory".

Take a look at step 3, where we are default constructing the `boost::filesystem::directory_iterator` class. It works just as a `std::istream_iterator` class, which acts as an end iterator when default constructed.

Step 4 is a tricky one, not because this function is hard to understand, but because lots of conversions are happening. Dereferencing the `begin` iterator returns `boost::filesystem::directory_entry`, which is implicitly converted to `boost::filesystem::path`, which is used as a parameter for the `boost::filesystem::status` function. Actually, we can do much better:

```
boost::filesystem::file_status fs = begin->status();
```

Read the reference documentation carefully to avoid unrequired implicit conversions.

Step 5 is obvious, so we are moving to step 6 where implicit conversion to the path happens again. A better solution would be the following:

```
std::cout << begin->path() << '\n';
```

Here, `begin->path()` returns a const reference to the `boost::filesystem::path` variable that is contained inside `boost::filesystem::directory_entry`.

There's more...

Unfortunately, `Boost.Filesystem` is not a part of C++11, but it is proposed for inclusion in the next C++ standard. `Boost.Filesystem` currently misses support for rvalue references, but still remains one of the simplest and most portable libraries to work with a filesystem.

See also

> ▸ The *Erasing and creating files and directories* recipe will show another example of the usage of `Boost.Filesystem`.

> ▸ Read Boost's official documentation for `Boost.Filesystem` to get more info about its abilities; it is available at the following link:
>   http://www.boost.org/doc/libs/1_53_0/libs/filesystem/doc/index.htm.

> ▸ The `Boost.Filesystem` library is proposed for inclusion in C++1y. The draft is available at http://www.open-std.org/jtc1/sc22/wg21/docs/papers/2012/n3399.html.

Erasing and creating files and directories

Let's consider the following lines of code:

```
std::ofstream ofs("dir/subdir/file.txt");
ofs << "Boost.Filesystem is fun!";
```

In these lines, we attempt to write something to `file.txt` in the `dir/subdir` directory. This attempt will fail if there is no such directory. The ability to work with filesystems is necessary for write a good working code.

In this recipe we'll construct a directory and a subdirectory, write some data to a file, and try to create symlink, and if the symbolic link's creation fails, erase the created file. We will also avoid using exceptions as a mechanism of error reporting, preferring some form of return codes.

Let's see how that can be done in an elegant way using Boost.

Getting ready

Basic knowledge of C++ and the std::ofstream class is required for this recipe. Boost.Filesystem is not a header-only library, so code in this recipe requires linking against the boost_system and boost_filesystem libraries.

How to do it...

We continue to deal with portable wrappers for a filesystem, and in this recipe we'll see how to modify the directory content:

1. As always, we'll need to include some headers:

```
#include <boost/filesystem/operations.hpp>
#include <cassert>
#include <fstream>
```

2. Now we need a variable to store errors (if any):

```
int main() {
    boost::system::error_code error;
```

3. We will also create directories, if required, as follows:

```
boost::filesystem::create_directories(
    "dir/subdir", error);
assert(!error);
```

4. Then we will write data to the file:

```
std::ofstream ofs("dir/subdir/file.txt");
ofs << "Boost.Filesystem is fun!";
assert(ofs);
ofs.close();
```

5. We need to attempt to create symlink:

```
boost::filesystem::create_directory_symlink("dir/subdir",
                       "symlink", error);
```

6. Then we need to check that the file is accessible through symlink:

```
if (!error) {
    std::cerr << "Symlink created\n";
    assert(boost::filesystem::exists("symlink/file.txt"));
```

7. Or remove the created file, if `symlink` creation failed:

```
    } else {
        std::cerr << "Failed to create a symlink\n";
        boost::filesystem::remove("dir/subdir/file.txt", error);
        assert(!error);
    } /*if (!error)*/
} /*main*/
```

How it works...

We saw `boost::system::error_code` in action in almost all of the recipes in *Chapter 6, Manipulating Tasks*. It can store information about errors and is widely used throughout the Boost libraries.

 If you do not provide an instance of `boost::system::error_ code` to the `Boost.Filesystem` functions, the code will compile well, but when an error occurs, an exception will be thrown. Usually a `boost::filesystem::filesystem_error` exception is thrown unless you are having trouble with allocating memory.

Take a careful look at step 3. We used the `boost::filesystem::create_directories` function, not `boost::filesystem::create_directory`, because the latter cannot create subdirectories.

The remaining steps are trivial to understand and should not cause any trouble.

There's more...

The `boost::system::error_code` class is a part of C++11 and can be found in the `<system_error>` header in the `std::` namespace. The classes of `Boost.Filesystem` are not a part of C++11, but they are proposed for inclusion in C++1y, which will probably be ready in 2014.

Finally, a small recommendation for those who are going to use `Boost.Filesystem`; when the errors occurring during filesystem operations are routine, use `boost::system::error_ codes`. Otherwise, catching exceptions is preferable and more reliable.

See also

▶ The *Listing files in a directory* recipe also contains information about `Boost. Filesystem`. Read Boost's official documentation to get more information and examples at `http://www.boost.org/doc/libs/1_53_0/libs/filesystem/doc/index.htm`.

Passing data quickly from one process to another

Sometimes we write programs that will communicate with each other a lot. When programs are run on different machines, using sockets is the most common technique for communication. But if multiple processes run on a single machine, we can do much better!

Let's take a look at how to make a single memory fragment available from different processes using the `Boost.Interprocess` library.

Getting ready

Basic knowledge of C++ is required for this recipe. Knowledge of atomic variables is also required (take a look at the *See also* section for more information about atomics). Some platforms require linking against the runtime library.

How to do it...

In this example we'll be sharing a single atomic variable between processes, making it increment when a new process starts and decrement when the process terminates:

1. We'll need to include the following header for interprocess communications:

   ```
   #include <boost/interprocess/managed_shared_memory.hpp>
   ```

2. Following the header, `typedef` and a check will help us make sure that atomics are usable for this example:

   ```
   #include <boost/atomic.hpp>

   typedef boost::atomic<int> atomic_t;
   #if (BOOST_ATOMIC_INT_LOCK_FREE != 2)
   #error "This code requires lock-free boost::atomic<int>"
   #endif
   ```

3. Create or get a shared segment of memory:

   ```
   boost::interprocess::managed_shared_memory
       segment(boost::interprocess::open_or_create, "shm-cache",
   1024);
   ```

4. Get or construct an `atomic` variable:

   ```
   atomic_t& atomic
       = *segment.find_or_construct<atomic_t> //1
           ("shm-counter") // 2
           (0)             // 3
   ;
   ```

5. Work with the `atomic` variable in the usual way:

```
std::cout << "I have index " << ++ atomic
    << "\nPress any key...";
std::cin.get();
```

6. Destroy the `atomic` variable:

```
int snapshot = -- atomic;
if (!snapshot) {
    segment.destroy<atomic_t>("shm-counter");
    boost::interprocess::shared_memory_object
            ::remove("shm-cache");
}
} /*main*/
```

That's all! Now if we run multiple instances of this program simultaneously, we'll see that each new instance increments its index value.

How it works...

The main idea of this recipe is to get a segment of memory that is visible to all processes, and place some data in it. Let's take a look at step 3, where we retrieve such a segment of memory. Here, `shm-cache` is the name of the segment (different segments differ in name); you can give any names you like to the segments. The first parameter is `boost::interprocess::open_or_create`, which says that `boost::interprocess::managed_shared_memory` will open an existing segment with the name `shm-cache`, or it will construct it. The last parameter is the size of the segment.

 The size of the segment must be big enough to fit the `Boost.Interprocess` library-specific data in it. That's why we used `1024` and not `sizeof(atomic_t)`. But it does not really matter, because the operating system will round this value to the nearest larger supported value, which is usually equal to or larger than 4 kilobytes.

Step 4 is a tricky one as we are doing multiple tasks at the same time here. In part 2 of this step, we will find or construct a variable with the name `shm-counter` in the segment. In part 3 of step 4, we will provide a parameter, which will be used for the initialization of a variable if it has not been found in step 2. This parameter will be used only if the variable is not found and must be constructed, otherwise it is ignored. Take a closer look at the second line (part 1). See the call to the dereference operator `*`. We are doing it because `segment.find_or_construct<atomic_t>` returns a pointer to `atomic_t`, and working with bare pointers in C++ is a bad style.

Note that we are using atomic variables in shared memory! This is required, because two or more processes can simultaneously work with the same `shm-counter` atomic variable.

You must be very careful when working with objects in shared memory; do not forget to destroy them! In step 6, we are destroying the object and segment using their names.

There's more...

Take a closer look at step 2 where we are checking for `BOOST_ATOMIC_INT_LOCK_FREE != 2`. We are checking that `atomic_t` won't use mutexes. This is very important, because usually, mutexes won't work in shared memory. So if `BOOST_ATOMIC_INT_LOCK_FREE` is not equal to 2, we'll get an undefined behavior.

Unfortunately, C++11 has no interprocess classes, and as far as I know, `Boost.Interprocess` is not proposed for inclusion in C++1y.

 Once a managed segment is created, it cannot increase in size! Make sure that you are creating segments big enough for your needs, or take a look at the *See also* section for information about increasing managed segments.

Shared memory is the fastest way for processes to communicate, and works for processes that can share memory. That usually means that the processes must run on the same host or on a **symmetric multiprocessing** (**SMP**) cluster.

See also

- The *Syncing interprocess communications* recipe will tell you more about shared memory, interprocess communications, and syncing access to resources in shared memory
- See the *Fast access to common resource using atomics* recipe in Chapter 5, *Multithreading* for more information about atomics
- Boost's official documentation for `Boost.Interprocess` may also help; it is available at `http://www.boost.org/doc/libs/1_53_0/doc/html/interprocess.html`
- How to increase managed segments is described at `http://www.boost.org/doc/libs/1_53_0/doc/html/interprocess/managed_memory_segments.html#interprocess.managed_memory_segments.managed_memory_segment_advanced_features.growing_managed_memory`

Syncing interprocess communications

In the previous recipe, we saw how to create shared memory and how to place some objects in it. Now it's time to do something useful. Let's take an example from the *Creating a work_queue class* recipe in *Chapter 5, Multithreading*, and make it work for multiple processes. At the end of this example, we'll get a class that can store different tasks and pass them between processes.

Getting ready

This recipe uses techniques from the previous one. You will also need to read the *Creating a work_queue class* recipe in *Chapter 5, Multithreading*, and get its main idea. The example requires linking against the runtime library on some platforms.

How to do it...

It is considered that spawning separate subprocesses instead of threads makes a program more reliable, because termination of a subprocess won't terminate the main process. We won't argue with that assumption here, and just see how data sharing between processes can be implemented.

1. A lot of headers are required for this recipe:

    ```cpp
    #include <boost/interprocess/managed_shared_memory.hpp>
    #include <boost/interprocess/containers/deque.hpp>
    #include <boost/interprocess/allocators/allocator.hpp>
    #include <boost/interprocess/sync/interprocess_mutex.hpp>
    #include <boost/interprocess/sync/interprocess_condition.hpp>
    #include <boost/interprocess/sync/scoped_lock.hpp>

    #include <boost/optional.hpp>
    ```

2. Now we need to define our structure, `task_structure`, which will be used to store tasks:

    ```cpp
    struct task_structure {
        // ...
    };
    ```

3. Let's start writing the `work_queue` class:

    ```cpp
    class work_queue {
    public:
        typedef task_structure task_type;
        typedef boost::interprocess::managed_shared_memory
            managed_shared_memory_t;
    ```

```
    typedef boost::interprocess::allocator<
        task_type,
        managed_shared_memory_t::segment_manager
    > allocator_t;
```

4. Write the members of `work_queue` as follows:

```
private:
    managed_shared_memory_t segment_;
    const allocator_t allocator_;

    typedef boost::interprocess::deque<task_type, allocator_t>
        deque_t;

    typedef boost::interprocess::interprocess_mutex mutex_t;
    typedef boost::interprocess::interprocess_condition
        condition_t;
    typedef boost::interprocess::scoped_lock<mutex_t>
        scoped_lock_t;

    deque_t& tasks_;
    mutex_t& mutex_;
    boost::interprocess::interprocess_condition& cond_;
```

5. Initialization of members should look like the following:

```
public:
    explicit work_queue()
        : segment_(
              boost::interprocess::open_or_create,
              "work-queue",
              1024 * 1024 * 64
          )
        , allocator_(segment_.get_segment_manager())
        , tasks_(
            *segment_.find_or_construct<deque_t>
              ("work-queue:deque")(allocator_)
          )
        , mutex_(
            *segment_.find_or_construct<mutex_t>
              ("work-queue:mutex")()
          )
        , cond_(
            *segment_.find_or_construct<condition_t>
              ("work-queue:condition")()
          )
    {}
```

6. We need to make some minor changes to the member functions of `work_queue`, such as using `scoped_lock_t` instead of the original unique locks:

```
boost::optional<task_type> try_pop_task() {
    boost::optional<task_type> ret;
    scoped_lock_t lock(mutex_);
    if (!tasks_.empty()) {
        ret = tasks_.front();
        tasks_.pop_front();
    }
    return ret;
}
```

How it works...

In this recipe, we are doing almost exactly the same things as in the *Creating a work_queue class* recipe in *Chapter 5*, *Multithreading*, but when we allocate the data in shared memory, additional care must be taken when doing memory allocations or using synchronization primitives.

Take additional care when storing shared memory objects that have pointers or references as member fields. We'll see how to cope with pointers in the next recipe.

Take a look at step 2. We did not use `boost::function` as a task type because it has pointers in it, so it won't work in shared memory.

Step 3 is interesting because of `allocator_t`. It is a type of allocator that all containers must use to allocate elements. It is a stateful allocator, which means that it will be copied along with the container. Also, it cannot be default constructed.

If memory is not allocated from the shared memory segment, it won't be available to other processes; that's why a specific allocator for containers is required.

Step 4 is pretty trivial, except that we have only references to `tasks_`, `mutex_`, and `cond_`. This is done because objects themselves are constructed in the shared memory. So, `work_queue` can only store references to them.

In step 5 we are initializing members. This code will be familiar to you; we were doing exactly the same things in the previous recipe. Note that we are providing an instance of allocator to `tasks_` while constructing it. That's because `allocator_t` cannot be constructed by the container itself.

> Shared memory is not destructed at the exit event of a process, so we can run the program once, post the tasks to a work queue, stop the program, start some other program, and get tasks stored by the first instance of the program. Shared memory will be destroyed only at restart, or if you explicitly call `segment.deallocate("work-queue");`.

There's more...

As was mentioned in the previous recipe, C++11 has no classes from `Boost.Interprocess`. Moreover, you must not use C++11 or C++03 containers in shared memory segments. Some of those containers may work, but that behavior is not portable.

If you look inside some of the `<boost/interprocess/containers/*.hpp>` headers, you'll find that they just use containers from the `Boost.Containers` library:

```
namespace boost { namespace interprocess {
    using boost::container::vector;
}}
```

Containers of `Boost.Interprocess` have all of the benefits of the `Boost.Containers` library, including rvalue references and their emulation on older compilers.

`Boost.Interprocess` is the fastest solution for communication between processes that are running on the same machine.

See also

- The *Using pointers in shared memory* recipe
- Read *Chapter 5, Multithreading*, for more information about synchronization primitives and multithreading
- Refer to Boost's official documentation for the `Boost.Interprocess` library for more examples and information; it is available at the following link:

  `http://www.boost.org/doc/libs/1_53_0/doc/html/interprocess.html`

Using pointers in shared memory

It is hard to imagine writing some C++ core classes without pointers. Pointers and references are everywhere in C++, and they do not work in shared memory! So if we have a structure like this in shared memory and assign the address of some integer variable in shared memory to `pointer_`, we won't get the correct address in the other process that will attempt to use `pointer_` from that instance of `with_pointer`:

```
struct with_pointer {
    int* pointer_;
    // ...
    int value_holder_;
};
```

How can we fix that?

Getting ready

The previous recipe is required for understanding this one. The example requires linking against the runtime system library on some platforms.

How to do it...

Fixing it is very simple; we need only to replace the pointer with `offset_ptr<>`:

```
#include <boost/interprocess/offset_ptr.hpp>
struct correct_struct {
    boost::interprocess::offset_ptr<int> pointer_;
    // ...
    int value_holder_;
};
```

Now we are free to use it as a normal pointer:

```
correct_struct& ref = *segment
    .construct<correct_struct>("structure")();

ref.pointer_ = &ref.value_holder_;
assert(ref.pointer_ == &ref.value_holder_);
assert(*ref.pointer_ == ref.value_holder_);

ref.value_holder_ = ethalon_value;
assert(*ref.pointer_ == ethalon_value);
```

How it works...

We cannot use pointers in shared memory because when a piece of shared memory is mapped into the address space of a process, its address is valid only for that process. When we are getting the address of a variable, it is just a local address for that process; other processes will map shared memory to a different base address, and as a result the variable address will differ.

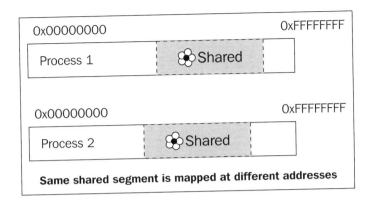

Same shared segment is mapped at different addresses

So how can we work with an address that is always changing? There is a trick! As the pointer and structure are in the same shared memory segment, the distance between them does not change. The idea behind `boost::interprocess::offset_ptr` is to remember that distance, and on dereference, add the distance value to the process-dependent address of the `offset_ptr` variable.

The offset pointer imitates the behavior of pointers, so it is a drop-in replacement that can be applied fast.

 Do not place classes that may have pointers or references into shared memory!

There's more...

An offset pointer works slightly slower than the usual pointer because on each dereference, it is required to compute the address. But this difference is not usually sufficient to bother you.

C++11 has no offset pointers.

See also

▶ Boost's official documentation contains many examples and more advanced `Boost.Interprocess` features; it is available at `http://www.boost.org/doc/libs/1_53_0/doc/html/interprocess.html`

▶ The *fastest way to read files* recipe contains information about some nontraditional usage of the `Boost.Interprocess` library

The fastest way to read files

All around the Internet, people are asking "What is the fastest way to read files?". Let's make our task for this recipe even harder: "What is the fastest and most portable way to read binary files?"

Getting ready

Basic knowledge of C++ and the `std::fstream` containers is required for this recipe.

How to do it...

The technique from this recipe is widely used by applications critical to input and output performance.

1. We'll need to include two headers from the `Boost.Interprocess` library:

   ```
   #include <boost/interprocess/file_mapping.hpp>
   #include <boost/interprocess/mapped_region.hpp>
   ```

2. Now we need to open a file:

   ```
   const boost::interprocess::mode_t mode =
   boost::interprocess::read_only;
   boost::interprocess::file_mapping fm(filename, mode);
   ```

3. The main part of this recipe is mapping all of the files to memory:

   ```
   boost::interprocess::mapped_region region(fm, mode, 0, 0);
   ```

4. Getting a pointer to the data in the file:

   ```
   const char* begin
       = reinterpret_cast<const char*>(region.get_address());
   ```

That's it! Now we can work with a file just as with normal memory:

```
const char* pos = std::find(begin, begin + region.get_size(), '\1');
```

How it works...

All popular operating systems have the ability to map a file to processes' address space. After such mapping is done, the process can work with those addresses just as with normal memory. The operating system will take care of all of the file operations, such as caching and read-ahead.

Why is it faster than traditional read/writes? That's because in most cases read/write is implemented as memory mapping and copying data to a user-specified buffer. So read usually does more work.

Just as in the case of STL, we must provide an open mode when opening a file. See step 2 where we provided the `boost::interprocess::read_only` mode.

See step 3 where we mapped a whole file at once. This operation is actually really fast, because the OS does not read data from the disk, but waits for the requests to be a part of the mapped region. After a part of the mapped region was requested, the OS loads that part of the file from the disk. As we can see, memory mapping operations are lazy, and the size of the mapped region does not affect performance.

> However, a 32-bit OS cannot memory-map large files, so you'll need to map them in pieces. POSIX (Linux) operating systems require `_FILE_OFFSET_BITS=64` to be defined for the whole project to work with large files on a 32-bit platform. Otherwise, the OS won't be able to map parts of the file that are beyond 4 GB.

Now it's time to measure the performance:

```
$ TIME="%E" time ./reading_files m

mapped_region: 0:00.08


$ TIME="%E" time ./reading_files r

ifstream: 0:00.09

$ TIME="%E" time ./reading_files a

C:
 0:00.09
```

Just as expected, memory-mapped files are slightly faster than traditional reads. We can also see that pure C methods have the same performance as that of the C++ `std::ifstream` class, so please do not use functions related to `FILE*` in C++. They are just for C, not for C++!

For optimal performance of `std::ifstream`, do not forget to open files in binary mode and read data by blocks:

```
std::ifstream f(filename, std::ifstream::binary);
// ...
char c[kilobyte];
f.read(c, kilobyte);
```

There's more...

Unfortunately, classes for memory mapping files are not part of C++11, and it looks like they won't be in C++14 either.

Writing to memory-mapped regions is also a very fast operation. The OS will cache the writes and won't flush modifications to the disc immediately. There is a difference between the OS and the `std::ofstream` data caching. If the `std::ofstream` data is cached by an application and it terminates, the cached data can be lost. When data is cached by the OS, termination of the application won't lead to data loss. Power failures and system crashes lead to data loss in both cases.

If multiple processes map a single file, and one of the processes modifies the mapped region, the changes are immediately visible to the other processes.

See also

▶ The `Boost.Interprocess` library contains a lot of useful features to work with the system; not all of them are covered in this book. You can read more about this great library at the official site:

```
http://www.boost.org/doc/libs/1_53_0/doc/html/interprocess.html
```

Coroutines – saving the state and postponing the execution

Nowadays, plenty of embedded devices still have only a single core. Developers write for those devices, trying to squeeze maximum performance out of them. Using `Boost.Threads` or some other thread library for such devices is not effective; the OS will be forced to schedule threads for execution, manage resources, and so on, as the hardware cannot run them in parallel.

So how can we make a program switch to the execution of a subprogram while waiting for some resource in the main part?

Getting ready

Basic knowledge of C++ and templates is required for this recipe. Reading some recipes about `Boost.Function` may also help.

How to do it...

This recipe is about coroutines, subroutines that allow multiple entry points. Multiple entry points give us an ability to suspend and resume the execution of a program at certain locations, switching to/from other subprograms.

1. The `Boost.Coroutine` library will take care of almost everything. We just need to include its header:

```
#include <boost/coroutine/coroutine.hpp>
```

2. Make a coroutine type with the required signature:

```
typedef boost::coroutines::coroutine<
    std::string&(std::size_t max_characters_to_process)
> corout_t;
```

3. Make a coroutine:

```
void coroutine_task(corout_t::caller_type& caller);

int main() {
    corout_t coroutine(coroutine_task);
```

4. Now we can execute the subprogram while waiting for an event in the main program:

```
    // Doing some work
    // ...
    while (!spinlock.try_lock()) {
        // We may do some useful work, before
        // attempting to lock a spinlock once more
        coroutine(10); // Small delays
    }
    // Spinlock is locked

    // ...
    while (!port.block_ready()) {
        // We may do some useful work, before
        // attempting to get block of data once more
        coroutine(300);  // Bigger delays
        std::string& s = coroutine.get();
        // ...
    }
```

5. The coroutine method should look like this:

```
void coroutine_task(corout_t::caller_type& caller) {
    std::string result;

    // Returning back to main program
    caller(result);

    while (1) {
        std::size_t max_characters_to_process = caller.get();
        // Do process some characters
        // ...

        // Returning result, switching back
        // to main program
        caller(result);
    } /*while*/
}
```

How it works...

At step 2, we are describing the signature of our subprogram using the function signature `std::string& (std::size_t)` as a template parameter. This means that the subprogram accepts `std::size_t` and returns a reference to a string.

Step 3 is interesting because of the `coroutine_task` signature. Note that this signature is common for all coroutine tasks. `caller` is the variable that will be used to get parameters from the caller and to return the result of the execution back.

Step 3 requires additional care because the constructor of `corout_t` will automatically start the coroutine execution. That's why we call `caller(result)` at the beginning of the coroutine task (it returns us to the `main` method).

When we call `coroutine(10)` in step 4, we are causing a coroutine program to execute. Execution will jump to step 5 right after the first `caller(result)` method, where we'll get a value `10` from `caller.get()` and will continue our execution until `caller(result)`. After that, execution will return to step 4, right after the `coroutine(10)` call. Next, a call to `coroutine(10)` or `coroutine(300)` will continue the execution of the subprogram from the place right after the second `caller(result)` method at step 5.

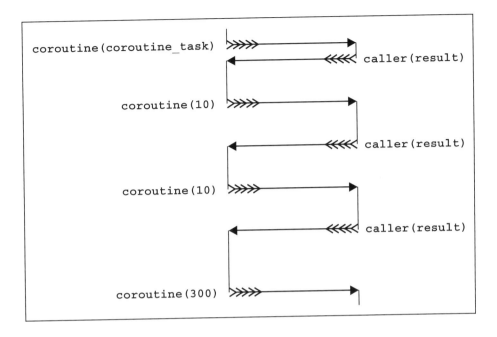

Take a look at `std::string& s = coroutine.get()` in step 4. Here, we'll be getting a reference to the `std::string` result from the beginning of `coroutine_task` described in step 5. We can even modify it, and `coroutine_task` will see the modified value. Let me describe the main difference between coroutines and threads. When a coroutine is executed, the main task does nothing. When the main task is executed, the coroutine task does nothing. You have no such guarantee with threads. With coroutines, you explicitly specify when to start a subtask and when to finish it. In a single core environment, threads can switch at any moment of time; you cannot control that behavior.

> Do not use thread's local storage and do not call `boost::coroutines::coroutine<>::operator()` from inside the same coroutine; do not call `boost::coroutines::coroutine<>::get()` when a coroutine task is finished. These operations lead to undefined behavior.

There's more...

While switching threads, the OS does a lot of work, so it is not a very fast operation. However, with coroutines, you have full control over switching tasks; moreover, you do not need to do any OS-specific internal kernel work. Switching coroutines is much faster than switching threads, however, it's not as fast as calling `boost::function`.

The `Boost.Coroutine` library will take care of calling a destructor for variables in a coroutine task, so there's no need to worry about leaks.

 Coroutines use the `boost::coroutines::detail::forced_unwind` exception to free resources that are not derived from `std::exception`. You must take care not to catch that exception in coroutine tasks.

C++11 has no coroutines. But coroutines use features of C++11 when possible, and even emulate rvalue references on C++03 compilers. You cannot copy `boost::coroutines::coroutine<>`, but you can move them using `Boost.Move`.

See also

▸ Boost's official documentation contains more examples, performance notes, restrictions, and use cases for the `Boost.Coroutines` library; it is available at the following link:

`http://www.boost.org/doc/libs/1_53_0/libs/coroutine/doc/html/index.htm`

▸ Take a look at recipes from *Chapter 3*, *Managing Resources*, and *Chapter 5*, *Multithreading*, to get the difference between the `Boost.Coroutine`, `Boost.Thread`, and `Boost.Function` libraries

12
Scratching the Tip of the Iceberg

In this chapter we will cover:

- ► Working with graphs
- ► Visualizing graphs
- ► Using a true random number generator
- ► Using portable math functions
- ► Writing test cases
- ► Combining multiple test cases in one test module
- ► Manipulating images

Introduction

Boost is a huge collection of libraries. Some of those libraries are small and meant for everyday use and others require a separate book to describe all of their features. This chapter is devoted to some of those big libraries and to give you some basics to start with.

The first two recipes will explain the usage of `Boost.Graph`. It is a big library with an insane number of algorithms. We'll see some basics and probably the most important part of it visualization of graphs.

We'll also see a very useful recipe for generating true random numbers. This is a very important requirement for writing secure cryptography systems.

Some C++ standard libraries lack math functions. We'll see how that can be fixed using Boost. But the format of this book leaves no space to describe all of the functions.

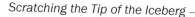

Writing test cases is described in the *Writing test cases* and *Combining multiple test cases in one test module* recipes. This is important for any production-quality system.

The last recipe is about a library that helped me in many courses during my university days. Images can be created and modified using it. I personally used it to visualize different algorithms, hide data in images, sign images, and generate textures.

Unfortunately, even this chapter cannot tell you about all of the Boost libraries. Maybe someday I'll write another book... and then a few more.

Working with graphs

Some tasks require a graphical representation of data. `Boost.Graph` is a library that was designed to provide a flexible way of constructing and representing graphs in memory. It also contains a lot of algorithms to work with graphs, such as topological sort, breadth first search, depth first search, and Dijkstra shortest paths.

Well, let's perform some basic tasks with `Boost.Graph`!

Getting ready

Only basic knowledge of C++ and templates is required for this recipe.

How to do it...

In this recipe, we'll describe a graph type, create a graph of that type, add some vertexes and edges to the graph, and search for a specific vertex. That should be enough to start using `Boost.Graph`.

1. We start with describing the graph type:

   ```cpp
   #include <boost/graph/adjacency_list.hpp>
   #include <string>

   typedef std::string vertex_t;
   typedef boost::adjacency_list<
       boost::vecS
       , boost::vecS
       , boost::bidirectionalS
       , vertex_t
   > graph_type;
   ```

2. Now we construct it:

   ```cpp
   graph_type graph;
   ```

3. Let's use a non portable trick that speeds up graph construction:

```
static const std::size_t vertex_count = 5;
graph.m_vertices.reserve(vertex_count);
```

4. Now we are ready to add vertexes to the graph:

```
typedef boost::graph_traits<graph_type>
            ::vertex_descriptor descriptor_t;

descriptor_t cpp
    = boost::add_vertex(vertex_t("C++"), graph);
descriptor_t stl
    = boost::add_vertex(vertex_t("STL"), graph);
descriptor_t boost
    = boost::add_vertex(vertex_t("Boost"), graph);
descriptor_t guru
    = boost::add_vertex(vertex_t("C++ guru"), graph);
descriptor_t ansic
    = boost::add_vertex(vertex_t("C"), graph);
```

5. It is time to connect vertexes with edges:

```
boost::add_edge(cpp, stl, graph);
boost::add_edge(stl, boost, graph);
boost::add_edge(boost, guru, graph);
boost::add_edge(ansic, guru, graph);
```

6. We make a function that searches for a vertex:

```
template <class GraphT>
void find_and_print(const GraphT& g, boost::string_ref name) {
```

7. Now we will write code that gets iterators to all vertexes:

```
typedef typename boost::graph_traits<graph_type>
            ::vertex_iterator vert_it_t;

vert_it_t it, end;
boost::tie(it, end) = boost::vertices(g);
```

8. It's time to run a search for the required vertex:

```
typedef
    boost::graph_traits<graph_type>::vertex_descriptor desc_t;
for (; it != end; ++ it) {
    desc_t desc = *it;
    if (boost::get(boost::vertex_bundle, g) [desc]
            == name.data()) {
        break;
```

```
            }
        }
        assert(it != end);
        std::cout << name << '\n';
    } /* find_and_print */
```

How it works...

In step 1, we are describing what our graph must look like and upon what types it must be based. `boost::adjacency_list` is a class that represents graphs as a two-dimensional structure, where the first dimension contains vertexes and the second dimension contains edges for that vertex. `boost::adjacency_list` must be the default choice for representing a graph; it suits most cases.

The first template parameter, `boost::adjacency_list`, describes the structure used to represent the edge list for each of the vertexes; the second one describes a structure to store vertexes. We can choose different STL containers for those structures using specific selectors, as listed in the following table:

Selector	STL container
boost::vecS	std::vector
boost::listS	std::list
boost::slistS	std::slist
boost::setS	std::set
boost::multisetS	std::multiset
boost::hash_setS	std::hash_set

The third template parameter is used to make an undirected, directed, or bidirectional graph. Use the `boost::undirectedS`, `boost::directedS`, and `boost::bidirectionalS` selectors respectively.

The fifth template parameter describes the datatype that will be used as the vertex. In our example, we chose `std::string`. We can also support a datatype for edges and provide it as a template parameter.

Steps 2 and 3 are trivial, but at step 4 you will see a non portable way to speed up graph construction. In our example, we use `std::vector` as a container for storing vertexes, so we can force it to reserve memory for the required amount of vertexes. This leads to less memory allocations/deallocations and copy operations during insertion of vertexes into the graph. This step is non-portable because it is highly dependent on the current implementation of `boost::adjacency_list` and on the chosen container type for storing vertexes.

At step 4, we see how vertexes can be added to the graph. Note how `boost::graph_traits<graph_type>` has been used. The `boost::graph_traits` class is used to get types that are specific for a graph type. We'll see its usage and the description of some graph-specific types later in this chapter. Step 5 shows what we need do to connect vertexes with edges.

> If we had provided a datatype for the edges, adding an edge would look as follows:
> ```
> boost::add_edge(ansic, guru,
>     edge_t(initialization_parameters), graph)
> ```

Note that at step 6 the graph type is a `template` parameter. This is recommended to achieve better code reusability and make this function work with other graph types.

At step 7, we see how to iterate over all of the vertexes of the graph. The type of vertex iterator is received from `boost::graph_traits`. The function `boost::tie` is a part of `Boost.Tuple` and is used for getting values from tuples to the variables. So calling `boost::tie(it, end) = boost::vertices(g)` will put the `begin` iterator into the `it` variable and the `end` iterator into the `end` variable.

It may come as a surprise to you, but dereferencing a vertex iterator does not return vertex data. Instead, it returns the vertex descriptor `desc`, which can be used in `boost::get(boost::vertex_bundle, g)[desc]` to get vertex data, just as we have done in step 8. The vertex descriptor type is used in many of the `Boost.Graph` functions; we saw its use in the edge construction function in step 5.

> As already mentioned, the `Boost.Graph` library contains the implementation of many algorithms. You will find many search policies implemented, but we won't discuss them in this book. We will limit this recipe to only the basics of the graph library.

There's more...

The `Boost.Graph` library is not a part of C++11 and it won't be a part of C++1y. The current implementation does not support C++11 features. If we are using vertexes that are heavy to copy, we may gain speed using the following trick:

```
vertex_descriptor desc = boost::add_vertex(graph);
boost::get(boost::vertex_bundle, g_)[desc] = std::move(vertex_data);
```

It avoids copy constructions of `boost::add_vertex(vertex_data, graph)` and uses the default construction with `move` assignment instead.

The efficiency of `Boost.Graph` depends on multiple factors, such as the underlying containers types, graph representation, edge, and vertex datatypes.

See also

▶ Reading the *Visualizing graphs* recipe can help you work more easily with graphs. You may also consider reading its official documentation at the following link:

```
http://www.boost.org/doc/libs/1_53_0/libs/graph/doc/table_of_
contents.html
```

Visualizing graphs

Making programs that manipulate graphs was never easy because of issues with visualization. When we work with STL containers such as `std::map` and `std::vector`, we can always print the container's contents and see what is going on inside. But when we work with complex graphs, it is hard to visualize the content in a clear way: too many vertexes and too many edges.

In this recipe, we'll take a look at the visualization of `Boost.Graph` using the **Graphviz** tool.

Getting ready

To visualize graphs, you will need a Graphviz visualization tool. Knowledge of the preceding recipe is also required.

How to do it...

Visualization is done in two phases. In the first phase, we make our program output the graph's description in a text format; in the second phase, we import the output from the first step to some visualization tool. The numbered steps in this recipe are all about the first phase.

1. Let's write the `std::ostream` operator for `graph_type` as done in the preceding recipe:

```
#include <boost/graph/graphviz.hpp>
std::ostream& operator<<(std::ostream& out, const graph_type& g) {
    detail::vertex_writer<graph_type> vw(g);
    boost::write_graphviz(out, g, vw);
    return out;
}
```

2. The `detail::vertex_writer` structure, used in the preceding step, must be defined as follows:

```
namespace detail {

    template <class GraphT>
    class vertex_writer {
```

```
            const GraphT& g_;

        public:
            explicit vertex_writer(const GraphT& g)
                : g_(g)
            {}

            template <class VertexDescriptorT>
            void operator()(std::ostream& out,
                const VertexDescriptorT& d) const
            {
                out << " [label=\""
                    << boost::get(boost::vertex_bundle, g_)[d]
                    << "\"]";
            }
        }; // vertex_writer
    } // namespace detail
```

That's all. Now, if we visualize the graph from the previous recipe using the `std::cout << graph;` command, the output can be used to create graphical pictures using the `dot` command-line utility:

```
$ dot -Tpng -o dot.png

digraph G {

0 [label="C++"];

1 [label="STL"];

2 [label="Boost"];

3 [label="C++ guru"];

4 [label="C"];

0->1 ;

1->2 ;

2->3 ;

4->3 ;

}
```

The output of the preceding command is depicted in the following figure:

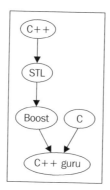

We can also use the **Gvedit** or **XDot** programs for visualization if the command line frightens you.

How it works...

The `Boost.Graph` library contains function to output graphs in Graphviz (DOT) format. If we write `boost::write_graphviz(out, g)` with two parameters in step 1, the function will output a graph picture with vertexes numbered from `0`. That's not very useful, so we provide an instance of the `vertex_writer` class that outputs vertex names.

As we can see in step 2, the format of output must be DOT, which is understood by the Graphviz tool. You may need to read the Graphviz documentation for more info about the DOT format.

If you wish to add some data to the edges during visualization, we need to provide an instance of the edge visualizer as a fourth parameter to `boost::write_graphviz`.

There's more...

C++11 does not contain `Boost.Graph` or the tools for graph visualization. But you do not need to worry—there are a lot of other graph formats and visualization tools and `Boost.Graph` can work with plenty of them.

See also

▶ The *Working with graphs* recipe contains information about the construction of `Boost.Graphs`

▶ You will find a lot of information about the DOT format and Graphviz at `http://www.graphviz.org/`

> ▶ Boost's official documentation for the `Boost.Graph` library contains multiple examples and useful information, and can be found at `http://www.boost.org/doc/libs/1_53_0/libs/graph/doc/table_of_contents.html`

Using a true random number generator

I know of many examples of commercial products that use incorrect methods for getting random numbers. It's a shame that some companies still use `rand()` in cryptography and banking software.

Let's see how to get a fully random uniform distribution using `Boost.Random` that is suitable for banking software.

Getting ready

Basic knowledge of C++ is required for this recipe. Knowledge of different types of distributions will also be helpful. The code in this recipe requires linking against the `boost_random` library.

How to do it...

To create a true random number, we need some help from the operating system or processor. This is how it can be done using Boost:

1. We'll need to include the following headers:

```
#include <boost/config.hpp>
#include <boost/random/random_device.hpp>
#include <boost/random/uniform_int_distribution.hpp>
```

2. Advanced random number providers have different names under different platforms:

```
    static const std::string provider =
#ifdef BOOST_WINDOWS
        "Microsoft Strong Cryptographic Provider"
#else
        "/dev/urandom"
#endif
    ;
```

3. Now we are ready to initialize the generator with `Boost.Random`:

```
boost::random_device device(provider);
```

4. Let's get a uniform distribution that returns a value between 1000 and 65535:

```
boost::random::uniform_int_distribution<unsigned short>
        random(1000);
```

That's it. Now we can get true random numbers using the `random(device)` call.

How it works...

Why does the `rand()` function not suit banking? Because it generates pseudo-random numbers, which means that the hacker could predict the next generated number. This is an issue with all pseudo-random number algorithms. Some algorithms are easier to predict and some harder, but it's still possible.

That's why we are using `boost::random_device` in this example (see step 3). That device gathers information about random events from all around the operating system to construct an unpredictable hardware-generated number. The examples of such events are delays between pressed keys, delays between some of the hardware interrupts, and the internal CPU random number generator.

Operating systems may have more than one such type of random number generators. In our example for POSIX systems, we used `/dev/urandom` instead of the more secure `/dev/random` because the latter remains in a blocked state until enough random events have been captured by the OS. Waiting for entropy could take seconds, which is usually unsuitable for applications. Use `/dev/random` to create long-lifetime `GPG/SSL/SSH` keys.

Now that we are done with generators, it's time to move to step 4 and talk about distribution classes. If the generator just generates numbers (usually uniformly distributed), the distribution class maps one distribution to another. In step 4, we made a uniform distribution that returns a random number of unsigned short type. The parameter `1000` means that distribution must return numbers greater or equal to `1000`. We can also provide the maximum number as a second parameter, which is by default equal to the maximum value storable in the return type.

There's more...

`Boost.Random` has a huge number of true/pseudo random generators and distributions for different needs. Avoid copying distributions and generators; this could turn out to be an expensive operation.

C++11 has support for different distribution classes and generators. You will find all of the classes from this example in the `<random>` header in the `std::` namespace. The `Boost.Random` libraries do not use C++11 features, and they are not really required for that library either. Should you use Boost implementation or STL? Boost provides better portability across systems; however, some STL implementations may have assembly-optimized implementations and might provide some useful extensions.

▶ The official documentation contains a full list of generators and distributions with descriptions; it is available at the following link:

```
http://www.boost.org/doc/libs/1_53_0/doc/html/boost_random.html
```

Using portable math functions

Some projects require specific trigonometric functions, a library for numerically solving ordinary differential equations, and working with distributions and constants. All of those parts of `Boost.Math` would be hard to fit into even a separate book. A single recipe definitely won't be enough. So let's focus on very basic everyday-use functions to work with float types.

We'll write a portable function that checks an input value for infinity and not-a-number (NaN) values and changes the sign if the value is negative.

Getting ready

Basic knowledge of C++ is required for this recipe. Those who know C99 standard will find a lot in common in this recipe.

How to do it...

Perform the following steps to check the input value for infinity and NaN values and change the sign if the value is negative:

1. We'll need the following headers:

```cpp
#include <boost/math/special_functions.hpp>
#include <cassert>
```

2. Asserting for infinity and NaN can be done like this:

```cpp
template <class T>
void check_float_inputs(T value) {
    assert(!boost::math::isinf(value));
    assert(!boost::math::isnan(value));
```

3. Use the following code to change the sign:

```cpp
    if (boost::math::signbit(value)) {
        value = boost::math::changesign(value);
    }

    // ...
} // check_float_inputs
```

That's it! Now we can check that `check_float_inputs(std::sqrt(-1.0))` and `check_float_inputs(std::numeric_limits<double>::max() * 2.0)` will cause asserts.

How it works...

Real types have specific values that cannot be checked using equality operators. For example, if the variable `v` contains NaN, `assert(v!=v)` may or may not pass depending on the compiler.

For such cases, `Boost.Math` provides functions that can reliably check for infinity and NaN values.

Step 3 contains the `boost::math::signbit` function, which requires clarification. This function returns a signed bit, which is 1 when the number is negative and 0 when the number is positive. In other words, it returns `true` if the value is negative.

Looking at step 3 some readers might ask, "Why can't we just multiply by `-1` instead of calling `boost::math::changesign`?". We can. But multiplication may work slower than `boost::math::changesign` and won't work for special values. For example, if your code can work with `nan`, the code in step 3 will be able to change the sign of `-nan` and write `nan` to the variable.

 The `Boost.Math` library maintainers recommend wrapping math functions from this example in round parenthesis to avoid collisions with C macros. It is better to write `(boost::math::isinf)(value)` instead of `boost::math::isinf(value)`.

There's more...

C99 contains all of the functions described in this recipe. Why do we need them in Boost? Well, some compiler vendors think that programmers do not need them, so you won't find them in one very popular compiler. Another reason is that the `Boost.Math` functions can be used for classes that behave like numbers.

`Boost.Math` is a very fast, portable, reliable library.

See also

▸ Boost's official documentation contains lots of interesting examples and tutorials that will help you get used to `Boost.Math`; browse to `http://www.boost.org/doc/libs/1_53_0/libs/math/doc/html/index.html`

Writing test cases

This recipe and the next one are devoted to auto-testing the `Boost.Test` library, which is used by many Boost libraries. Let's get hands-on with it and write some tests for our own class.

```
#include <stdexcept>
struct foo {
    int val_;

    operator int() const;
    bool is_not_null() const;
    void throws() const; // throws(std::logic_error)
};
```

Getting ready

Basic knowledge of C++ is required for this recipe. The code of this recipe requires linking against the static version of the `boost_unit_test_framework` library.

How to do it...

To be honest, there is more than one test library in Boost. We'll take a look at the most functional one.

1. To use it, we'll need to define the macro and include the following header:

   ```
   #define BOOST_TEST_MODULE test_module_name
   #include <boost/test/unit_test.hpp>
   ```

2. Each set of tests must be written in the test case:

   ```
   BOOST_AUTO_TEST_CASE(test_no_1) {
   ```

3. Checking some function for the `true` result is done as follows:

   ```
   foo f1 = {1}, f2 = {2};
   BOOST_CHECK(f1.is_not_null());
   ```

4. Checking for nonequality is implemented in the following way:

   ```
   BOOST_CHECK_NE(f1, f2);
   ```

5. Checking for an exception being thrown will look like this:

   ```
   BOOST_CHECK_THROW(f1.throws(), std::logic_error);
   } // BOOST_AUTO_TEST_CASE(test_no_1)
   ```

That's it! After compilation and linking, we'll get an executable file that automatically tests `foo` and outputs test results in a human-readable format.

How it works...

Writing unit tests is easy; you know how the function works and what result it should produce in specific situations. So you just check if the expected result is the same as the function's actual output. That's what we did in step 3. We know that `f1.is_not_null()` will return `true` and we checked it. At step 4, we know that `f1` is not equal to `f2`, so we checked it too. The call to `f1.throws()` will produce the `std::logic_error` exception and we check that an exception of the expected type is thrown.

At step 2, we are making a test case – a set of checks to validate correct behavior of the `foo` structure. We can have multiple test cases in a single source file. For example, if we add the following code:

```
BOOST_AUTO_TEST_CASE(test_no_2) {
    foo f1 = {1}, f2 = {2};
    BOOST_REQUIRE_NE(f1, f2);
    // ...
} // BOOST_AUTO_TEST_CASE(test_no_2)
```

This code will run along with the `test_no_1` test case. The parameter passed to the `BOOST_AUTO_TEST_CASE` macro is just a unique name of the test case that will be shown in case of error.

```
Running 2 test cases...
main.cpp(15): error in "test_no_1": check f1.is_not_null() failed
main.cpp(17): error in "test_no_1": check f1 != f2 failed [0 == 0]
main.cpp(19): error in "test_no_1": exception std::logic_error is
expected
main.cpp(24): fatal error in "test_no_2": critical check f1 != f2
failed [0 == 0]

*** 4 failures detected in test suite "test_module_name"
```

There is a small difference between the `BOOST_REQUIRE_*` and `BOOST_CHECK_*` macros. If the `BOOST_REQUIRE_*` macro check fails, the execution of the current test case will stop and `Boost.Test` will run the next test case. However, failing `BOOST_CHECK_*` won't stop the execution of the current test case.

Step 1 requires additional care. Note the `BOOST_TEST_MODULE` macro definition. This macro must be defined before including the `Boost.Test` headers, otherwise linking of the program will fail. More information can be found in the *See also* section of this recipe.

There's more...

Some readers may wonder, "Why did we write `BOOST_CHECK_NE(f1, f2)` in step 4 instead of `BOOST_CHECK(f1 != f2)`?". The answer is simple: the macro at step 4 provides a more readable and verbose output.

C++11 lacks support for unit testing. However, the `Boost.Test` library can be used to test C++11 code. Remember that the more tests you have, the more reliable code you get!

See also

▸ The *Combining multiple test cases in one test module* recipe contains more information about testing and the `BOOST_TEST_MODULE` macro

▸ Refer to Boost's official documentation for a full list of test macros and information about advanced features of `Boost.Test`; it's available at the following link:

`http://www.boost.org/doc/libs/1_53_0/libs/test/doc/html/index.html`

Combining multiple test cases in one test module

Writing auto tests is good for your project. But managing test cases is hard when the project is large and many developers are working on it. In this recipe, we'll take a look at how to run individual tests and how to combine multiple test cases in a single module.

Let's pretend that two developers are testing the `foo` structure declared in the `foo.hpp` header and we wish to give them separate source files to write a test to. In that way, the developers won't bother each other and can work in parallel. However, the default test run must execute the tests of both developers.

Getting ready

Basic knowledge of C++ is required for this recipe. This recipe partially reuses code from the previous recipe and it also requires linking against the static version of the `boost_unit_test_framework` library.

How to do it...

This recipe uses the code from the previous one. This is a very useful recipe for testing large projects; do not underestimate it.

1. Of all the headers in `main.cpp` from the previous recipe, leave only these two lines:

```
#define BOOST_TEST_MODULE test_module_name
#include <boost/test/unit_test.hpp>
```

2. Let's move the tests cases from the previous example into two different source files:

```
// developer1.cpp
#include <boost/test/unit_test.hpp>
#include "foo.hpp"
BOOST_AUTO_TEST_CASE(test_no_1) {
    // ...
}


/////////////////////////////////////////////////////////////


// developer2.cpp
#include <boost/test/unit_test.hpp>
#include "foo.hpp"
BOOST_AUTO_TEST_CASE(test_no_2) {
    // ...
}
```

That's it! Thus compiling and linking all of the sources and both test cases will work on program execution.

How it works...

All of the magic is done by the `BOOST_TEST_MODULE` macro. If it is defined before `<boost/test/unit_test.hpp>`, `Boost.Test` thinks that this source file is the main one and all of the helper testing infrastructure must be placed in it. Otherwise, only the test macro will be included from `<boost/test/unit_test.hpp>`.

All of the `BOOST_AUTO_TEST_CASE` tests are run if you link them with the source file that contains the `BOOST_TEST_MODULE` macro. When working on a big project, each developer may enable compilation and linking of only their own sources. That gives independence from other developers and increases the speed of development—no need to compile alien sources and run alien tests while debugging.

There's more...

The `Boost.Test` library is good because of its ability to run tests selectively. We can choose which tests to run and pass them as command-line arguments. For example, the following command will run only the `test_no_1` test case:

`./testing_advanced -run=test_no_1`

The following command will run two test cases:

`./testing_advanced -run=test_no_1,test_no_2`

Unfortunately, C++11 standard does not have built-in testing support and it looks like C++1y won't adopt the classes and methods of `Boost.Test` either.

See also

▶ The *Writing test cases* recipe contains more information about the `Boost.Test` library. Read Boost's official documentation for more information about `Boost.Test`, at http://www.boost.org/doc/libs/1_53_0/libs/test/doc/html/utf. html.

▶ Brave readers can take a look at some of the test cases from the Boost library. Those test cases are allocated in the `libs` subfolder located in the `boost` folder. For example, `Boost.LexicalCast` tests cases are allocated at `boost_1_53_0\libs\conversion\test`.

Manipulating images

I've left you something really tasty for dessert – Boost's **Generic Image Library** (**GIL**), which allows you to manipulate images and not care much about image formats.

Let's do something simple and interesting with it; let's make a program that negates any picture.

Getting ready

This recipe requires basic knowledge of C++, templates, and `Boost.Variant`. The example requires linking against the PNG library.

How to do it...

For simplicity, we'll be working with only PNG images.

1. Let's start with including the header files:

```
#include <boost/gil/gil_all.hpp>
#include <boost/gil/extension/io/png_dynamic_io.hpp>
#include <string>
```

2. Now we need to define the image types that we wish to work with:

```
typedef boost::mpl::vector<
        boost::gil::gray8_image_t,
        boost::gil::gray16_image_t,
        boost::gil::rgb8_image_t,
        boost::gil::rgb16_image_t
> img_types;
```

3. Opening an existing PNG image can be implemented like this:

```
std::string file_name(argv[1]);
boost::gil::any_image<img_types> source;
boost::gil::png_read_image(file_name, source);
```

4. We need to apply the operation to the picture as follows:

```
boost::gil::apply_operation(
    view(source),
    negate()
);
```

5. The following code line will help you to write an image:

```
boost::gil::png_write_view("negate_" + file_name,
    const_view(source));
```

6. Let's take a look at the modifying operation:

```
struct negate {
    typedef void result_type; // required

    template <class View>
    void operator()(const View& source) const {
        // ...
    }
}; // negate
```

7. The body of `operator()` consists of getting a channel type:

```
typedef typename View::value_type value_type;
typedef typename boost::gil::channel_type<value_type>::type
    channel_t;
```

8. It also iterates through pixels:

```
const std::size_t channels
    = boost::gil::num_channels<View>::value;
const channel_t max_val = (std::numeric_limits<channel_t>::max)();

for (unsigned int y = 0; y < source.height(); ++y) {
    for (unsigned int x = 0; x < source.width(); ++x) {
        for (unsigned int c = 0; c < channels; ++c) {
            source(x, y)[c] = max_val - source(x, y)[c];
        }
    }
}
```

Now let's see the results of our program:

The previous picture is the negative of the one that follows:

How it works...

In step 2, we are describing the types of images we wish to work with. Those images are gray images with 8 and 16 bits per pixel and RGB pictures with 8 and 16 bits per pixel.

The `boost::gil::any_image<img_types>` class is a kind of `Boost.Variant` that can hold an image of one of the `img_types` variable. As you may have already guessed, `boost::gil::png_read_image` reads images into image variables.

The `boost::gil::apply_operation` function at step 4 is almost equal to `boost::apply_visitor` from the `Boost.Variant` library. Note the usage of `view(source)`. The `boost::gil::view` function constructs a light wrapper around the image that interprets it as a two-dimensional array of pixels.

Do you remember that for `Boost.Variant` we were deriving visitors from `boost::static_visitor`? When we are using GIL's version of variant, we need to make a `result_type` typedef inside `visitor`. You can see it in step 6.

A little bit of theory: images consist of points called pixels. Single images have pixels of the same type. However, pixels of different images can differ in channel count and color bits for a single channel. A channel represents a primary color. In the case of an RGB image, we'll have a pixel consisting of three channels—red, green, and blue. In the case of a gray image, we'll have a single channel representing gray.

Back to our image. In step 2, we described the types of images we wish to work with. In step 3, one of those image types is read from file and stored in the source variable. In step 4, the `operator()` method of the `negate` visitor is instantiated for all image types.

In step 7, we can see how to get the channel type from the image view.

In step 8, we iterate through pixels and channels and negate them. Negation is done via `max_val - source(x, y)[c]` and the result is written back to the image view.

We write an image back in step 5.

There's more...

C++11 has no built-in methods for working with images.

The `Boost.GIL` library is fast and efficient. The compilers optimize its code very well and we can even help the optimizer using some of the `Boost.GIL` methods to unroll loops. But this chapter talks about only some of the library basics, so it is time to stop.

See also

- More information about `Boost.GIL` can be found at Boost's official documentation; go to `http://www.boost.org/doc/libs/1_53_0/libs/gil/doc/index.html`
- See the *Storing multiple chosen types in a variable/container* recipe in *Chapter 1, Starting to Write Your Application*, for more information about the `Boost.Variant` library

Index

Thank you for buying
Boost C++ Application Development Cookbook

About Packt Publishing

Packt, pronounced 'packed', published its first book "*Mastering phpMyAdmin for Effective MySQL Management*" in April 2004 and subsequently continued to specialize in publishing highly focused books on specific technologies and solutions.

Our books and publications share the experiences of your fellow IT professionals in adapting and customizing today's systems, applications, and frameworks. Our solution based books give you the knowledge and power to customize the software and technologies you're using to get the job done. Packt books are more specific and less general than the IT books you have seen in the past. Our unique business model allows us to bring you more focused information, giving you more of what you need to know, and less of what you don't.

Packt is a modern, yet unique publishing company, which focuses on producing quality, cutting-edge books for communities of developers, administrators, and newbies alike. For more information, please visit our website: www.packtpub.com.

About Packt Open Source

In 2010, Packt launched two new brands, Packt Open Source and Packt Enterprise, in order to continue its focus on specialization. This book is part of the Packt Open Source brand, home to books published on software built around Open Source licenses, and offering information to anybody from advanced developers to budding web designers. The Open Source brand also runs Packt's Open Source Royalty Scheme, by which Packt gives a royalty to each Open Source project about whose software a book is sold.

Writing for Packt

We welcome all inquiries from people who are interested in authoring. Book proposals should be sent to author@packtpub.com. If your book idea is still at an early stage and you would like to discuss it first before writing a formal book proposal, contact us; one of our commissioning editors will get in touch with you.

We're not just looking for published authors; if you have strong technical skills but no writing experience, our experienced editors can help you develop a writing career, or simply get some additional reward for your expertise.

[PACKT] open source ✿
PUBLISHING
community experience distilled

Boost.Asio C++ Network
Programming

ISBN: 978-1-782163-26-8   Paperback: 156 pages

Enhance your skills with practical examples for C++
network programming

1. Augment your C++ network programming using
   Boost.Asio

2. Discover how Boost.Asio handles synchronous
   and asynchronous programming models

3. Practical examples of client/server applications

4. Learn how to deal with threading when writing
   network applications

jQuery Tools UI Library

ISBN: 978-1-849517-80-5   Paperback: 112 pages

Learn jQuery Tools with clear, practical examples and get
inspiration for developing your own ideas with the library

1. Learn how to use jQuery Tools, with clear, practical
   projects that you can use today in your websites

2. Learn how to use useful tools such as Overlay,
   Scrollable, Tabs and Tooltips

3. Full of practical examples and illustrations, with
   code that you can use in your own projects,
   straight from the book

Please check **www.PacktPub.com** for information on our titles

Building Machine Learning Systems with Python

ISBN: 978-1-782161-40-0   Paperback: 290 pages

Master the art of machine learning with Python and build effective mahine learning system with this intensive hands-on guide

1. Master Machine Learning using a broad set of Python libraries and start building your own Python-based ML systems

2. Covers classification, regression, feature engineering, and much more guided by practical examples

3. A scenario-based tutorial to get into the right mind-set of a machine learner (data exploration) and successfully implement this in your new or existing projects

OpenCV Computer Vision with Python

ISBN: 978-1-782163-92-3   Paperback: 122 pages

Learn to capture, videos, manipulate images, and track objects with Python using the OpenCV Library

1. Set up OpenCV, its Python bindings, and optional Kinect drivers on Windows, Mac or Ubuntu

2. Create an application that tracks and manipulates faces

3. Identify face regions using normal color images and depth images

Please check **www.PacktPub.com** for information on our titles

11580964R00196

Made in the USA
San Bernardino, CA
21 May 2014